Shuk

Shuk

From Market to Table,
the Heart of Israeli Home Cooking

EINAT ADMONY & JANNA GUR

PHOTOGRAPHS BY QUENTIN BACON

ARTISAN | NEW YORK

Library of Congress Cataloging-in-Publication Data
Names: Admony, Einat, author. | Gur, Janna, author. | Bacon, Quentin,
    photographer.
Title: Shuk / Einat Admony and Janna Gur ; photographs by Quentin Bacon.
Description: New York : Artisan Books, a division of Workman Publishing Co.,
    Inc., [2019] | Includes index.
Identifiers: LCCN 2019018638 | ISBN 9781579656720 (hardcover : alk. paper)
Subjects: LCSH: Cooking, American. | LCGFT: Cookbooks.
Classification: LCC TX715 .A2425 2019 | DDC 641.5973--dc23
LC record available at https://lccn.loc.gov/2019018638

Design by Laura Palese
Cover and art direction by Michelle Ishay-Cohen

Artisan books are available at special discounts when purchased in bulk for
premiums and sales promotions as well as for fund-raising or educational use.
Special editions or book excerpts also can be created to specification. For
details, contact the Special Sales Director at the address below, or send an
e-mail to specialmarkets@workman.com.

For speaking engagements, contact speakersbureau@workman.com.

Published by Artisan
A division of Workman Publishing Co., Inc.
225 Varick Street
New York, NY 10014-4381
artisanbooks.com

Artisan is a registered trademark of Workman Publishing Co., Inc.

Published simultaneously in Canada by Thomas Allen & Son, Limited

Printed in China

First printing, August 2019

10 9 8 7 6 5 4 3 2 1

**To my parents, whose cultures
informed all of my cooking**

—E. A.

**To my children, Amit and Noa,
my best creation**

—J. G.

Contents

Shuk *(noun)* **1.** An open-air marketplace. **2.** A lively maze of stalls and stands selling all manner of vegetables and fruits, spices, meats and fish, breads and baked goods, olives and pickles, cheeses and yogurts, dried fruit and nuts, and vibrant herbs by the handful, plus cafés, restaurants, and food vendors serving the best hummus, flaky *bourekas*, meat-stuffed pitas, Iraqi *kubbeh* soup, and fresh-squeezed pomegranate juice. **3.** The bustling heart of Israel's towns and cities, each shuk a crossroads where Israelis of myriad descent (Persian, Yemenite, Moroccan, Iraqi, Tunisian, Lebanese, Syrian, Russian, and more) as well as Palestinians jostle alongside tourists, pilgrims, students, the religious and the secular, retirees and children, in their quest for nourishment, community, and the foods of their childhood.

The Spirit of Shuk

EINAT ADMONY

When I was growing up, my dad was the one who shopped at the shuk, not my mother, as you might think. He was the unusual husband who was happy to take his wife's shopping list and then head out to pick up the day's groceries: glossy *baladi* eggplant, fragrant bunches of cilantro and parsley, dates, creamy *gvina levana*, and perhaps more freshly toasted and ground *baharat* spice mix, which seemed to make its way into so many of my mom's recipes.

I would often go with my father when he shopped. Shuk HaCarmel in Tel Aviv (page 80) was not far from our home in the suburbs and was also right near the Yemenite quarter in which my dad spent his childhood. We would do the shopping and then wander into the shuk's Yemenite quarter, which housed a handful of simple restaurants serving Yemenite classics, the kind of food you'd otherwise find only in a family's home.

My dad was happy to take on the shopping because he knew he'd be rewarded by my mother's fantastic cooking (plus he was a nice guy). But he also might have volunteered for the shuk because he could indulge in some of the food he loved best–especially *lachuch*, a springy, moist Yemenite flatbread that was the one dish from his culture that my mom never mastered; see my version on page 320.

My Persian mom was born in Iran, and was eventually raised in an Iraqi household. In Israel, our family would be called "Mizrahi," meaning Jews who came from the Middle East rather than those with roots in Spain (Sephardic) or elsewhere in Europe (Ashkenazi).

Mizrahi dishes are the foods of my childhood, and I learned to make them starting at about age eleven, when I became my mom's assistant. She was always cooking something intriguing and delicious–Persian rice dishes fragrant with handfuls of herbs; *kubbaneh*, a delicious Yemenite bread she'd bake overnight for Shabbat lunch; chicken in *fassenjan*, a sauce made from ground walnuts and pomegranate juice and flavored with crazy-looking dried Persian limes. Our next-door neighbor was Moroccan, and she would let me help her with the hand-rolled couscous and all the spicy, tangy accompaniments for it–pumpkin *chirshi*, pepper and tomato *matboucha*, sweet and savory lamb tagine.

While my mom and neighbor were getting free labor, I was getting an education, and I ended up as a professional chef (with a stop at cooking school along the way). It's those foods of my multicultural childhood that I crave the most and that I now cook most often here in New York City. I've even built restaurants around my favorite Mizrahi dishes: My fast-casual Israeli chain, Taïm, was one of the first in the United States to serve *sabich*, an Iraqi Jewish, deliciously sloppy fried eggplant sandwich . . . something that just a few years ago you'd never have seen outside the neighborhood. (I've turned it into a salad on page 106.) And my couscous restaurant, Kish-Kash, celebrates all the influences of North African cuisine that surrounded me throughout my childhood.

I'm gratified to see that the rest of the world is catching on. So many of the wonderful dishes I grew up cooking and eating are no longer considered *ochel shel bayit*–food you would only eat at home–but are being featured on restaurant menus all over Israel and in the United States.

Food like this, whether Persian, Moroccan, Ethiopian, or Yemenite, represents not only my childhood and my heart but also Israeli cuisine as a whole–a multicultural mosaic of traditions from literally all over the globe, served in the spirit of generosity, hospitality, and joy, evolving as Israel grows as a nation. Israeli cuisine is young but with ancient roots, and I'm happy to be a part of its evolution. Now you can cook these dishes, too, and join me as we continue to create new traditions.

A Short Story of Israeli Food

JANNA GUR

I still remember my first visit to a shuk. A teenager, in Israel barely a month, still reeling from the merciless heat of the Israeli summer, I found myself at the Carmel Market in Tel Aviv. For someone fresh from the Nordic, polite Latvia, it was almost too much to bear–the hassle, the crowds, the smells–but the food, oh my God! It was early August, and the shuk was an orgy of peaches and watermelons, figs and grapes, all even more fragrant because of the heat. To this day, when I go to a shuk, for the first few minutes, I abandon myself to the memories of this shockingly sensual visit.

Food was one of the things I liked best about my new homeland, yet turning it into a career never crossed my mind. I wanted to be a literary translator and eventually became one, but at the age of twenty-six, I met Ilan, my future husband, and he introduced me to the crazy and fascinating world of magazine publishing.

At first, I helped him out with a marine sports magazine he was publishing at the time; then in 1991, we launched a culinary magazine called *Al Hashulchan* ("On the Table" in Hebrew). That was supposed to be a temporary stint before I went back to my "real" career, but within a few months, I realized that I was totally in love with the world of food. Today, after producing 387 issues of the magazine, editing almost forty cookbooks and authoring three, I still feel the same way.

I was also very lucky–the three decades of my career in food writing coincided with the dramatic revolution of the Israeli food culture and the birth of Israeli cuisine. Being an editor of a food magazine at such a time gave me an opportunity to document and champion this revolution as it unfolded right before my eyes.

WHAT IS ISRAELI CUISINE?

Israel has been a country for just over seventy years, not nearly enough time to form anything resembling a cuisine. In recent years, this not-yet-cuisine has evolved into one of the hottest global culinary trends. Tourists fall hard for the fresh, sexy, colorful food served in our restaurants. Adventurous foodies revel in the fact that there are so many cuisines to choose from. Health buffs admire our love of vegetables and penchant for starting every meal with a salad.

But is this enough to qualify as a cuisine? Very roughly, the contemporary Israeli food scene is a fusion of the local (Levantine/Palestinian) cuisine with foods brought to Israel by Jewish immigrants. Jewish resettlement in Palestine started in the late nineteenth century and gained momentum over the course of the twentieth century. The first settlers came from Eastern Europe, followed by a large wave of immigrants from central Europe. In the 1950s, shortly after the creation of the State of Israel, the population almost tripled, with the arrival of hundreds of thousands of immigrants from North African and Middle Eastern countries. The recent and most significant wave occurred in the 1990s, when almost a million immigrants came from the former Soviet Union. Each community brought to Israel its customs, language, music, memories, and, of course, food.

Everywhere Jews settled during two thousand years of the Diaspora, they created some kind of autonomous food system. Kosher laws prevented them from using certain foods and food combinations, so they adapted local dishes to their needs, often coming up with a completely new set of dishes. Many of those were designed to solve the challenge of serving your best meal on Shabbat–the day when you cannot cook. Others celebrated Jewish holidays, all of which involve at least one huge meal.

Now imagine this universe of culinary traditions landing in a tiny place, driven by an ambition to build a home for the Jewish people in their historic homeland. There was an even bigger ambition, and that was to create a new Jew–an Israeli, to be exact, who would be proud, strong, and connected to the land. It is not surprising that initially, the feeling was that in this promising new world, there was no place for anything reeking of the "sorrowful Diaspora," including its food.

It took decades for Israelis to feel confident enough as a nation to allow ourselves to embrace our diverse backgrounds. Only toward the end of the previous century did Jewish ethnic foods finally take center stage and become the driving force of our nascent cuisine.

There are over sixty ethnic communities that make up the Jewish population of Israel, but not all of them have a strong presence on the local food scene. When you visit Israel, you'll be surprised (perhaps disappointed) to find so little Ashkenazi food. With a few exceptions, like chicken soup, chopped liver, or babka, the unique cuisine of Eastern European Jews never became part of mainstream Israeli cooking. Like plants that have a better chance of survival in a new habitat if it is similar to their native one, so too cuisines that make up the Israeli food scene come from regions that are close to us geographically: North Africa, the Middle East, and the Balkans.

North African Jews brought couscous, shakshuka, and *chraime*. Persian cooks exposed us to exquisite rice dishes. Yemenites contributed a range of unique breads. Kurdish and Iraqi cooks made us fall for *kubbeh* dumplings and taught us about *silan*, the ancient date honey. The list of ethnic Jewish dishes that have become part of local gastronomy is long and is getting longer, but even today, there are so many more dishes (and even entire cuisines) waiting to be discovered.

Because Israel is such a small country and intermarrying among different communities is the norm, the cuisines are in a constant state of interplay. Israeli cooks, both professional and amateur, wouldn't think twice about garnishing Tripolitan shakshuka with Balkan feta or pairing Austrian schnitzel with Moroccan couscous.

The connection to the global roots of Jewish cooking was joined by another important connection—to the food traditions of the local population. Early on, Israelis fell in love with Palestinian hummus, labneh, tahini,

and grilled skewered meats, but beyond that, our knowledge of the food culture of Palestine and that of the neighboring countries of the Levant remained superficial. The change came during the 1990s, the formative decade of the Israeli food renaissance. It was then that local chefs realized that the first step in creating a cuisine is connecting to the terroir and learning from the people who have been living and cooking there for centuries.

In this time of bitter conflict between the two peoples attempting to share this land, the connection of Israelis to Palestinian food culture is fraught with controversy and sometimes viewed as a form of culinary colonialism. To put it bluntly: First you take our land, then you take our hummus. The reality, as always, is more nuanced. The fact that Jews and Arabs who live in Israel love the same food could be seen as a unifying rather than dividing factor. Even during times when the conflict flares into violence, ties between Israeli and Palestinian chefs remain strong. Restaurants serving authentic Palestinian and Levantine dishes are increasingly popular and influence Jewish Israeli chefs, but just as in the case of Jewish ethnic cooking, there's still much to be learned and discovered.

Both Jewish immigrant cuisines (let's call them "grandmothers' cooking") and Palestinian cuisine ("our neighbors' cooking") are steeped in age-old traditions. Israeli chefs and home cooks borrow freely from both but are not bound by either. This lack of commitment to tradition is one of the defining features of our young food culture. Unlike Lebanese, Greek, or Moroccan chefs who can get to the top of their profession by creating perfect renditions of traditional dishes, Israeli chefs are expected and encouraged to experiment and produce innovative flavor combinations.

Speaking of flavors and ingredients, it's time to bring another element of the Israeli food scene into the equation: our passion for vegetables. Farming the land and eating what you grow are at the core of the

Zionist project, and they spurred Israel to become an agricultural superpower. Practically everything we eat and cook is grown locally, and the variety is dizzying!

Naturally, the best place to celebrate this plenty is a shuk. Even though seasons become blurred due to the advances of modern agriculture, at the markets, we can still feel their rhythm. In winter, stalls are brimming with leafy greens, crunchy tubers, and golden mounds of oranges and tangerines. Spring brings green garlic, fresh fava beans, and tons of juicy strawberries. Come summer, the shuk becomes a celebration of fruit; apricots, cherries, grapes, and peaches come first, followed by figs, pomegranates, apples, and pears, which stay with us throughout autumn.

THE ISRAELI TABLE

Another important reason that our food culture is so vital has to do with the fact that Israelis actually cook . . . a lot! Because distances are short and family ties are strong, having a multigenerational Shabbat meal is the norm. And mind you, the food is expected to be cooked from scratch. On holidays, the whole country is afflicted by a cooking craze: Markets are packed, recipes swapped, grandmothers consulted, and the preparations–usually involving a few family members– continue for days on end.

With a society as eclectic as ours, every holiday table is different, yet they share a few common traits. First, there will be a lot of food. We take the expression "cooking for a crowd" quite literally. A typical festive meal will start with what we call in Israel *shulchan hasalatim* (the salads table). These are not just green or chopped salads–almost any combination of cooked, grilled, or pickled vegetables qualifies as salad. In the colder months, this will be followed by a fish course or a soup (or both). We really need to pace ourselves to make room for the main course, which might be roasted chicken, stuffed vegetables, or braised lamb with sides of rice, couscous, or potatoes . . . and more salads. When it's time for dessert, everybody is stuffed, but Israelis wouldn't say no to a slice of homemade cake to round out the evening.

Weekday cooking is naturally more basic. Many of our meals are eaten outside the home, yet there always will be something cooked and homey (a pot of soup, meatballs in a sauce, a bowl of rice and lentils) waiting in the fridge. As in most Mediterranean countries, lunch is the main meal of the day, though today, with longer working hours, many families have their biggest meal together in the evening.

Breakfast is equally important. During the busy weekday morning it is often nothing more than a bowl of cereal or a slice of toast, but on weekends we would take the time to prepare a proper Israeli breakfast: fried eggs, good bread, tahini, and–most important–a salad. This custom of having salad for breakfast is a uniquely Israeli tradition. We can't imagine our breakfast without a salad. Actually, we can't imagine any meal without a salad.

Given our passionate relationship with food, it is not surprising that Israelis love eating out. Our restaurant scene shares a lot of traits with home cooking–it is generous, innovative, casual, and extremely eclectic. And like in home cooking, vegetables reign supreme! It's no surprise that some of our favorite restaurants are located at the markets, or that even many of those that are not have an unmistakably shuk-like vibe.

And so we are back where we started–at a shuk, a simple place brimming with joy for life, fantastic produce, and intriguing foods from many different cultures. I hope that this book will bring some of this happy spirit into your kitchen. Einat's food and culinary wisdom will speak to you throughout, while I will be here to give it context, to tie the dishes to their roots and tell the stories behind them.

CHAPTER 1

Bringing the Shuk to Your Kitchen

Good news: You won't need to buy a lot of hard-to-find ingredients to cook Israeli food. The backbone of our kitchens is fresh produce (shuk-fresh, if possible). As for the pantry items and basic ingredients, you probably have much of what you need in your kitchen now, and you can easily find most of the rest in mainstream supermarkets. A few more unusual ingredients could require a trip to a Middle Eastern grocery, but that is always a fun adventure. And, of course, everything is available online. Many of the products you'll find in this chapter are discussed in more detail throughout the book, but this guide will give you a nice taste of Israeli cuisine. There are also recipes for some of our favorite spice blends, condiments, and relishes: preserved lemons, fiery harissa, crunchy dukkah, and more.

The Pantry

OLIVE OIL. Just like everywhere else in the Mediterranean, Israeli cooking relies heavily on olive oil for every possible use in the kitchen–dressing salads, making marinades, drizzling on finished dishes, and of course cooking, frying, and baking. You should have two different kinds of oil on hand: a strongly aromatic oil for seasoning and finishing dishes, and a more delicate, neutral-tasting one for cooking, frying, baking, and making marinades. A good–and more economical–option for a cooking oil is to use a blend of half olive and half canola or other vegetable oil. Make sure your olive oil is as fresh as possible, ideally from the current year's harvest. Good oils will always list the harvest date on the bottle.

TAHINI. If there is one ingredient you absolutely need in order to cook like an Israeli, tahini is it. This flavorful sesame paste is a staple of Middle Eastern cooking and is used in countless ways–from various tahini-based sauces and dressings to cult dishes such as baba ghanoush and hummus. But that's just the

beginning: We drizzle tahini on roasted vegetables, transform it into delicious crusts for roasted meats and fish, and even use it in desserts and pastries. The key to success is using good-quality raw tahini. Taste it straight from the jar–the flavor should be nutty, deep, and without a hint of bitterness. For more about this magical ingredient, see page 112.

SILAN (DATE HONEY). This dark brown syrup made from boiled dates is a wonderful way to add a sweet element to salad dressings, glazes, marinades, and of course desserts. It's vegan, which contributes to its current popularity. It's similar to honey but is darker, with a distinct caramel flavor. Make sure you buy pure *silan*, without any sugar added. Read more about its curious history and uses on page 57.

PRESERVED LEMONS. Originally designed to replace fresh lemons when they were not in season, this North African treat is so much more. The curing process makes the lemons considerably less tart and packs them with rich and evocative flavors along with some heat.

You can buy preserved lemons, but of course it's better to make your own. See recipes for both a traditional and a quick version on pages 30 and 31.

HARISSA. In addition to fresh chiles, it's a good idea to always have some kind of spicy relish on hand to zing up a variety of dishes during cooking or for serving. Harissa is the most popular of these spicy condiments (known collectively as *hareef*) and is widely available, but once again, it's simple to make your own (page 26) and so much better than store-bought.

POMEGRANATE MOLASSES. Made from reduced pomegranate juice, pomegranate molasses (also known as pomegranate syrup) is widely used in Middle Eastern cooking, especially in Syrian, Lebanese, and Persian cuisines. It adds complexity and deep sweet-tart flavor to sauces and dressings, and is often used along with fresh pomegranate juice. Look for a variety with no added sugar.

AMBA. This bright yellow relish is made from mangoes, crushed fenugreek seeds, lemon, and salt. Originally from India, *amba* arrived in Israel with Iraqi immigrants and became a local staple. It is especially popular as a condiment for street food, such as *sabich*, falafel, and shawarma. *Amba* is sold as a prepared relish or as a powder that has to be mixed with water. Read more on *amba* on page 71.

The Fresh Stuff

YOGURT. For Israeli cooks, yogurt is far more than a healthy snack. It's an essential cooking ingredient used for sauces, dressings, and sweet and savory baking and adds a fresh creamy element to countless dishes. For more on yogurt, see page 143.

LABNEH. This easy-to-make fresh cheese is basically strained yogurt that is at once very tart and very creamy, and therefore lends itself to many creative uses in the kitchen. Think of it as a Levantine counterpart to sour cream or low-fat cream cheese. To try your hand at making homemade labneh, see page 140.

FETA CHEESE. Locally called *gvina melucha* (salty cheese), this is the most useful cheese for both cooking and baking. Even neighborhood grocery stores in Israel carry a dozen varieties of this semi-hard savory cheese. The differences come from the kind of milk used (cow, sheep, or goat) and the texture, which ranges from crumbly to velvety.

FRESH LEMONS. Generous use of lemon juice is one of the defining features of Levantine cuisine; vinegar is rarely used. Needless to say, nothing beats freshly squeezed lemon juice, which combines tartness with the lovely aroma of the etheric oils found in the rind.

FRESH HERBS, LOTS OF THEM. The basic set of herbs found in most Israeli households includes parsley (flat-leaf), cilantro, dill, and mint. All four are used copiously, so when we shop, we always toss a bunch of each into our cart. For more about the joys of fresh herbs, see page 210.

CHILES. Even though chiles are used quite often in our cooking, Israelis aren't fussy about using specific varieties. The go-to chile sold at Israeli markets is the relatively mild Anaheim. Israelis refer to it simply as *pilpel hareef*–hot pepper. But this doesn't mean that you shouldn't take advantage of the variety of chiles available in your own markets. Make your choice based on how fresh the chiles look and how much heat you want in your dish.

A uniquely Israeli product that is great to have on hand is tiny pickled chiles called *shipka*. These delicious tiny peppers are part of the traditional *hamutzim* (pickles) plate that also contains cracked bitter olives and pickled cucumbers, and is offered at no extra cost in many restaurants and street-food eateries. Finely chopped pickled *shipka* are part of the garlicky, lemony dressing often served with hummus.

The Spice Rack

Salt. The recipes in this book were developed and tested using kosher salt, but you can use whatever salt you prefer. Just remember: Kosher salt is less salty by volume than table salt or fine sea salt; the grains of kosher salt are fluffier, so they take up more space in the measuring spoon. A rule of thumb is that 1 tablespoon of Diamond Crystal kosher salt equals about 2 heaping teaspoons of table salt. Other brands of kosher salt have different densities.

BLACK PEPPER. Please, please only use freshly ground. Black pepper is all about the aroma.

PAPRIKA. The basic style of paprika in Israeli cuisine is Hungarian sweet paprika, but feel free to use a hotter variety if you'd like.

CUMIN. This popular spice is ubiquitous in Middle Eastern cooking, both as whole seed and ground into powder. It can be overpowering, so use with caution and taste as you go.

TURMERIC. This spice adds a beautiful golden color and elusive aroma to whatever dish it's in, not to mention notable anti-inflammatory health benefits. Turmeric's flavor is slightly bitter, so use it with a light hand.

CINNAMON. In Middle Eastern cooking, cinnamon isn't just for sweets. Many savory dishes, including meat stews, rice, and even some salads, are perfumed with cinnamon.

SUMAC. This bright and sour spice is made from the berries of a local bush. A sprinkle of purple-red sumac wakes up flavors in salads and is also a popular addition to chicken, fish, and vegetable dishes.

CARDAMOM. This is a favored spice for meat and fish dishes, and we love adding it to marinades for the grill. Using whole cracked pods will yield a more delicate flavor, while ground cardamom is potent–use sparingly.

ORANGE BLOSSOM WATER. As it sounds, this flavoring is made from the essential oil of orange blossoms. It adds flowery and fruity notes to desserts and can also be used for savory dishes; see page 169.

ROSE WATER. A by-product of the perfume industry, rose water's aroma is quite similar to that of the orange blossom but is even more floral and sweet. Add a few drops to a cream or custard, or sprinkle over cut fruit.

DRIED MINT. In a culture that relies so heavily on fresh herbs, the use of dried ones can be unexpected. Dried mint is an exception–it brings lemony, woody notes and tones down excessive sweetness in dishes containing *silan*, honey, or pomegranate molasses. Read more about dried mint on page 259.

BAHARAT. This is the most renowned and commonly used spice mix in Middle Eastern cooking. The blend can change dramatically according to use and the country of origin. A well-stocked Israeli spice shop would carry several *baharat* mixtures for various uses–for meat patties, grilled food, stuffed vegetables, and more. Almost all *baharat* blends include warm spices such as cinnamon, allspice, and ginger, and many also contain caraway, cumin, and even dried ground rosebuds, which add an elusive floral whiff. Because it's so versatile and useful, we strongly recommend making your own (see page 22).

RAS EL HANOUT. This rich spice mix hails from Morocco and can contain a few dozen spices. As implied by its name ("head of the shop" in Arabic), each shop owner would make their own secret blend. Use the recipe on page 23 as a starting point for your own.

HAWAIJ. These two fragrant spice blends hail from the Yemenite kitchen. Soup *hawaij* is the more common of the two and is indeed great for soups, but it is also handy for seasoning meat, chicken stews, and braises. Coffee *hawaij* got its name because it was originally intended to spice up Yemenite white coffee, but it can be used for various sweet confections. Look for recipes for both blends as well as suggested uses on page 23.

ZA'ATAR. Za'atar in Arabic refers to an herb called wild oregano (also Lebanese oregano) as well as to a spice mix originally made from dried crushed za'atar, sesame seeds, sumac, salt, and sometimes fennel, cumin, and a dash of olive oil. Because original za'atar is a rare and protected plant, more common herbs, such as thyme, marjoram, or hyssop, are often substituted. Well-made za'atar mix is wonderfully aromatic–at once herbal and earthy. It's great sprinkled on a plate of labneh or tahini, goes well with local salty cheeses, and is a perfect addition to all kinds of savory pastries. See the za'atar recipe on page 24.

CUMIN

CARAWAY

HAWAIJ

SUMAC

CARDAMOM

BLACK PEPPER

Pistachio Dukkah

PISTACHIO

SESAME

COCONUT

CUMIN

CORIANDER

SALT

Spice Blends
Making Your Own

For best results—and this goes for all spices or spice blends—start with the freshest whole spices you can find, and roast and grind them yourself. Though the process takes more effort than just opening a jar of ground spices, which are not necessarily fresh, the results are worth it—fragrant, intriguing, memorable dishes.

Toasting is a simple procedure: Put the spices (each one separately) in a dry skillet and heat over medium heat, stirring continuously, until fragrant, usually 3 to 4 minutes. Transfer to a dry, cold plate to stop the cooking and let cool.

As for grinding, you can buy a nice spice grinder for around $35, or you can use a coffee grinder, but reserve it only for spices so the lingering savory aromas don't flavor your coffee. Most of the spices used in blends here can be ground at home, but there are a few exceptions, such as paprika, ginger, turmeric, and cinnamon. For those spices, starting from the chile, rhizome, or bark would require special equipment. Nutmeg kernels can be easily grated on a fine grater or a Microplane zester. As for black pepper, if you love to cook and eat, you should have a pepper mill in your kitchen. Use it. Ground pepper loses its aroma very fast.

If, despite your best intentions, toasting and grinding your own spices is just too inconvenient, then be sure to buy small batches of ground spices from reliable sources.

Store your spices and spice blends in small containers with tight-fitting lids, and keep them in a cool, dark place. Glass is better than plastic, which will absorb the flavors and thereby perfume whatever else you store in that container in the future.

Baharat with Dried Rosebuds

MAKES ABOUT ½ CUP (45 G)

Perhaps the most popular Middle Eastern spice blend around, *baharat* (the plural of "spices" in Arabic) comes in many versions, depending on the origin and intended use. You can easily find it in spice shops and online, but I suggest you take the time to make your own. This version was created by Lior Lev Sercarz, an Israeli chef and spice expert based in New York. In addition to the allspice, cinnamon, and pepper found in most *baharat* mixes, it contains ground rosebuds for pretty color and floral notes, as well as caraway for a savory touch. If you can't find rosebuds, don't worry—the flavor will still be wonderful.

2½ tablespoons allspice berries

1 teaspoon caraway seeds

2 heaping tablespoons dried rosebuds (available at Middle Eastern stores)

2 tablespoons ground ginger

2 tablespoons ground cinnamon

1 teaspoon freshly ground black pepper

Heat a small dry skillet over medium heat. Add the allspice and toast, stirring continuously, until just fragrant, about 2 minutes. Transfer to a small plate and let cool. In the same pan, toast the caraway until fragrant, 1 to 2 minutes. Transfer to a separate small plate and let cool.

Grind the allspice and caraway seeds separately in a spice or coffee grinder and transfer them to a small bowl. Grind the dried rosebuds (if using) and add them to the bowl. Add the ginger, cinnamon, and pepper and stir to combine. Store in an airtight jar in a cool, dark place up to 1 year.

Soup Hawaij

MAKES ABOUT ⅓ CUP (32 G)

One of the most popular spice mixes in an Israeli kitchen, *hawaij* actually comes in two distinct blends, both hailing from Yemen. Soup *hawaij* (or savory *hawaij*) tastes like Indian garam masala spiked with bright yellow turmeric. Use it for soups and stews, especially those based on legumes (see, for example, the white bean Yemenite soup on page 235).

1 tablespoon ground coriander

3 tablespoons ground cumin

2 teaspoons ground turmeric

1½ teaspoons freshly ground black pepper

1 teaspoon ground cardamom

½ teaspoon ground cloves

Combine all the ingredients in a small glass jar, seal, and store in a cool, dark place for up to 1 year.

Sweet Coffee Hawaij

MAKES ABOUT ½ CUP (45 G)

Coffee *hawaij* (or sweet *hawaij*) was originally used as a flavoring for Yemenite "white coffee," so named for its lightly roasted beans. Made with sweet, warm, aromatic spices, coffee *hawaij* works deliciously in a variety of cakes and cookies (like the tahini cookies on page 357), and it's a perfect match for pumpkin pies.

1 tablespoon ground cloves

2 tablespoons freshly grated nutmeg

2 tablespoons ground cinnamon

2 tablespoons ground ginger

1 tablespoon ground cardamom

Combine all the ingredients in a small glass jar, seal, and store in a cool, dark place for up to 1 year.

Ras el Hanout

MAKES ABOUT ¼ CUP (23 G)

Yes, this North African spice mix uses a lot of ingredients, but that's what creates the complexity of flavor and aroma. The cinnamon stick can be difficult to grind, so break it into smaller pieces before you add it to the spice grinder.

1 tablespoon whole cumin seeds

1 tablespoon whole coriander seeds

1 teaspoon whole black peppercorns

½ stick cinnamon

1 piece mace

½ teaspoon whole fennel seeds

½ teaspoon whole cloves

Seeds from 6 cardamom pods

½ teaspoon crushed dried rose petals (optional)

½ teaspoon ground allspice

1 teaspoon ground ginger

½ teaspoon turmeric

¾ teaspoon paprika

½ teaspoon freshly grated nutmeg

Heat a small, dry skillet over medium heat. Add the whole cumin, coriander, peppercorns, cinnamon stick, mace, fennel seeds, cloves, cardamom seeds, and rose petals (if using) and toast, stirring constantly, until just fragrant, 4 to 6 minutes. Transfer to a small plate and let cool. Grind together in a spice grinder.

Transfer to a small bowl, add the allspice, ginger, turmeric, paprika, and nutmeg, and mix thoroughly. Store in an airtight jar in a cool, dark place up to 2 months.

Za'atar

MAKES ABOUT ¾ CUP (70 G)

This classic Palestinian herb-based seasoning should definitely become a pantry staple. Sprinkle it on vegetables, over yogurt or labneh, on hummus, or on warm flatbread brushed with a touch of olive oil.

2 small bunches oregano

½ bunch thyme

½ cup (75 g) sesame seeds, lightly toasted

1 teaspoon ground sumac

1 teaspoon kosher salt

2 teaspoons extra-virgin olive oil

Lay the oregano and thyme on a rack over a tray (for airflow) and leave in a sunny place to dry for a few days, or in a 200°F (93°C) oven or a dehydrator for a few hours.

Strip the leaves from the stems and grind in a food processor. You want to end up with about ¼ cup (7 g). Mix the ground oregano and thyme with the sesame seeds, sumac, and salt in a small bowl. Add the oil and mix with your fingers until everything is lightly coated with the oil. Store in an airtight container; try to use within a month.

Shawarma Spice Rub

MAKES ABOUT 2 CUPS (180 G)

Use this lively blend as a rub for almost any meat or vegetable destined for the grill.

½ cup (145 g) whole cumin seeds

⅓ cup (100 g) whole coriander seeds

5 cardamom pods

⅓ cup (32 g) ground turmeric

⅓ cup (32 g) sweet paprika

1½ teaspoons freshly ground black pepper

2 tablespoons baharat (see page 22)

1 tablespoon amba powder (see page 71)

⅓ cup (32 g) granulated onion

Heat a small dry skillet over medium heat. Toast the cumin seeds just until fragrant. Transfer to a small plate and let cool. Repeat with the coriander seeds and cardamom pods, keeping the toasted spices separate. Grind the spices separately in a spice or coffee grinder, transferring them to a small bowl as you go. Add the turmeric, paprika, pepper, baharat, amba, and granulated onion and stir to combine. Store in a sealed jar in the pantry for up to 6 months.

HAREEF MEANS "HOT"

Hareef means "hot or spicy" in Hebrew. The word is also used as a slang term to describe someone very sharp, but if a falafel vendor or a restaurant waiter asks you if you would like *hareef*, he's referring to some kind of spicy condiment or relish to zing up your plate or your pita.

Which condiment? Good question. Usually it would be some kind of North African red harissa (see page 26), perhaps a bright green Yemenite *s'chug* (see page 25), or, if you eat at a Tripolitan restaurant, tart and garlicky *filfel chuma* (see page 27). All three are pantry items and keep well in the fridge, and all three contain chiles and garlic, but there are differences in color, flavor, and character.

Classic Green S'chug

MAKES ABOUT 1½ CUPS (360 ML)

Yemenite cooking is the spiciest of all ethnic cuisines in Israel, and the heat usually comes from this fiery bright green condiment. Take *s'chug* away from a Yemenite, and you take away his appetite. When I was growing up, my dad was the one who made it; my mother wasn't allowed to help. From shopping for the herbs at the shuk to grinding all the ingredients in an old-fashioned meat grinder, he was the *s'chug* master.

Heat masks *s'chug*'s lovely herbiness, so only add it at the very last moment or serve it in a separate bowl with the meal.

15 garlic cloves, coarsely chopped

4 dried red chiles, such as chiles de àrbol

3 jalapeño chiles, cored, seeded, and coarsely chopped

1 teaspoon kosher salt

½ teaspoon ground cumin

¼ teaspoon ground cardamom

¾ cup (180 ml) vegetable oil or extra-virgin olive oil

2 cups (100 g) packed fresh cilantro leaves

Put the garlic, dried chiles, jalapenos, salt, cumin, cardamom, and oil in a food processor and process to a homogenous but slightly chunky paste. Add the cilantro and pulse a few times until it's chopped and combined with the rest of the ingredients, but don't overprocess; you want to retain some texture.

Store in a glass container with a tight-fitting lid in the fridge for up to 2 weeks.

VARIATION

Mix grated tomatoes (see page 50) with a bit of *s'chug* and you have an instant salsa that goes great with hard-boiled eggs and famous Yemenite pastries, such as *kubaneh* (see page 315) or *lachuch* (see page 320).

Red S'chug

MAKES ABOUT ½ CUP (120 ML)

Red *s'chug* is perfect for those who don't like cilantro. Less spicy than the green version, it resembles North African harissa but with a thinner texture and an aromatic cardamom twist. You can mellow the spice heat even more by adding a roasted and peeled red pepper to the mix. Since it doesn't contain much oil, its keeping time is short—just a few days.

9 small or 4 or 5 medium Fresno or other medium-hot fresh red chiles, stemmed, ribs and seeds left intact

10 medium garlic cloves

¼ teaspoon ground cardamom

1 teaspoon freshly ground black pepper

1 teaspoon ground cumin

1 teaspoon sweet paprika

1 teaspoon kosher salt

¼ cup (60 ml) vegetable oil

Put all the ingredients in a food processor and process until almost smooth. Store in a glass container with a tight-fitting lid in the fridge for up to 2 weeks.

Red Harissa

MAKES ABOUT 2½ CUPS (600 ML)

Without a doubt, this is the most popular *hareef* across North Africa and the Middle East and as such has hundreds of variations. I've probably tasted most of them having grown up with Moroccan neighbors. In my version, sweet roasted red peppers form the basis of its flavor, with garlic, cumin, and caraway adding complexity. Feel free to use harissa as both a condiment and an ingredient in cooking.

10 medium garlic cloves

2 large red bell peppers, roasted, peeled, and seeded (see page 155)

1¼ cups (300 ml) vegetable or extra-virgin olive oil

½ cup (48 g) ground cumin

⅓ cup (32 g) cayenne

⅓ cup (32 g) sweet paprika

¼ cup (24 g) ground caraway

2 tablespoons kosher salt

Put all the ingredients in a food processor and process to an almost smooth paste, stopping to scrape down the sides of the processor bowl every now and then. Store in a glass container with a tight-fitting lid in the fridge for up to 1 month.

Yellow Harissa

MAKES ABOUT 1½ CUPS (360 ML)

More sauce than condiment, yellow harissa—made with roasted yellow bell peppers—is slightly less spicy and more aromatic than red harissa, and is especially good with fish and lamb.

3 yellow bell peppers, roasted, peeled, and seeded (see page 155)

½ small habanero pepper, roasted and seeded (see page 155)

2 medium garlic cloves, minced or grated

2 teaspoons ground coriander

2 teaspoons ground cumin

2 teaspoons ground caraway

2 teaspoons ground turmeric

1½ teaspoons kosher salt

¼ cup (60 ml) vegetable or extra-virgin olive oil

Put the bell pepper, habanero, garlic, coriander, cumin, caraway, turmeric, and salt in a food processor and process to a smooth paste. With the motor running, stream in the oil and process just until the mixture becomes smooth and emulsified. Store in a glass container with a tight-fitting lid in the fridge for up to 1 week.

Filfel Chuma

MAKES ABOUT 1½ CUPS (360 ML)

A close relative of harissa, this condiment hails from Jewish Libyan (Tripolitan) cuisine. *Filfel* means "pepper" (or "chile," in this case) in Arabic, and *chuma* means "garlic," so its dominant flavors should come as no surprise. A generous splash of lemon juice adds a bright sour note. Use this in any recipe that calls for harissa (particularly to spice up salads, pasta, and legumes), but keep its garlicky, lemony flavor profile in mind. Mostly used as an ingredient in cooking rather than as a condiment, it's the official *hareef* for Tripolitan shakshuka (see page 149) and *chraime* (spicy fish stew).

30 to 40 garlic cloves

5 small dried chiles, such as chiles de àrbol

3 tablespoons sweet paprika

1 tablespoon cayenne

½ cup (120 ml) vegetable oil

1½ teaspoons kosher salt

1½ teaspoons ground cumin

1½ teaspoons ground caraway

½ cup (120 ml) fresh lemon juice

Put all the ingredients in a food processor and pulse until fully combined but still a bit chunky, stopping to scrape down the sides of the processor bowl every now and then. Store in a glass container with a tight-fitting lid in the fridge for up to 1 week.

Spiced Olives

MAKES 1 QUART (560 G) OLIVES

This recipe will turn even supermarket olives into a delicacy.

¾ cup (170 ml) extra-virgin olive oil

4 garlic cloves, smashed

½ medium fennel bulb, sliced thin

2 preserved lemons (see page 30), sliced thin

2 dried hot chiles, such as chile de árbol

1 tablespoon fresh lemon juice

Two 5-inch (12.5 cm) sprigs rosemary

2 bay leaves

2 (3-by-1-inch/7.5 by 2.5 cm) strips pared orange zest

1 quart (560 g) drained mixed olives, such as Kalamata, Castelvetrano, or Niçoise

Put all the ingredients except the olives in a sterile jar and stir to mix. Add the olives, give them a shake, and refrigerate for at least 2 days or up to 1 month to allow the flavors to develop.

Take the olives out of the refrigerator and let them come to room temperature before serving, so the texture is luscious and the flavors more pronounced.

Preserved lemons, sometimes called Moroccan or pickled lemons, may have been developed originally as a way to preserve fresh lemons past their season, but for the modern cook, preserved lemons are a treat unto themselves to be enjoyed year-round. Tart, salty, and made more complex with added spices, preserved lemons bring a sort of citrusy sunshine to all manner of dishes.

Here we're presenting the classic preserving method, which takes around three months and produces a pickled lemon that will last in the fridge for many months beyond that. But if your timeline doesn't stretch that far into the future, you can make a quick version that's still plenty tasty. And the preserved lemon paste—it's a game changer! Whip up a batch with either store-bought or homemade preserved lemons (see below), and then use it as your secret weapon to bring vibrancy to just about anything you can think of.

Mix crushed, preserved lemons with yogurt or tahini to make exciting dressings and spreads or add them to stews, braises, and soups or as a genius addition to salads. Next time you make a tuna, pasta, or legume-based salad, add a spoonful of chopped preserved lemon and see for yourself. If you plan to chop the lemons and use them as a garnish or in salad, discard the mushy pulp and use only the rind. If you're adding them to stews, roasts, or braises, or pureeing them into a dressing, you can use the whole (chopped) wedge. Either way, before using the lemons, rinse them to make them less salty and remove all the bitter seeds.

Preserved Lemons

MAKES 15 LEMONS

If you have a lot of lemons, feel free to double or triple these amounts. Once you discover their magic, you won't stop using them; plus, they make great presents. Make sure the glass jars you'll pack them in are squeaky clean.

3 cups (720 g) kosher salt

½ cup (100 g) sugar

1½ teaspoons coriander seeds

1½ teaspoons whole black peppercorns

¼ teaspoon ground turmeric

¼ teaspoon sweet paprika

About 15 lemons, washed and quartered lengthwise

2 bay leaves

1 cinnamon stick

Mix the salt, sugar, coriander, peppercorns, turmeric, and paprika in a large bowl. Spread half the mixture over the bottom of a 1-gallon (4 L) glass jar with a tight-fitting lid.

Put the lemon wedges in the jar, squeezing their juices into the jar as you throw them in. Pack the lemons tightly to remove all the air, which would cause them to oxidize. Add the bay leaves, cinnamon stick, and the remaining spice mixture and pour in just enough water to fill the jar to the rim. Seal and leave at room temperature for at least 2 months (3 months is even better), until the rinds are very soft. Every couple of weeks, flip the jar a couple of times to make sure all the flavors and spices are distributed evenly. To check for doneness, use a clean fork to remove one lemon wedge from the bottom part of the jar and make sure the rind is completely soft.

Once the lemons are ready, move them to the fridge (this will slow down the pickling process), where they will keep for at least 6 months. To prevent spoilage, don't be tempted to remove the lemons from the jar with your fingers (even if you are convinced those fingers are clean)—always use a clean, dry spoon, fork, or tongs. Give them a quick rinse and remove any seeds before using.

Quick Preserved Lemons

MAKES ABOUT 2 CUPS (500 G)

Don't have any preserved lemons at the ready? No problem. This speedy version yields a comparable flavor in a fraction of the time. Use them in any recipe that calls for preserved (Moroccan) lemons. They won't keep as long, though—just a month in the fridge.

5 lemons, washed and quartered lengthwise

3 tablespoons kosher salt

¼ teaspoon ground turmeric

3 tablespoons sugar

Extra-virgin olive oil, for storing

Combine the lemons, salt, turmeric, sugar, and 3 cups (720 ml) water in a medium saucepan and bring the water to a boil. Reduce the heat to low and simmer, stirring occasionally, for about 1 hour, until the lemons' flesh has broken down and the rinds are very soft.

Drain thoroughly and transfer to a clean, dry jar with a lid. Pour in just enough oil to cover the lemons. Seal the jar and store in the fridge for up to 1 month. Use a clean, dry spoon or fork (never your fingers) to remove the lemons from the jar as needed. Give them a quick rinse and remove any seeds before using.

Preserved Lemon Paste

MAKES ABOUT 1½ CUPS (360 ML)

Use some of your preserved lemons to make this vividly yellow, brightly sour and fragrant paste. Enlivened with lemon juice, honey, and turmeric, the paste adds a boost of flavor to a wide range of dressings and spreads. Try mixing it into soups, chicken braises, yogurt, or tahini. You can even add a few teaspoons to a sandwich instead of mustard.

12 wedges preserved lemon (see opposite), rinsed and seeded

¾ cup (180 ml) fresh lemon juice

2 tablespoons honey, plus more as needed

1 tablespoon ground turmeric

3 tablespoons extra-virgin olive oil

Put all the ingredients in a blender or food processor and process thoroughly until you have a smooth paste. Taste and adjust the flavorings until you have a bright, intense, salty-sour condiment. Transfer to a clean, dry glass jar with a tight-fitting lid. Store in the fridge for up to 1 month, though you may find yourself making a new batch sooner than you expected!

Pistachio Dukkah

MAKES ABOUT 2½ CUPS (350 G)

A whole host of toasted nuts, seeds, and even coconut come together in this redolent Egyptian spice blend. Traditionally mixed with oil and used for dipping bread, it's actually far more versatile than that. Sprinkle it over anything and everything that can use a nutty boost, from eggs to salads to yogurt. You can even use it to make a crunchy coating for pan-fried meats or vegetables. Want to change things up? See the variations for almond and sunflower dukkahs below.

2 tablespoons cumin seeds

2½ tablespoons coriander seeds

½ cup (75 g) sesame seeds

1½ cups (195 g) shelled pistachios

¾ cup (65 g) unsweetened coconut flakes

1 teaspoon kosher salt

Freshly ground black pepper

Preheat the oven to 300°F (145°C). Line a rimmed baking sheet with parchment paper.

Heat a small dry skillet over medium heat. Toast the cumin and coriander, stirring frequently with a wooden spoon, until just fragrant, 2 to 3 minutes (this happens quickly, so stick around and make sure the spices don't burn). Transfer to a small plate and let cool. Toast the sesame seeds in the same pan, stirring frequently, until lightly golden, 3 to 4 minutes. Transfer to a small plate and let cool.

Scatter the pistachios on the baking sheet in a single layer. Toast in the oven until slightly fragrant and drier, 15 to 20 minutes. Keep an eye on them–toasted pistachios should retain their green color; if they turn brown, you've toasted them too long and must start again with a new batch of nuts. (Don't worry, it happens.) Transfer the pistachios to a plate and let cool; leave the oven on.

Scatter the coconut flakes on the baking sheet and toast in the oven until they turn golden, 6 to 8 minutes, stirring halfway through to make sure the coconut toasts evenly.

Grind the toasted cumin and coriander in a spice or coffee grinder or using a pestle and mortar; in both cases, you want the texture to remain slightly coarse. Transfer to a medium bowl.

Pulse the cooled pistachios in a food processor until finely chopped, then transfer to the bowl with the cumin and coriander. Add the toasted sesame seeds, toasted coconut flakes, salt, and a few twists of black pepper. Stir thoroughly to combine.

Store in an airtight container in a cool, dark place for up to 2 months.

TIP *If your dukkah gets stale over time, don't throw it away! Scatter it on a baking sheet lined with parchment paper and heat for 5 to 7 minutes in a 250°F (120°C) oven. It will be as good as new. Let it cool before returning it to the storage container.*

VARIATIONS

Almond Dukkah: Use 2 cups (220 g) slivered almonds in place of the pistachios. Toast them in the oven at 300°F (145°C) for 20 to 25 minutes, let cool, then pulse in the food processor until evenly and finely chopped. Be careful not to overpulse or you'll end up with almond flour (or almond butter, if you really get distracted!).

Sunflower Dukkah: Use 2 cups (280 g) hulled sunflower seeds in place of the pistachios. Toast the sunflower seeds in a large dry skillet over medium-high heat, stirring frequently, until lightly toasted, 2 to 3 minutes.

Chermoula

MAKES 2 CUPS (480 ML)

This North African condiment is used almost exclusively with fish, because it has everything the fish needs—aromatics, herbs, tartness, and some heat (but much less heat than harissa). Serve it with whole grilled or baked fish, fish fillets, or fish cakes, or try chermoula with hummus (see page 121).

1 tablespoon cumin seeds

1 tablespoon coriander seeds

¾ cup (40 g) coarsely chopped fresh parsley

¾ cup (30 g) coarsely chopped fresh cilantro

1 jalapeño chile, cored, seeded, and finely chopped

½ teaspoon sweet paprika

1 teaspoon kosher salt

Zest and juice of 2 lemons

1 cup (240 ml) extra-virgin olive oil

Heat a small dry skillet over medium heat. Toast the cumin and coriander seeds until fragrant, about 2 minutes. Transfer to a plate and let cool. Grind in a spice or coffee grinder and transfer to a small bowl.

Add the parsley, cilantro, jalapeño, paprika, salt, lemon zest, lemon juice, and oil. Taste and adjust the seasoning.

If not using at once, store in an airtight container in the fridge for up to 2 days.

TIP *If you don't have time (or a grinder), you can use preground spices, as long as they are fresh and of good quality.*

Preserved Lemon and Mint Pesto

MAKES 1⅓ CUPS (320 ML)

This bold pesto is delicious with semisoft Mediterranean cheeses. Try it with burrata, manouri, or halloumi.

8 preserved lemon quarters (see page 30)

2 medium garlic cloves, minced or grated

¼ cup (60 ml) fresh lemon juice

⅓ cup (45 g) pine nuts, toasted or fried (see page 69)

⅓ cup (80 ml) silan or honey

⅓ cup (80 ml) extra-virgin olive oil

¼ cup finely chopped fresh mint leaves or 2 teaspoons dried

Kosher salt

Rinse the preserved lemons, remove the seeds and most of the pulp, and chop the rinds finely. Don't worry if they turn mushy.

Put the garlic, lemon juice, pine nuts, silan, oil, and dried mint (or if using fresh, add it just before serving) in a food processor and process thoroughly until well blended. Stir in the preserved lemons and fresh mint (if using). Taste and decide whether you need to add salt—the preserved lemons are quite salty, so you may not. Store in an airtight container in the fridge for up to 1 week.

Garlic Confit and Sumac Mayonnaise

MAKES 1 CUP (240 ML)

Slowly cooking garlic in oil mellows its sharp edges and turns it sweet and rich, perfect for dressing up creamy mayonnaise.

20 medium garlic cloves, peeled, plus 1 small garlic clove, minced or finely grated

About ½ cup (120 ml) extra-virgin olive oil (or half olive oil and half canola oil)

1 cup (240 ml) best-quality mayonnaise

½ teaspoon ground sumac

1 teaspoon fresh lemon juice, plus more as needed

Kosher salt

Put the garlic cloves in a small pan, add oil to cover, and cook over very low heat until they turn golden brown, about 30 minutes. Drain the garlic cloves, but don't throw the oil away—it's great for frying or brushing onto bread to make bruschetta; store it in the refrigerator for up to 2 weeks.

Mash the softened garlic cloves with a spoon or a fork in a medium bowl. Add the grated fresh garlic, mayonnaise, sumac, lemon juice, and a pinch of salt and stir to blend. Taste and adjust the seasoning with more salt and lemon juice to your liking. Store in an airtight container in the fridge for up to 1 week. Use it in any way you would mayonnaise—as a condiment for meat, chicken, or french fries, or as a sandwich spread.

Za'atar Goat Cheese Dip

MAKES ABOUT 1 CUP (240 ML)

Adding a little yogurt to soft goat cheese makes the cheese creamy and dippable. A little lemon zest and herby za'atar make it irresistible.

- 6 ounces (170 g) soft fresh goat cheese, at room temperature
- ¼ cup (60 ml) whole-milk Greek yogurt (we like Fage)
- 1 teaspoon finely grated lemon zest
- 1 small garlic clove, minced or grated
- 1 tablespoon za'atar, store-bought or homemade (page 24)

- 2 tablespoons extra-virgin olive oil
- 1 teaspoon honey, plus more for serving if desired
- Kosher salt and freshly ground black pepper
- Silan, for serving (optional)

Combine the goat cheese, yogurt, lemon zest, garlic, za'atar, oil, and honey in a medium bowl and beat with a spoon to blend and lighten the texture a little. Taste and add salt–most goat cheeses are salty, so you shouldn't need much–and pepper. Drizzle with silan (if using) or more honey and serve.

The dip can be stored in an airtight container in the fridge for 3 to 4 days–it will firm up a bit and needs to be beaten again before serving. You can also add a little water or yogurt to reach the desired consistency. Use whatever is left as a snack with crackers or pita or as a sauce for making a boureka (page 322).

Pistachio-Yogurt Dressing

MAKES ABOUT ¾ CUP (180 ML)

Use this pale green dressing on roasted vegetables. Beets look especially pretty.

- ½ cup (65 g) shelled pistachios (ideally Sicilian), toasted
- 2 tablespoons vegetable oil
- 2 tablespoons water

- 1 teaspoon kosher salt, plus more as needed
- ½ cup (120 ml) whole-milk Greek yogurt (we like Fage)

Combine the pistachios, vegetable oil, water, and salt in a food processor and process to a smooth paste similar in consistency to thin nut butter. Add a little bit more water if it's too thick. Pour the mixture into a medium bowl and whisk in the yogurt until blended. Taste and adjust the seasoning.

TIP *Instead of buying expensive Sicilian pistachios, use this simple trick to obtain vividly green nuts: Bring 2 cups (480 ml) water to a boil with 1 teaspoon kosher salt. Add shelled pistachios and blanch them for 2 minutes. Drain and let cool for a couple of minutes. While they are still warm, rub them in a clean and odorless kitchen towel–this will separate the nuts from the skins. Discard the skins and spread the nuts on a baking sheet. Toast for 7 minutes in a preheated 300°F (145°C) oven; the color should stay green–you don't want to brown them. Cool completely and store in an airtight jar at room temperature.*

Shuk Levinsky/Levinsky Market

The story

Levinsky is not a market in the traditional sense of the word. There are no stalls and no fresh produce, just a maze of little shops spilling onto the narrow sidewalks in the dusty commercial area of downtown Tel Aviv. The story of Levinsky begins in Salonika (Thessaloniki in Greek), an ancient city in northern Greece that has been a center of Jewish life since the expulsion from Spain in 1492. In mid-1930, a few thousand Salonikan Jews arrived in Palestine. Most settled in Tel Aviv, in the newly established Florentin Quarter, and were instrumental in launching the first Hebrew Port in Tel Aviv. A small, lively market sprang up spontaneously on nearby Levinsky Street, and, as it catered mainly to Salonikans, it offered, in addition to fruits and vegetables, all kinds of cured or dried fish, olives, *bottarga* (dried fish roe), and other imported Balkan foodstuffs. About a decade later, the municipality decided to close down this improvised market and moved the vendors into shops across the street. Some stayed on; others left, and the shops they vacated were taken up in the 1950s by a new wave of immigrants—this time from Iran. And so it came to be that next to Balkan delis, the Levinsky shuk now offered exotic foodstuffs never seen before in Israel: dried lemons, saffron, pomegranate molasses, and every imaginable kind of rice, legume, nut, and dried fruit. In the 1980s, a bunch of restaurant supply stores opened on the neighboring streets, which put the market on the radar of enthusiastic amateur cooks. The problem was that the more Levinsky had to offer, the tougher it became to shop there, with narrow streets chronically crammed with trucks and pickups and practically no parking options. Spacious air-conditioned gourmet stores, which started to pop up across the country, drove away most of the clientele, and by the beginning of the 2000s, it seemed that the days of Levinsky were numbered. But then, miraculously, it was given a new lease on life, as young Tel Avivians seeking affordable housing started to move into the neighborhood.

The vibe

The aging market now has a new pool of shoppers who adore its shabby-chic atmosphere, understand good food, and are keen to try new things. Many veteran shops, now run by the grandchildren of the founders, have been recently revamped and modernized, while a crop of new businesses—restaurants, bars, cafés, bakeries, and organic stores—complete the makeover. Levinsky is still crammed and dusty, and finding a parking spot is harder than ever, but its culinary treasures and singular mix of old and new are worth the trouble.

When to come

If you plan some serious shopping or just dislike crowds, come during the week, preferably in the morning. The shopkeepers will be more obliging and more likely to offer you a taste and an explanation. On Fridays, Levinsky turns into one big street party. Prepare to wait in lines, run into friends (even if you're a tourist), and be entertained by spontaneous live music and colorful characters.

חיים רפאל מאז 1958 ... בלוינסקי

Olives, pickles, and other treats from
the Balkans at Haim Rafael deli (ABOVE);
Happy hour at Pimpinella market bar
(OPPOSITE)

Our Favorite Spots

HAVSHUSH SPICES
18 Hahalutzim Street

Levinsky is famous for its spice shops, also selling dried fruit and herbs, legumes, and other interesting dry goods. You'll find quite a few of those on Levinsky Street, but we prefer to head straight to Havshush, which hides away on a street that runs parallel to Levinsky. It seems that the owners do everything to discourage curious walk-ins–the green metal door is usually half shut, and the dimly lit store is cramped and uninviting. At first sight you won't even see spices, but you will definitely smell them. The selection here is excellent, and so is the quality. If the place is not too busy, ask one of the shopkeepers to show you some of what they call "mystical stuff": all kinds of sinister-looking potions, roots, stones, and powders that are bound to drive away an evil eye, lift a curse, or help you find your soul mate.

HAIM RAFAEL
36 Levinsky Street

YOM TOV
43 Levinsky Street

Through pure coincidence, two of the most popular delis at the market are located right across from each other on opposite sides of Levinsky Street. Both have been in

Freshly roasted seeds and nuts at Moshe & Sons Pitzuchim (TOP); Dried limes, secret ingredient of Persian cooks (ABOVE); Gorgeous gazoz drinks at Café Levinsky 41 (RIGHT); dried fish at Victor's, the oldest shop at the market (OPPOSITE TOP); "Mystical stuff" at Havshush Spices (OPPOSITE BOTTOM)

business for more than half a century, and both are now run by the grandchildren of their founders. Haim Rafael was born in Salonika, while Yom Tov Levi came from Istanbul. Given the famous age-old animosity between the Greeks and the Turks, the comparison between these two places is almost inevitable, but if truth be told, the selection is quite similar and–judging by the length of the lines–both have their faithful fans. You can find all manner of cured, dried, or smoked fish; olives; pickles; cheeses from all over the world; deli salads and spreads; and, on Fridays, prepared food to take home for weekend meals.

CAFÉ LEVINSKY 41
41 Levinsky Street

Good strong espresso and dainty homemade cakes are on offer here, but the main reason people are lining up at all hours in front of this tiny café is the unique *gazoz* drinks. Before canned sugary sodas became the norm, generations of Israelis quenched their thirst on summer days with a glass of *gazoz*–soda water mixed with fruit syrup heavy on sugar and artificial colorings. Benny Briga, the owner of this charming hole-in-the-wall, turned this nostalgic drink into a quirky work of art: Chunks of macerated fruit and homemade syrups, not at all reminiscent of the mass-produced stuff, are topped with soda water and garnished with a bunch of aromatic herbs. First you drink the water, then you dig out the fruit with a straw that doubles as a spoon. You're then left with a little bouquet of sweet-smelling herbs that you can sniff as you walk around the market.

MOSHE & SONS PITZUCHIM
51 Levinsky Street

This is the best place at the market for *pitzuchim*, a collective name for roasted seeds and nuts that Israelis (especially male) love to munch on, especially during weekend soccer games or in front of the television. Buying a few paper bags of *pitzuchim* for Shabbat is a time-honored tradition, which explains long lines in front of *pitzuchiyot* (places that sell *pitzuchim* and other munchables). Here the selection is especially tempting, everything is freshly and expertly roasted, and the lines are accordingly long.

OUZERIA
44 Matalon Street

We love Avivit Priel, the chef-owner of this cheerful tavern, because of her bubbly personality and her seriously good food. Ouzeria was the first of the new wave of restaurants to open at Levinsky Market, and it was the first one to stay open late (now there's a whole scene at Levinsky by night). Just like Levinsky itself, the food blends Balkan and Levantine dishes that go perfectly with an East-meets-West playlist and a groovy ambience.

CHAPTER 2

Salad All Day

In Hebrew, the word for "salad" is often used to describe something thrown together in a hurry. This is funny, given that we take our salads quite seriously. We can't imagine a meal—be that lunch, dinner, or breakfast (yes, we start our day with a bowl of salad)—without a salad. The most famous one is the classic Israeli chopped salad, but there are many others that we love to cook and serve: herby tabboulehs, filling grain-based salads, leafy salads packed with crunchy goodies.

A word of advice (and one that goes for all vegetable dishes): Leave the decision on which salad to serve with your meal until you get to the market, where you can be inspired by the mounds of fragrant herbs, meaty red tomatoes, slender squash, spicy greens, or any of the array of fresh produce that is the heart of shuk shopping. The more exciting the vegetable, the more delicious your salad.

Israeli Salad

4 ripe but firm medium
tomatoes, cut into
½-inch (1.5 cm) chunks,
or 1 pint (455 g) sweet
cherry tomatoes, halved

3 Persian cucumbers,
cut into ½-inch (1.5 cm)
chunks

½ large or 1 small red bell
pepper, cored and cut
into ½-inch (1.5 cm)
chunks

1 medium carrot, cut into
½-inch (1.5 cm) dice

1 small red onion,
finely chopped

2 tablespoons finely
chopped fresh parsley
and/or mint

3 tablespoons fresh lemon
juice

3 tablespoons flavorful
extra-virgin olive oil

1 teaspoon ground sumac

Kosher salt and freshly
ground black pepper

I've probably eaten a chopped salad every day of my life (once I moved past baby food). My mother, who added carrot and kohlrabi to hers, took great pains to chop her salad finely and evenly. As she got older, her "chopped" became more like "chunked," but it still tasted great. If you've never made an Israeli salad before, this recipe will serve you well as a guide to the flavor profile. Use it as a template for your own variations . . . and challenge yourself to cut everything into a perfect quarter-inch. Learn more tricks to perfect Israeli salad in the guide on page 44.

Put the tomatoes, cucumbers, bell pepper, carrot, onion, parsley, and/or mint in a large salad bowl and toss with the lemon juice and oil. Season with the sumac. Taste and season with salt and black pepper. Serve right away.

Israeli Salad Rules

Israel is a nation of salad eaters, and we are happy to call countless dishes by that name—from green salads to deli-style spreads to relishes. But if you just ask for a "salad" in Israel, you will most likely be served a tomato-cucumber chopped salad. It was not invented in Israel—Israelis encountered it through their Palestinian neighbors, and similar salads can be found in many Levantine and Balkan cuisines. But what makes it uniquely Israeli is the way it pops up at every meal: in a pita with falafel or shawarma, on a lunch plate next to schnitzel or grilled chicken, or with hard-boiled eggs and cottage cheese for a light supper.

Most notably—and uniquely—this chopped salad is part of a classic Israeli breakfast. The custom of eating chopped salad in the morning, born in a kibbutz dining hall, has become the hallmark of the Israeli morning. We know that most people would find starting their day with a salad a bit weird, but for us, it's the most natural thing in the world.

The recipe for Israeli salad couldn't be simpler, but you must follow some rules to make one worthy of its reputation.

VEGETABLES

There's no point in making Israeli salad from less-than-great vegetables. Tomatoes are the most crucial. They need to be ripe and flavorful, but not so soft that they get mushy when you cut them. If you can't find suitable full-size tomatoes, try cherry tomatoes, which have a longer season and are usually quite sweet and firm. Can't find either? Sorry–try another salad.

Close to tomatoes in importance are the cucumbers. If possible, use smaller Persian cucumbers, which are sweeter, crispier, and better tasting than English ones. In Israel, we usually don't peel cucumbers for salad, but if the skin looks too thick or wax-coated, it's better to peel them. If the cucumbers seem watery, halve them lengthwise and scoop out the seeds with a teaspoon before cutting them up.

Tomatoes and cucumbers are the backbone of all Israeli salads, but they're just the beginning. The following vegetables will make your salad more delicious and add crunch and flavor: red bell peppers, red onion, small radishes, carrots, kohlrabi, or jicama (though you'll not find jicama in Israel). Because of their decidedly crunchy texture, these last two are especially handy if cucumbers are not at their best.

FRESH HERBS

The most popular are flat-leaf (also called Italian) parsley and mint. If you're a fan of cilantro or dill, please include them as well. Chopped chives or scallions are also great accents for Israeli salad.

SEASONING

The essential seasonings are good, vivacious extra-virgin olive oil, fresh lemon juice, kosher salt, and freshly ground black pepper. You can also sprinkle the salad with some ground sumac, which will add an intriguing tang. A tiny dash of ground cinnamon–odd as it sounds–adds a little something that's hard to describe yet delicious . . . the alchemy of spices! Try it and taste for yourself.

If you're feeling adventurous, add a spoonful of finely chopped lemon rind, which will give your salad a lovely citrusy aroma. Another popular addition is very finely chopped or grated garlic–just a bit, or the flavor will dominate. And if you're a fan of spicy heat, add a sprinkling of chopped seeded fresh chile or a few drops of harissa (see page 26).

The most important thing is to respond to the character of your ingredients. Season with a very light hand and let the natural flavors take the lead. Always taste as you go, and keep in mind that you can always add more.

TIMING

After the quality of the vegetables, timing is the most important salad rule: Chop, dress, and serve the salad at once. Even half an hour in the fridge, and the magic is gone. If you're cooking for a crowd and must make your salad ahead, cut up the vegetables but keep the tomatoes in a separate bowl. If they bleed a lot of juices, drain them before combining them with the rest of the vegetables. If you're using onions, scallions, or garlic, keep them separate; add them to the salad just before serving and toss. If you store your vegetables in the fridge, take them out half an hour before you make the salad, which will allow the flavors to wake up.

CHOPPING

Here the rules are a little more flexible. Finely chopped salad is highly praised and considered a sign of a meticulous cook, but coarsely chopped, chunky salad has its charm, especially if the vegetables are amazing.

Whichever method you choose, use a very sharp knife–especially for tomatoes, so you don't crush them.

Make Your Salad More Substantial

- Serve the salad with a dollop of tahini sauce (see pages 114-117); make the sauce relatively thin.

- Sprinkle some crumbled feta cheese on top.

- Sprinkle a coarsely grated hard-boiled egg on top (egg is especially delicious with tahini dressing).

- To make a fatoush-style salad, toss the salad with chunks of fried or toasted pita and let it sit for a few minutes before serving so the bread soaks up some of the delicious salad juice.

- Serve the salad on a bed of labneh (yogurt cheese; see page 140). This works best with a coarsely cut salad.

- If you have some cooked rice (white or brown) or bulgur wheat, mix it with your salad. This will not only make your salad more filling, it will give it staying power, because the grains will absorb the juices and keep the salad from getting soggy–a smart move for picnics.

Israeli Ceviche

Chopped Salad with Raw Salmon on a Bed of Labneh

1 pound (455 g) best-quality fresh skinless salmon fillet, cut into ¼-inch (6 mm) chunks, nice and cold

3 tablespoons fresh lemon juice

½ teaspoon kosher salt, plus more as needed

2 tablespoons extra-virgin olive oil

4 ripe but firm tomatoes (about 1 pound/455 g), cut into ¼-inch (6 mm) chunks

2 Persian or 1 large regular cucumber, cut into ¼-inch (6 mm) chunks (peeled if the skin is thick or waxed)

1 Fresno or other medium-hot fresh red chile, cored, seeded, and thinly sliced

2 tablespoons chopped fresh cilantro

2 tablespoons chopped fresh mint

3 tablespoons thinly sliced scallions

1½ cups (360 ml) labneh, store-bought or homemade (see page 140)

Ground sumac, for garnish (optional)

As far as most Israelis are concerned, "ceviche" is another name for a chopped salad, but one with chunks of raw fish in it. Labneh (yogurt cheese) takes this fresh and super-easy dish farther away from its ancestral home in South America into the Levant and adds a layer of tart creaminess.

Right before serving, put the fish in a large bowl and toss with the lemon juice and salt. Add the oil, tomatoes, cucumber, chile, cilantro, mint, and scallions. Mix everything together gently. Taste and add more salt if you like.

Using a large spoon, spread a nice swoosh of the labneh on individual plates or a large serving platter. Top with the ceviche and give it a light sprinkle of sumac (if using). Serve at once.

VARIATIONS

If you can't find sweet and delicious larger tomatoes, use halved cherry tomatoes (using different colors will make the salad look more vibrant).

Instead of salmon, use another very fresh fish, such as bass, snapper, tuna, fluke, or mackerel.

For more creamy goodness—or to make the salad vegetarian—use cubes of ripe but firm avocado in addition to or instead of the fish.

Chopped Avocado, Cucumber, and Kohlrabi Salad

4 Persian or 2 large regular cucumbers, cut into ½-inch (1.5 cm) chunks

1 medium kohlrabi or small jicama, peeled and cut into ½-inch (1.5 cm) chunks

1 medium red onion, finely chopped

1 jalapeño chile, cored, seeded, and minced

½ cup (20 g) chopped fresh cilantro

¼ cup (13 g) chopped fresh mint

¼ cup (60 ml) fresh lemon juice

1 teaspoon kosher salt, plus more as needed

Freshly ground black pepper

2 ripe but firm medium avocados, cut into ½-inch (1.5 cm) chunks

Lemon wedges, for serving

This irresistibly crunchy salad is a celebration of the shuk in a bowl. Israelis adore kohlrabi, with its crisp texture and subtle sweet-spicy flavor, and of course cucumbers bring crunch and juiciness together in every bite. Couple all that texture with the velvety softness of the avocado, another favorite of ours, and you've got a compelling salad. Red onion, cilantro, and mint add welcome pops of flavor. Be sure to pick an avocado that is ripe yet firm, or it will turn mushy when diced. Serve this salad alongside almost any meat course, from schnitzel to grilled fish.

Combine the cucumbers, kohlrabi, onion, jalapeño, cilantro, and mint in a large bowl. Add the lemon juice, salt, and a few twists of pepper. Toss, then add the avocados and toss gently once more, taking care not to mash the avocados. Taste and adjust the seasoning. Serve at once with lemon wedges, for squeezing.

Tomato Love

Once upon a time, tomatoes in Israel—like everywhere else—had seasons. They were juicy and sweet in the summer, bland and pale in the winter. Then, shortly before the end of the millennium, the food world began to hear about incredible candy-sweet cherry tomatoes that grow year-round in the Israeli desert. But they were in such high demand in Europe that most were exported.

Years went by, the scale of production increased, the export decreased due to fierce competition, and now practically all Israeli tomatoes are sold locally. They're spectacular and now available year-round. Large (regular) tomatoes come mostly from the Eshkol and HaBesor regions on the northern tip of the desert, while cherry tomatoes thrive in the hot, dry, and sunny terrain of the Negev Mountains. Right in the heart of the desert, but relatively high up, this area is the site of cutting-edge desert agriculture. Grapes, olives, watermelons, potatoes, and many other fruits and vegetables grow in the computer-monitored futuristic orchards and hothouses, and cherry tomatoes are the leading crop. They are irrigated by a cocktail of sweet and saline (brackish) water drawn from deep artesian wells. This salinity is what makes the fruit so sweet and bright colored. Because the area is so remote and dry, almost no pesticides are needed, which makes the produce very clean, even when it is not certified organic.

Having wonderful tomatoes year-round is great news for local cooks, because for us, cooking without tomatoes is inconceivable. Their color, juiciness, and perfect balance of sweet and tart make them the backbone of local cuisine.

Here is some tomato wisdom:

- *Store them at room temperature.* Tomatoes and the refrigerator don't get along. Only store your tomatoes in the fridge if they are super ripe and need to be reined in a bit by the cold so that they don't turn to mush.

- *Mix different types of tomatoes.* Every variety will bring its special flavor. Your salad will look prettier; your sauce or soup will have a deeper, more complex flavor.

- *Grate them!* This technique is so simple and rewarding. Cut away a thin slice of skin and grate the tomato flesh on the large holes of a box grater held over a bowl. In less than a minute, you'll have frothy, juicy pulp in the bowl and a sheet of tomato skin in your hand. If the tomatoes are ripe and sweet, the pulp will be so delicious, you won't need anything except a dash of salt, but if you like, you can also stir in extra-virgin olive oil, freshly ground black pepper, and some finely chopped herbs–basil, cilantro, parsley, mint, or even more assertive herbs such as dill, tarragon, or oregano. Serve this instant salsa as a dip for pita or focaccia, or swirl it on a plate with sour cream or yogurt. Shabbat breakfasts at Sephardic and Yemenite homes always feature a bowl of grated tomatoes and a smaller bowl of *s'chug* (see page 25) or harissa (see page 26)–both go beautifully with rich, buttery pastries such as *kubaneh*–and hard-boiled eggs.

- *Roast them.* When you turn on the oven to roast fish, chicken, or root vegetables, add a bunch of cherry tomatoes (or, even better, a cluster of tomatoes on the vine). Serve them alongside other veggies or fish or meat, and squeeze a bit of roasted tomato pulp on top to get a drop of summer sweetness.

- When tomatoes are not at their best, you can cook with good-quality Italian canned tomatoes. But even then, add one or two chopped fresh tomatoes. Even if they're bland and pale, they'll add a layer of freshness to your sauce or soup.

- Speaking of soups, next time you make chicken soup or a chicken stock, throw a whole tomato into the pot (score the skin first to release the juices)–it will deepen the color of the soup or stock and add some fresh acidity.

- *Grill them.* When you're having a barbecue, put a few whole tomatoes on the grill. Sear them until soft and their skin is charred. Don't bother peeling them; just smash, season with a bit of salt, pepper, and olive oil, and serve as a warm salsa for grilled meats.

- *Don't forget the seeds.* Many classic tomato recipes call for discarding their little clusters of seeds. Don't! They're delicious, a little bit crunchy, and lovely as a garnish.

Spicy Tomato and Garlic Salad with Tahini Dressing

GARLIC CONDIMENT

2 medium garlic cloves, finely grated or minced

1 teaspoon fresh lemon juice

1 teaspoon extra-virgin olive oil

Small pinch of sugar

Small pinch of kosher salt

TAHINI DRESSING

½ cup (120 ml) best-quality raw tahini

3 tablespoons fresh lemon juice

½ garlic clove, finely grated or minced

6 tablespoons (90 ml) ice water

¾ teaspoon kosher salt

Freshly ground black pepper

SALAD

1 pint (455 g) cherry tomatoes, halved

½ to 1 jalapeño chile (depending on the jalapeño and how spicy you want the salad), cored, seeded, and sliced paper-thin

1½ teaspoons fresh lemon juice

1½ teaspoons extra-virgin olive oil

1 teaspoon kosher salt

This spicy, garlicky tomato salad enriched with tahini sauce goes deep on flavor. I've eaten it at M25 restaurant at the Carmel market in Tel Aviv, where it is served with *arayes* (see page 304), but it's also delicious with all kinds of grilled meat.

Make the garlic condiment: Combine the garlic and lemon juice in a small bowl. Stir to blend, then stir in the oil, sugar, and salt. Set aside for 30 minutes. This will mellow the strong flavor of the raw garlic.

Make the tahini dressing: Pour the tahini into a medium bowl. Whisk in the lemon juice and garlic, followed by the ice water, a couple of tablespoons at a time. Keep whisking until the mixture is creamy with a consistency similar to a creamy hummus; you may not use all the water. Whisk in the salt and several twists of pepper and set aside.

Assemble the salad: Toss the cherry tomatoes and jalapeño in a medium bowl with the lemon juice, oil, and salt. Spread the tahini dressing around the rim of a serving dish as you would hummus, leaving a well in the center for the tomatoes. Pile the tomatoes and jalapeño into the well, then spoon the garlic condiment over them. Serve at once, before the tomatoes become soupy.

Three-Tomato Salad

1 pint (455 g) cherry
    tomatoes (ideally mixed
    colors)

1 tablespoon extra-virgin
    olive oil

Kosher salt

**SUN-DRIED TOMATO
DRESSING**

5 sun-dried tomatoes
    packed in oil, drained and
    coarsely chopped

¼ cup (60 ml) white wine
    vinegar

1 teaspoon honey

1 medium garlic clove,
    minced or grated

½ teaspoon kosher salt,
    plus more as needed

Freshly ground black pepper

¼ cup (60 ml) extra-virgin
    olive oil

5 halved Oven-Dried
    Tomatoes (recipe follows)

Handful of whole fresh
    mint or cilantro leaves,
    or small handful of
    fresh oregano leaves,
    microgreens, or a mix, for
    garnish

Picture a late-summer day at a farmers' market, when the stalls are bursting with ripe, juicy tomatoes of all sizes, shapes, and colors. That's pretty much the scene at a typical Israeli shuk throughout the year (yes, even in winter—more about that on page 50). But no matter where I'm cooking, tomato season inspires me. This recipe uses a combination of fresh tomatoes and roasted tomatoes, all dressed in a sun-dried tomato vinaigrette. The result is a juicy, bright red celebration.

Preheat the oven to 450°F (230°C). Line a baking sheet with parchment paper.

Set half the cherry tomatoes aside. Toss the remainder with the oil and a generous pinch of salt in a large bowl. Spread them on a baking sheet and roast until they're wrinkled and their skins are slightly charred, about 20 minutes. Let cool slightly.

Meanwhile, prepare the dressing:
Combine the sun-dried tomatoes, vinegar, honey, garlic, salt, and several twists of pepper in a food processor and process until the sun-dried tomatoes are crushed. With the motor running, slowly stream in the olive oil and process until almost smooth, though the dressing should remain slightly chunky.

Cut the reserved fresh cherry tomatoes in half and transfer them to a large salad bowl. Add the warm roasted cherry tomatoes and the oven-dried tomatoes. Drizzle with about half the dressing and season with a few twists of pepper. Taste and adjust the seasoning; add more dressing, if you like. Garnish with the fresh herbs and serve at once, while the roasted cherry tomatoes are still warm.

Oven-Dried Tomatoes

In Israel, we call these "moist tomatoes," and that's exactly what they are. Halfway between fresh and sun-dried, they're still quite juicy and can be enjoyed on their own or added to salads, pastas, and sandwiches. Roma (plum) tomatoes are good for oven-drying because they're meaty and firm. They taste bland when fresh, but long, slow baking concentrates the flavors. Oven-dried tomatoes keep well in the fridge, covered with olive oil, so I always make a large batch. **MAKES 15 TO 20 TOMATOES**

15 to 20 plum or other small ripe tomatoes
3 tablespoons extra-virgin olive oil
Kosher salt
5 fresh rosemary sprigs
4 fresh thyme sprigs

Preheat the oven to 250°F (120°C). Line a baking sheet with parchment paper.

Cut out the stem end of the tomatoes and halve them lengthwise. Scoop out the seeds with a teaspoon.

Toss the tomatoes with the oil (add a touch more, if necessary, to gloss them all nicely) and a generous sprinkle of salt. Arrange them cut-side up in a single layer on the prepared baking sheet. Scatter the rosemary and thyme sprigs over the tomatoes. Bake until the tomatoes look shriveled, especially around the edges, but are still quite moist; depending on your tomatoes, this could take between 2 and 3 hours.

Remove from the oven and set aside until they're cool enough to handle. Try to peel them: If the skins come off easily, go ahead and remove them; if not, leave them on—the tomatoes will still be good. If not using at once, transfer the tomatoes to an airtight container and cover with oil to prevent spoilage. Store in the fridge for up to 2 weeks.

Fresh Herb Salad

SERVES 4 TO 6

Picked leaves from 1 bunch parsley

Picked leaves from 1 bunch cilantro

Small handful of fresh mint leaves, torn if large

Small handful of fresh dill sprigs

Small handful of other tender herbs or baby greens

1 Fresno or other fresh hot red or green chile, cored and sliced into very thin rings

About 2 tablespoons finely diced lemon peel (including the white pith)

Fresh lemon juice

Kosher salt and freshly ground black pepper

Extra-virgin olive oil

This type of salad reminds me of growing up, when my Persian mom would always have a plate of fresh herbs on the dinner table, usually with scallions and some Israeli watercress.

Make this salad when you have young, tender herbs from the market. Treat them like baby greens and use the leaves whole, rather than chopped. Rinse the whole herbs thoroughly and dry them in a salad spinner, then pick the leaves, including a few tender stems.

The salad is super refreshing—like a tonic—so serve as a green foil to grilled fish or rich meat dishes.

Make sure your herbs and greens have been thoroughly washed and totally dried in a salad spinner. Pile them all into a bowl along with the chile rings and lemon peel.

Squeeze on 1 tablespoon of lemon juice, season with salt and pepper, and drizzle on about 3 tablespoons oil. Toss to distribute the oil and seasoning, taste, and adjust with more salt, pepper, lemon juice, or oil until the salad is bright and refreshing.

SERVES 4

Salt-Roasted Beet Carpaccio with Tahini and Silan

2 cups (480 g) kosher salt or other coarse salt

3 small, even-sized beets, unpeeled, trimmed, and scrubbed

Fresh lemon juice

1 heaping tablespoon best-quality raw tahini (stir well before using), plus more if you like

½ teaspoon silan

Maldon or other flaky salt, for serving

Salt-roasting turns beet flesh slightly translucent and almost jewel-like. I slice them thin and arrange them in a single layer to look like carpaccio. Here, tahini is used straight from the jar, so choose the best quality. *Silan*—date syrup—is thinner and darker than honey with a mild caramel flavor. Find it in the kosher sections of supermarkets and in Middle Eastern groceries, or order it online. Only buy natural *silan*, with no sugar added. If you can't find *silan*, you can use honey, but it's sweeter, so reduce the amount slightly.

Preheat the oven to 375°F (190°C). Line a baking dish that fits the beets in one even layer (without too much crowding) with parchment paper.

Spread the kosher salt in an even layer over the bottom of the prepared baking dish. Arrange the beets on the salt and roast until very tender when prodded with a knife or skewer, 35 to 45 minutes. Remove from the oven and let cool for a few minutes until you can handle them. Peel the beets (you may need to use a paring knife) and slice them into very thin rounds, ideally ⅛ inch (3 mm) or thinner.

Arrange the beets in one layer on a large shallow serving plate. Squeeze a generous teaspoon of lemon juice over the top. With a spoon, lightly drizzle on the tahini and silan, adding a bit more if needed to be sure every slice gets some of the flavorings, and sprinkle with Maldon salt. Serve warm or at room temperature.

SILAN: THE NEW-OLD ISRAELI HONEY

A couple of decades ago, *silan*—a glossy, chocolate-colored date syrup—was a rarity, familiar only within the Jewish Iraqi community. Iraqi grandmothers would cook *silan* from scratch and use it as *haroset*, a sweet dip served at the ritual Passover meal.

Commercial production of *silan* in Israel started on the shores of Lake Kinneret (the Sea of Galilee), one of the leading date-growing regions. The story has it that employees of Iraqi origin at one of the fruit-packing plants in the area would ask permission to take home date scraps. This went on for years, until the plant manager got curious and asked what they did with all those scraps. To this day, most Israeli *silan* comes from the Galilee region and the neighboring Jordan Valley.

Jewish Iraqi *silan* may be relatively new in Israel, but date molasses has been around for millennia, widely used to sweeten food and wine. Biblical scholars and food historians believe that the honey in the famous expression "the land of milk and honey" refers to date molasses.

Salad of Caramelized Fennel and Radicchio with Arak Vinaigrette

5 tablespoons extra-virgin olive oil

1 large or 2 small fennel bulbs (about 1¼ pounds/285 g), trimmed, cored, and cut crosswise into ¼-inch (6 mm) slices

Kosher salt and freshly ground black pepper

1 large head radicchio, quartered lengthwise

2 tablespoons arak, ouzo, or pastis

1 tablespoon honey

1 tablespoon white wine vinegar

1 tablespoon lemon juice

French goat cheese, crumbled

2 tablespoons pomegranate seeds (optional)

I love the way the anise flavor of the fennel is amplified by the same flavor in the arak vinaigrette. When I was growing up, every household made their own arak, a Levantine anise-based spirit similar to ouzo or pastis, but it was only the old guys who drank it. Now you'll find trendy young Tel Avivians sipping artisanal arak at craft cocktail bars.

Heat 2 tablespoons of the oil in a medium skillet over medium heat. Add the fennel slices, season lightly with salt and pepper, and cook gently, stirring occasionally, until the fennel softens and turns golden brown and sweet, about 20 minutes. Cool.

In the same pan, add another tablespoon of oil, increase the heat to medium-high, and add the radicchio, cut-side down. Sauté until slightly wilted and browned around the edges, but still crunchy, about 2 minutes per side.

Make the dressing by whisking together the arak, honey, vinegar, lemon juice, and ½ teaspoon salt, then whisking in the remaining 2 tablespoons oil. Taste and adjust the seasoning.

Toss the fennel and radicchio with the dressing and arrange on a platter. Top with the goat cheese and pomegranate seeds (if using). Serve warm or at room temperature.

Whole Romaine Leaves with Fenugreek-Yogurt Dressing and Ja'ala

DRESSING

1½ tablespoons fresh lemon juice

2 teaspoons extra-virgin olive oil

2 teaspoons honey

½ cup (120 ml) plain yogurt (not Greek-style)

1 tablespoon dried fenugreek leaves

1 teaspoon kosher salt, plus more as needed

SALAD

2 or 3 romaine hearts, separated into leaves, any wilted outer leaves removed

1 to 1½ cups (115 to 170 g) Yemenite Ja'ala (recipe follows)

Two elements make this simple green salad stand out. The first is *ja'ala*, a Yemenite Jewish snack of spiced nuts and seeds that adds flavor and crunch. The other key element? The lush yogurt-based dressing. Perfumed with fenugreek, the essence of Yemenite cuisine, it adds a layer of exotic, currylike aroma to the salad. Find fenugreek at Middle Eastern and Indian groceries and online.

Make the dressing: Whisk together the lemon juice, oil, honey, yogurt, fenugreek leaves, and salt in a small bowl. Taste and adjust the seasoning.

Assemble the salad: Arrange the romaine leaves attractively in a large, shallow serving bowl. Spoon the fenugreek-yogurt dressing over the lettuce and scatter the ja'ala on top. Serve at once.

Yemenite Ja'ala

My Yemenite grandmother always served a big bowl of *ja'ala* at the end of every meal. As a kid, I, of course, would have preferred chocolate, but now I'm crazy about it. The scrumptious, savory mix of roasted nuts, seeds, and spices is still largely unknown beyond the Jewish Yemenite community. Historically, Yemenite Jews were poor and ate a frugal diet of breads, legumes, soups, and an occasional meat stew. *Ja'ala* represented wealth and luxury and was reserved for important guests and festive family gatherings. Nowadays it's often served on its own or as a pre- or post-dinner snack. But it's just as delicious as a component in salads, or even as a savory topping to your morning yogurt. **MAKES ABOUT 3 CUPS (380 G)**

½ cup (70 g) raw almonds (with skins)

½ cup (70 g) raw hazelnuts

½ cup (60 g) raw cashews

½ cup (65 g) shelled raw pistachios

¼ cup (40 g) shelled raw peanuts

¼ cup (35 g) hulled raw pumpkin seeds (pepitas)

¼ cup (35 g) hulled raw sunflower seeds

¼ cup (40 g) raw sesame seeds

1 teaspoon sugar

1 teaspoon sweet paprika

1 teaspoon granulated onion

½ teaspoon kosher salt

¼ cup (60 ml) boiling water

1 teaspoon extra-virgin olive oil

Preheat the oven to 250°F (120°C). Line a large baking sheet with parchment paper.

Put the almonds, hazelnuts, cashews, pistachios, peanuts, pumpkin seeds, sunflower seeds, sesame seeds, sugar, paprika, granulated onion, and salt in a large bowl. Mix well, then add the boiling water and oil and toss until the nuts are well coated.

Spread in a single layer on the prepared baking sheet—you want the nuts a bit crowded so they stick and clump together a little as they roast. Roast for 20 to 30 minutes, until the nuts feel dry to the touch and taste toasted. (They may still be a little chewy, but they'll crisp up as they cool.) Don't worry about stirring during cooking, but you can rotate the baking sheet halfway through if it looks like the nuts aren't roasting evenly. Let cool.

Store in a glass jar or other airtight container at room temperature for a week or longer. After a week, they might become stale, but if that happens, don't worry—to restore their crunch, just spread them over a baking sheet and toast in a preheated 250°F (120°C) oven for about 10 minutes.

Bulgur Tabbouleh with Raw Beets, Dill, and Walnuts

2 cups (280 g) coarse bulgur wheat

1 large beet, coarsely grated

½ cup (60 g) chopped walnuts, toasted or fried (see page 69)

⅔ cup (35 g) finely chopped fresh dill

¼ cup (60 ml) fresh lemon juice

2 tablespoons extra-virgin olive oil

Kosher salt and freshly ground black pepper

I love this salad because it's another way to serve raw beets, a favorite of mine from childhood. Bulgur wheat provides a hearty backdrop to the classic combination of beets and dill, with toasted walnuts enhancing the bulgur's nutty flavor.

Put the bulgur in a medium bowl and add hot tap water just to cover, probably 3 to 4 cups (720 to 960 ml). Set aside until the grains are tender but still a bit al dente, 12 to 15 minutes. Drain the bulgur thoroughly and return it to the bowl.

Add the beet, walnuts, dill, lemon juice, and oil and season well with salt and some pepper. Taste and adjust the seasoning.

Serve at once or store in an airtight container in the fridge for up to 3 days; bring to room temperature before serving so the flavors wake up.

THE RIGHT RATIO FOR TABBOULEH

If you order a tabbouleh in any Palestinian restaurant in Israel—or anywhere else across the Middle East, for that matter—you will get a bowl of finely chopped herbs (mostly parsley and some mint) sparsely dotted with bulgur wheat. Sometimes there will also be some chopped tomatoes and a light sprinkle of pomegranate seeds, if they're in season. If you come across a tabbouleh at, say, a lunch buffet in an Israeli hotel, expect the opposite: a bowl of bulgur dotted with herbs and chopped vegetables and maybe even some feta cheese crumbled on top. Authentic tabbouleh is all about herbs, with bulgur playing a second fiddle, but in contemporary kitchens around the world, this Middle Eastern classic has come to signify almost any salad made with bulgur and/or chopped herbs. In fact, even bulgur is not a must—couscous is fine too, and why not seeds or even grated raw cauliflower? The three salads featured here (see also pages 66 and 69) are tabbouleh in a very broad sense of the word. All three are juicy, delicious, super nutritious, and great destinations for your seasonal vegetables from the market.

Pomegranates
The New Kings of the Market

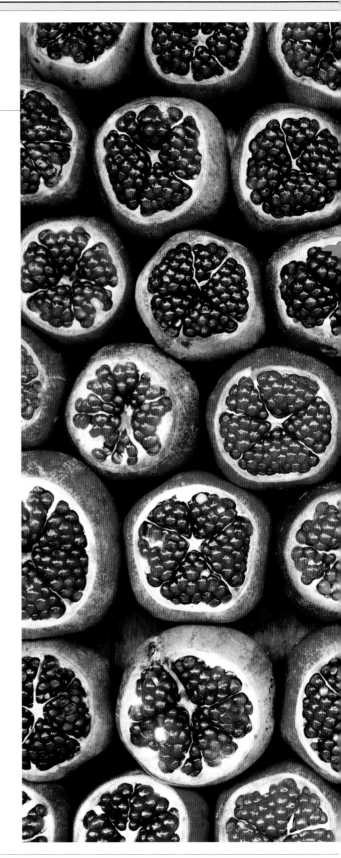

It seems that with every passing year, we see more pomegranates at the shuks and their season gets progressively longer. Up until a decade ago, they would pop for a month or so, just before Rosh Hashanah (the Jewish New Year, celebrated in September), and disappear shortly afterward. Israelis would buy a few of these regal-looking fruits to decorate the holiday table and sprinkle their crunchy jewel-like seeds on some of the dishes. A traditional Rosh Hashanah menu is heavy on symbolism, and pomegranates are laden with symbols—they signify knowledge, learning, wisdom, but most of all righteousness because, allegedly, each fruit has 613 seeds that correspond with the 613 commandments of the Torah. (Some folks actually took the trouble to count, and it turns out that an average fruit has between 400 and 500 seeds . . . myths are better left untested.)

In the last decade, the demand for pomegranates has increased dramatically, mainly because of their newly gained status as one of the healthiest fruits on Earth: They are packed with antioxidants and extremely beneficial for your heart. Many Israeli farmers have uprooted their citrus groves and planted pomegranate trees instead. Concurrently, new varieties were developed, each ripening at a different time, making pomegranate season last from August to December. Because pomegranates are very shelf stable, they stay at the markets well into February.

One of the welcome results of pomegranate popularity is that every juice stand (and we have lots of them at every shuk) now offers freshly pressed pomegranate juice—our favorite energy drink. It is slightly tannic, extremely invigorating, and ranges from tart to quite sweet, depending on the variety of the fruit. The juice is squeezed with a manual tool identical to one used to squeeze oranges.

Cauliflower Tabbouleh with Crunchy Seeds

3 tablespoons sesame seeds

Olive oil, for frying

3 tablespoons pine nuts

3 tablespoons hulled pumpkin seeds (pepitas)

3 tablespoons hulled sunflower seeds

1 medium cauliflower, cored and cut into large florets

1 tablespoon nigella seeds

2 tablespoons finely chopped fresh cilantro

2 tablespoons finely chopped fresh mint

2 tablespoons finely chopped fresh parsley

3 tablespoons fresh lemon juice, plus more as needed

3 tablespoons extra-virgin olive oil, plus more as needed

1 teaspoon kosher salt, plus more as needed

Freshly ground black pepper

⅓ cup (60 g) fresh pomegranate seeds, for garnish (optional)

I have no idea who came up with the idea of breaking cauliflower into tiny bits and using them as a gluten-free couscous of sorts, but I'd like to give her a Nobel Prize. Some recipes call for blanching the cauliflower before crushing it, but I think raw is better for salads since it has a fresher taste and a crunchy, bulgurlike texture. Just be sure to use a perfect head of cauliflower—snowy white, tightly closed, and unblemished. Feel free to change up the seeds with different varieties, combinations, and ratios. When pomegranates are in season, add some of their seeds for extra crunch, flavor, and color.

Toast the sesame seeds in a dry medium skillet over medium heat, stirring continuously, for a couple of minutes, until golden. Transfer to a small plate and let cool.

Line a plate with paper towels. Heat a thin layer of oil in the same skillet over medium-low heat. Add the pine nuts and sauté, shaking the skillet frequently, until they just turn light golden, 3 to 4 minutes. Use a slotted spoon to transfer them to the paper towels. Fry the pumpkin and sunflower seeds in the same manner; transfer them to the paper towels as well.

Pulse the cauliflower florets in a food processor until they are broken down to couscous-size crumbles. Transfer the cauliflower to a large bowl. If there are any large pieces left, return them to the food processor and pulse until they reach the desired size, then add them to the bowl.

Add the sesame seeds, pine nuts, pumpkin seeds, sunflower seeds, nigella seeds, cilantro, mint, and parsley to the bowl with the cauliflower. Add the lemon juice, oil, salt, and some energetic twists of pepper and toss to combine. Taste and adjust the seasoning, adding more salt, pepper, lemon juice, and/or oil as needed to make the salad yummy and bright.

Sprinkle the pomegranate seeds on top (if using) and serve promptly.

Quinoa Tabbouleh with Kale and Dried Cranberries

1 cup (170 g) quinoa, rinsed

3 cups chopped baby kale or shredded Tuscan kale leaves

¼ cup (60 g) fresh lemon juice

1 teaspoon kosher salt, plus more as needed

3 tablespoons extra-virgin olive oil

½ cup (20 g) chopped fresh cilantro

⅓ cup (45 g) sweetened dried cranberries, roughly chopped

½ cup (60 g) sliced almonds, toasted or fried (see page 69)

Freshly ground black pepper

Built on three superfoods, this easy salad is as good to eat as it is good for you. Both kale and quinoa are slightly on the bitter side, but sweetened dried cranberries offer a tangy-sweet counterpoint. Tuscan kale is tender and delicious. It's also known as cavolo nero, lacinato, or dinosaur kale.

Fill a large saucepan with about 3 quarts (3 L) water and bring to a boil over high heat. Add the quinoa, give it a stir, and cook, uncovered, until the grains are tender but not mushy, about 12 minutes. Drain and rinse under cold water to stop the cooking. Drain thoroughly, transfer to a large bowl, and let cool completely.

Put the kale in a large bowl, add the lemon juice and salt, toss, and massage briefly with your fingertips—this will slightly break down the fibers of the kale and make its texture less chewy. Let the kale sit for a few minutes before serving to blend the flavors and soften the kale a bit. Add the quinoa, oil, cilantro, cranberries, almonds (reserve a few for decoration), and several twists of pepper and toss to combine. Taste and adjust the seasoning, if needed. The salad is best fresh, but will keep in an airtight container in the fridge for up to 2 days.

FRIED, NOT TOASTED

The most common method of crisping nuts and seeds is toasting them in a hot, dry skillet. The problem with this is that you need to watch them closely, and even when you do, the exterior tends to brown or burn before the interior gets crispy. The following method is easy and effective and turns out evenly golden, crisp nuts or seeds. It works for pine nuts, hazelnuts, pumpkin seeds, and sunflower seeds, as well as halved or slivered almonds.

Line a plate with paper towels. Pour a thin layer of olive oil into a small skillet and heat over medium heat for a minute. Add a handful of nuts or seeds and fry, shaking the skillet and stirring the nuts or seeds, for a minute or two, until they start turning golden and smelling tasty. Immediately remove from the heat. Strain the oil (it can be reused for the next batch of nuts) and spread the nuts on the paper towels. You'll notice that their color turns a shade deeper from the residual heat, and the texture crisps up as they cool. Use promptly or store in an airtight container for up to a week.

Fresh Mango Salad with Amba and Mustard Vinaigrette

3 large ripe, firm mangoes

AMBA DRESSING

1 tablespoon yellow mustard seeds

1 tablespoon amba powder (see opposite)

¼ cup (60 ml) fresh lemon juice

1½ tablespoons honey

3 tablespoons extra-virgin olive oil

2 tablespoons cold water

Chile flakes

Kosher salt

Just like the sauce that inspired it (see opposite), this salad is a multilayered bombshell of flavors. At once sour and sweet, spicy and exotically fragrant, it's a great partner for grilled meats and the *pargiyot* recipe on page 301. Make sure the mangoes you pick are firm or you won't be able to slice them thin.

Peel one of the mangoes using a vegetable peeler or a paring knife. Cut a slice off the bottom to make it stable and position the fruit vertically on a work surface. Cut the flesh into wedges around the pit—you should have two bigger and two smaller semicircular wedges. Cut each wedge into very thin slices; if you have a mandoline slicer, this is a good time to break it out. Repeat with the 2 remaining mangoes.

Make the dressing: Heat a dry skillet over medium-high heat. Add the mustard seeds and toast them, stirring continuously, for a minute or so, until fragrant. Set aside on a plate to cool.

Mix the amba powder and lemon juice in a medium bowl until the powder dissolves. Add the honey, oil, cold water, a pinch of chile flakes, and the mustard seeds and whisk vigorously until smooth (it may take some time for the honey to dissolve). Taste and add salt if you like; amba powder is pretty salty, so you may not need much.

Add the mango to the bowl with the dressing and toss. Serve the salad at once or store in an airtight container in the refrigerator for 3 to 4 days. The salad will develop a pickled flavor, making it more similar in character to the original amba relish.

The Story of Amba

A Journey from Bombay to Baghdad to Ramat Gan

During the Gulf War of 1991, Israel was under attack from Iraqi Scud missiles for months, and the city that suffered the most was Ramat Gan, home to the largest community of Iraqi Jews (and the birthplace of *sabich*–see page 109). According to a popular joke, the explanation for this mysterious phenomenon was that Iraqi missiles homed in on Ramat Gan because they smelled *amba*. (Wartime brings out our dark humor.)

Amba is a spicy sauce made from pickled mangoes seasoned with salt, mustard seeds, turmeric, chiles, and fenugreek–this last being largely responsible for its pungent aroma. There are two theories as to the origin of *amba*. According to one, *amba* is a variation on a South Indian mango chutney; according to another, it was developed in the late nineteenth century by members of the Sassoon family, a clan of Baghdadi Jewish merchants residing in Bombay.

What is indisputable is that *amba* made its way to Israel–and to the rest of the world, for that matter–via the Iraqi Jewish community, which had long-standing ties to Indian Jews. *Amba* arrived in Israel in the 1950s with large waves of Iraqi immigrants and gradually made its way into the pantheon of Israeli spices and condiments, next to Yemenite *s'chug* and North African harissa.

Everything about *amba* is over the top–the gaudy yellow color, the slightly gooey texture, the flavor that is at once fruity, salty, sour, and hot . . . and the funky smell. But this is exactly what makes it special; if used in moderation, *amba* has the ability to brighten up so many foods. *Amba* is indispensable for a proper *sabich* sandwich, but the sauce can also be found at falafel and shawarma stalls and is often served with grilled meats. If you want to tone it down a bit, use *amba* as a seasoning and mix it with mild-tasting spreads such as labneh, yogurt, or mayonnaise.

Amba is sold in two formats–a prepared sauce and a powder. The powder, which is mixed with water to make the relish, is more convenient, especially if you plan to mix it with mayonnaise or yogurt. Both forms are available in Middle Eastern and Indian groceries and online.

Orange and Olive Salad with Harissa Vinaigrette

2 blood oranges

2 navel oranges

½ small red onion, halved crosswise and thinly sliced

¼ cup Moroccan (oil-cured) or Kalamata olives, pitted

¼ to ⅓ cup (60 to 80 ml) Harissa Vinaigrette (recipe follows)

Kosher salt (optional)

Handful of fresh cilantro leaves, for garnish

This sweet, savory, citrusy, spicy, vibrantly colored Moroccan classic, part of the traditional meze table, brightens up any meal, especially fish. If you can get your hands on Jaffa oranges—one of the jewels of an Israeli shuk in winter and exported all over the world—this salad is a perfect showcase. I like pairing regular oranges with a blood orange to make the salad especially stunning.

Slice the top and the bottom off the oranges so they will sit flat on your work surface. Stand them upright and, working from the top down, pare away the skin with a sharp knife, removing as much of the white pith as possible. Go around the fruit twice, if needed. Slice the oranges crosswise into ⅓-inch-thick (9 mm) rounds.

Gently toss the oranges, onion, olives, and ¼ cup (60 ml) of the vinaigrette in a large bowl. Taste and add more vinaigrette or salt, if you like, though the olives are salty, so you probably won't need much. Garnish with the cilantro leaves and serve at once.

Harissa Vinaigrette

This bright red vinaigrette offers a gentle heat balanced by a touch of sweetness, making it much more than just a salad dressing. Serve a small bowl of it with grilled fish, add it to chicken glaze, or use it to spice up roasted potatoes. **MAKES ABOUT 1 CUP (240 ML)**

3 tablespoons red harissa, store-bought or homemade (see page 26), plus more to taste

6 tablespoons (90 ml) fresh lemon juice

2 teaspoons honey

1 teaspoon kosher salt

6 tablespoons (90 ml) extra-virgin olive oil

Whisk together the harissa, lemon juice, honey, and salt in a medium bowl until smooth. While whisking, slowly stream in the oil and whisk until the dressing is emulsified. Taste and add more harissa if you like it spicier. Store in an airtight container in the fridge for up to 5 days. Shake before using.

Melon Salad with Mint and Crispy Bread Crumbs

2 cups chunks of ripe cantaloupe or other orange melon

2 cups chunks of ripe honeydew or other green melon

½ cup Fresh Mint Vinaigrette

Basil Bread Crumbs (page 241)

Fresh mint leaves, for garnish

This refreshing salad will be delicious with any ripe melon, but if you can find Galia melons, you'll really be eating like an Israeli. Developed in the 1960s by Israeli plant breeders and now widely available, Galias are sweet and succulent with a pretty, pale green flesh. I love them in any dish. Here, my mint vinaigrette plays so well with the fragrant melons, and the crunchy crumbs are a textural surprise. You'll have more vinaigrette than you need for this salad . . . which is a good thing, because you can enjoy it on other fruit salads, cabbage slaws, or roasted vegetable salads. Store it in the fridge for up to 4 days; shake before using.

Chill the melon chunks until just before serving. Toss both melons together with about ⅓ cup of the dressing. Arrange on a platter and sprinkle with about ½ cup of the bread crumbs. Garnish with the mint leaves. Serve right away so the crumbs don't get soggy.

Fresh Mint Vinaigrette

Fragrant and dotted with lovely specks of green, this bracing vinaigrette works with any green salad. **MAKES 1½ CUPS (360 ML)**

½ cup (120 ml) fresh lemon juice

1 teaspoon Dijon mustard

1 tablespoon honey

½ teaspoon kosher salt

1 medium garlic clove, coarsely chopped

1 cup (240 ml) delicate extra-virgin olive oil, or ½ cup (120 ml) vegetable oil and ½ cup (120 ml) olive oil

15 large fresh mint leaves

Combine the lemon juice, mustard, honey, salt, and garlic in a food processor and pulse briefly to combine. With the motor running, slowly stream in the oil and process until the mixture is emulsified. Add the mint leaves and pulse very briefly, just until they are chopped. Store in a glass jar with a tight-fitting lid in the fridge for up to 4 days. Shake vigorously before using.

Autumn Salad with Farro, Apple, and Roasted Persimmons

Kosher salt

1 cup (140 g) farro

3 large or 4 smaller Fuyu persimmons, peeled, quartered, and pitted

5 tablespoons extra-virgin olive oil

½ cup toasted walnuts

2 tablespoons fresh lemon juice

1½ teaspoons silan or honey

⅛ teaspoon freshly ground black pepper

¼ small red onion, finely diced

1 Granny Smith apple or other tart green apple, cored and cut into tiny dice (leave the skin on)

¼ cup dill sprigs

Persimmons start showing up at local markets in late September and stay until March. When very ripe, they're quite soft, extremely juicy, and delicious for snacking; the flavor is like a cross between a really sweet melon and a carrot. When not ripe, however, they can be astringent . . . and awful. My first taste of persimmon was of an underripe one, which kept me away from them until I moved to the States. Now I love them. Persimmons hold up beautifully in the oven and develop a lovely caramel flavor. Here, I'm pairing them with apples, another icon of the Israeli autumn, and adding farro and walnuts, which turn this brightly colored salad into a light meatless main. Farro isn't very Israeli, but I love it. However, if you can't find farro, wheat berries or barley will be fine substitutes.

Bring a medium pot of water to a boil, season generously with salt, and add the farro. Boil the farro until it's fully tender but not mushy, 17 to 30 minutes. Drain thoroughly, spread onto a large plate or tray, and let cool.

Meanwhile, preheat the oven to 350°F (175°C). Toss the persimmons with 2 tablespoons of the oil and a light sprinkling of salt. Spread onto a baking sheet and roast the persimmons until tender and lightly browned, about 20 minutes.

Roughly chop half the walnuts and then grate or very finely chop the other half.

Whisk together the lemon juice, silan, ½ teaspoon salt, black pepper, and the remaining 3 tablespoons oil.

Toss the farro with the grated or finely chopped walnuts, the onion, apple, and the dressing. Taste and season with more salt or pepper if needed.

Arrange a bed of the farro on a platter, top with the roasted persimmons, and finish with the roughly chopped walnuts and dill. Serve at room temperature.

Watermelon and Feta with Beer Glaze

BEER CARAMEL GLAZE

5 tablespoons (65 g) sugar

5 tablespoons (75 ml) white wine vinegar

3 tablespoons white wine or water

3 tablespoons light beer, such as a lager like Goldstar (popular in Israel) or Budweiser

SALAD

½ small or ⅓ large red seedless watermelon

One 6-ounce (170 g) chunk best-quality feta cheese (Valbreso is delicious)

Nothing says "Israeli summer" like sweet, cold watermelon with slices of creamy, salty feta. Add a bottle of chilled beer and you have our favorite beachside treat. Here, the beer becomes a bittersweet glaze to drizzle over the fruit and cheese, elevating this dish beyond a simple snack to dinner-party status.

Make the beer glaze: Put the sugar in a medium skillet and heat over medium heat, stirring often, until the sugar dissolves and turns frothy and light brown, 4 to 5 minutes. Add the vinegar and wine and cook, stirring often, for another 4 minutes, or until the mixture thickens and coats the back of a spoon. Pour in the beer and cook for another minute or two to reduce it slightly. Transfer the glaze to a small bowl and let cool.

Assemble the salad: Just before serving, remove the watermelon from the fridge and cut it into long wedges. Then cut each wedge into slices to make triangles and slice the triangles from the rind. Cut the feta into ¼-inch (6 mm) slices and cut across to make triangles; aim to have an equal number of watermelon and feta pieces.

Drizzle half the glaze over a flat serving plate. Arrange the watermelon and feta slices in an alternating pattern on the plate and drizzle the rest of the gastrique over them. Serve promptly.

Shuk HaCarmel/The Carmel Market

The story

In 1913, a group of affluent Russian Jewish families were talked into buying some land in the newly founded city of Tel Aviv. They were moved to do so for idealistic reasons–immigrating to Palestine was the last thing on their minds. But a few years later, in the wake of the October Revolution in 1917, they were forced to flee Russia, leaving their fortunes behind. They arrived in Tel Aviv penniless, except for the land they had purchased, which turned out to be nothing more than a bare patch of sand next to the Mediterranean seafront. To help them find a livelihood in their new home, the mayor of Tel Aviv allowed the group to set up a small market on the land they owned. Nobody believed that a bunch of formerly privileged refugees would make successful shopkeepers, but surprisingly, the market did well and soon spilled onto the adjoining streets of Kerem HaTeimanim–one of the oldest neighborhoods in Tel Aviv, founded in 1906 and populated by Yemenite Jews.

In 1920, Carmel was officially named the central city market of Tel Aviv, and for many years, it remained the main shopping destination for Tel Avivians. Today, the shuk is flanked by the beach on the west, fancy hotels on the south, and some of the most elegant neighborhoods all around.

The streets around it might be in the midst of massive gentrification, but the market itself is pretty shabby. Major renovation plans are under way, but we have mixed feelings about them–while the market can definitely use some cleaning up, many are worried it will lose much of its charm in the process.

The vibe

At eight o'clock in the morning, most of the stalls are still closed–like a true Tel Avivian, Carmel sleeps late. Toward noon, the market starts to fill up, mostly with people who come to eat rather than shop. Carmel today has everything you would expect to find in a big-city market–from designer clothing knockoffs to gorgeous (and quite pricey) fruits and vegetables, but its main draw, for visitors and locals alike, are the eateries that mushroom at such speed that it is impossible to keep track of them. In a way, the goings-on here mimic the hyperactive and dizzyingly eclectic Tel Aviv restaurant scene, but on a smaller and much cheaper scale. Opening a new restaurant in Tel Aviv has become insanely expensive, while setting up a casual eatery at one of the market stalls costs next to nothing. Every time we come, we discover another produce stall repurposed as a makeshift diner, which might serve anything from grilled *kofta kebabs* to Peruvian arepas. We would gladly recommend a paper-thin Druze pita smeared with labneh that we ate standing up at one of the back alleys or a crispy Turkish *lahmajun* we gobbled down at a pretty, bright blue stall on the market's main drag, but these places might not be around for the next visit. On the quiet little streets of the Yemenite Quarter, the pace is slower, and even new places look like they've been around for years. The food is local, homey, and unpretentious– Yemenite calf leg soup, beef patties in a gravy, stuffed vegetables, or a bowl of white rice topped with bean stew.

When to come

For a true Carmel experience, come on Wednesday, Thursday, or Friday and make sure you're hungry and in a mood to play.

M25 restaurant–prime cuts, hard-core offal, and addictive arayes (meat-stuffed pitas) **(ABOVE)**; Kofta kebab and handmade sausage at a typical market grill **(RIGHT)**; Herb stalls are always the prettiest at any shuk **(BELOW)**; Shuk HaCarmel is a favorite with tourists **(OPPOSITE)**

Our Favorite Spots

It's hard to recommend the cool little hot spots, because new ones pop up constantly. Here's a taste of the more established places at the shuk and in the neighboring Yemenite Quarter.

HABEN SHEL HASURI
("THE SON OF THE SYRIAN")
10 Hillel HaZaken Street

For twenty-five years, Zaki Mashaniya (aka the Syrian) ran one of the best hummus joints in the Yemenite Quarter. When he passed away in 2013, the place closed down, and a few years later his son opened a new restaurant a stone's throw from the original one. The décor is almost too elegant for a *hummusiya*, but the famous "hummus complet" (light creamy hummus, tahini, hard-boiled egg, warm fava bean stew) is just as good as it used to be when the father was in charge.

BOUREKAS TURKI ORIGINAL

39 HaCarmel Street

This no-frills *boureka* shop tucked away behind clothing stalls at the main entrance to the market is worth seeking out. *Bourekas* are baked on the premises and include classic pies stuffed with spinach, cheese, a combo of spinach and cheese, or potatoes. Without your even asking, the shopkeeper will cut up the warm pie you chose from the tray, add a sliced egg, and throw in some bitter olives and a tiny plastic container filled with spicy grated tomato salsa. If he offers you a glass of chilled *ayran* (a Turkish yogurt drink) to wash down your *boureka* breakfast, say yes—it's refreshing and delicious.

M25

Simtat HaCarmel 30

Don't let its scruffy looks fool you—M25 is a destination for carnivores from all over Israel. Choose the cuts that catch your fancy from the large glass display (go for the hardcore offal if you dare). Whatever you order, don't miss the *arayes*—crunchy golden grilled meat-stuffed pitas (see our recipe on page 304).

BEER BAZAAR

1 Rambam Street
36 Yishkon Street

If you're interested in the local microbrewery scene or just thirsty, this place is a must. Over one hundred beer brands are on offer, most of them local and artisanal, to drink on the spot or to take home. The place is so successful, it now has two outlets at the Carmel and one more at Mahane Yehuda Shuk.

Trays of freshly baked cheese baklava (**TOP**); *Radishes add a splash of red to a field of greens* (**ABOVE**); *Our favorite* bourekas *shop, tucked away at the entrance to the shuk* (**LEFT**); *Spices speak in three languages: Hebrew, English, and Russian* (**OPPOSITE TOP**); *A produce stall repurposed as a makeshift eatery* (**OPPOSITE BOTTOM**)

83

CHAPTER 3

Cauliflower and Eggplant: Our Vegetable Heroes

In a food culture where vegetables reign supreme, these two stunners stand out. One is snowy white and crisp; the other taut, shiny, and almost black. One peaks in winter; the other is at its best in summer. Cauliflower, native to the Mediterranean, has been around since Roman times; eggplant arrived in the region from India about a thousand years later but quickly assumed cult status on Levantine tables. Both are immensely versatile and can be cooked in countless ways, yet they are at their very best roasted and served whole.

Crispy Cauliflower with Bamba and Peanut Tahini Sauce

2 cups (320 g) rice flour

1 cup (240 ml) water

Vegetable oil, for deep-frying

1 large head cauliflower, cored and cut into 1-inch (2.5 cm) florets

½ cup Peanut Tahini Sauce (page 117), plus more as needed

One 5.6-ounce (160 g) bag Bamba, broken into pieces or sliced into coins

I wanted to create a cauliflower dish that was decidedly Israeli, and there's probably no food item more Israeli than Bamba—a crunchy, sweet-savory snack made from corn puffs and peanut butter. Every Israeli kid eats it growing up, and there's even scientific research suggesting that eating Bamba from a tender age is the reason for the relatively low occurrence of peanut allergies among kids in Israel.

In this dish, I pair the actual Bamba puffs with a peanut tahini sauce, which echoes the flavors. Look for Bamba at Middle Eastern markets, in the kosher sections of grocery stores, and at Trader Joe's! Israelis in the U.S. rejoiced when TJ's began importing their own Bamba and packaging it under their own label.

Whisk the rice flour with the water in a medium bowl to make a thin batter. Set aside.

Line a tray with paper towels. Fill a large wide pan with vegetable oil to a depth of about 2 inches (5 cm) (make sure the pan is at least 4 inches/10 cm deep, or deep enough to contain the oil once you add the cauliflower). Heat the oil over medium-high heat until it registers between 350° and 375°F (175° and 190°C) on a deep-fry thermometer. If you don't have a thermometer, give the oil a few minutes to get hot and then test it by adding a small drop of batter to the oil: If you see lots of small rapid bubbles, you're ready to go. Repeat this test throughout frying to make sure your oil is consistently hot.

Dip the cauliflower florets in the batter, making sure they're evenly coated. Working in batches to avoid overcrowding the pan, use a slotted spoon to slide the florets into the hot oil (frying too much at once can lower the oil temperature, which would make the cauliflower greasy). Give the florets a quick stir to make sure they don't stick together and fry until golden brown and just tender when poked with a paring knife, 3 to 4 minutes. Use the slotted spoon to transfer the fried cauliflower to the paper towels to drain. Repeat to cook the remaining cauliflower.

Transfer the hot cauliflower to a large serving bowl. Add the peanut tahini and toss to coat. Taste and add more tahini or salt if desired. Sprinkle with the Bamba pieces and serve at once.

Roasted Cauliflower with Parsley, Garlic, and Lemon Juice

1 large head cauliflower, cored and broken into 2-inch (5 cm) florets

3 tablespoons extra-virgin olive oil

1½ teaspoons kosher salt

2 or 3 garlic cloves, chopped

2 tablespoons chopped fresh parsley

Juice of 1 lemon

Roasting cauliflower brings out its sweet side, turning the edges golden and crisp. Just a bit of lemon juice, garlic, and parsley are all it needs to get a little dressed up. The trick is to season it right when it emerges from the oven—this way the flavors will be better absorbed.

Preheat the oven to 425°F (220°C). Line a baking sheet with parchment paper.

Toss the cauliflower with the oil and salt in a large bowl. Arrange on the prepared baking sheet in one layer and roast until the florets are tender and the tips are golden brown, about 30 minutes.

While the cauliflower is still hot, pile it into a bowl and toss with the garlic, parsley, and lemon juice (start with a small amount of juice and add more until you love the level of tanginess). Serve hot or at room temperature.

VARIATION
Use finely sliced fresh basil or chopped cilantro instead of–or in addition to–the parsley. A sprinkling of fried pine nuts would be tasty too.

Cauliflower
The New Eggplant?

In less than a decade, cauliflower has managed to reinvent itself, going from somewhat dreaded to celebrated in magazines, at home, and on restaurant menus. It didn't just happen in Israel; it happened pretty much everywhere. The obvious question is: Why have we changed our attitude toward a vegetable we previously regarded as bland and boring? But a more interesting question is: Why did it take us so long to realize how wonderful cauliflower can be if we put it in the center of the plate? It seems the cauliflower revealed its star quality when Israeli chefs started to serve whole roasted heads–meltingly soft and sweet inside and sexily scorched and crispy on the outside.

Today, cauliflower tends to pop up on almost every menu–sometimes whole, sometimes thickly sliced or broken into large florets, but almost always grilled or roasted (two methods that bring out its natural sweetness while retaining some of its bite). Roasted cauliflower is delicious with tahini, yogurt, or sour cream, but just a drizzle of extra-virgin olive oil and a sprinkle of salt are enough to bring out its beauty.

Cauliflower is so popular today that it looks like it's giving the eggplant–our king of local vegetables–a good run for its money. Eggplant and cauliflower do share some common qualities: They're both neutral-tasting and thus very versatile, both love roasting and grilling, and both look their best when served whole. But there is one major difference: Cauliflower is more user-friendly–no salt-curing required. Just make sure you pick a good one: snowy white, compact, and unblemished.

Whole Cauliflower Buried in Embers

2 to 3 tablespoons extra-virgin olive oil

2 garlic cloves, minced or grated

2 to 3 tablespoons chopped fresh herbs (oregano, thyme, rosemary, or a mix)

1 teaspoon honey

Kosher salt and freshly ground black pepper

1 small cauliflower

This is my contribution to the whole-cauliflower craze and an homage to Israeli childhood memories of get-togethers around a bonfire. Called *kumzitz* ("come, sit" in Yiddish), these gatherings always involved sing-alongs, telling outrageous stories (*chizbatim*), and baking potatoes (*kartoshkes*) at the bottom of the fire. Digging them up from the smoldering coals and burning your fingers in the process was part of the fun and somehow made them taste even more delicious. For this recipe, pick a small cauliflower that you can completely bury in the coals. If you're having a large party, make a few and cook them one by one. It doesn't take long.

Build a fire in a charcoal grill, using plenty of coals so you'll end up with a deep bed of embers.

Stir together the oil, garlic, herbs, and honey and season generously with salt and pepper in a small bowl. Put the cauliflower in the middle of a large sheet of aluminum foil, pour the herb mixture on top, and roll the cauliflower around, massaging the herb mixture into the cauliflower. Wrap the cauliflower in the foil to make a nice compact package.

When the coals are white with ash on the exterior and glowing red on the inside, push the wrapped cauliflower into the coals, under the rack, trying to get it as deep as you can. Unless you have a large, deep grill, you won't be able to bury it completely, but it's okay if it peeks out a bit.

Leave the cauliflower in the coals for 15 to 20 minutes, turning it occasionally with tongs. To check for doneness, prick the cauliflower through the foil with a skewer or a knife—it should go in and out without any resistance. Carefully lift out of the coals, set on a platter, unwrap (careful of the steam), and dig in.

SERVES 4 TO 6

Spice-Crusted Grilled Cauliflower Steaks

1 large cauliflower (look for one that's especially dense)

2½ tablespoons Shawarma Spice Rub (page 24)

1 teaspoon honey

¼ cup (60 ml) blended oil (equal parts extra-virgin olive oil and vegetable oil)

1 teaspoon kosher salt

Chilled yogurt

Tahini sauce (see pages 114–117)

We're used to seeing cauliflower in floret-form, so a whole head of cauliflower sliced into a neat slab—a "steak"—makes this dish a standout. Just be gentle with the steaks so the floret ends don't crumble. You'll still end up with a few pieces that don't hold together in slab form, but don't worry, just season them and let them come along for the delicious ride.

Trim the bottom part of the cauliflower so it sits upright on the counter. Using a large sharp knife, slice it horizontally into ¾-inch-thick (2 cm) slices. The slices on the sides will be smaller and might crumble—no need to worry about that. You should still be able to get 6 or 7 nice steaks.

Stir together the shawarma rub, honey, oil, and salt in a wide, shallow bowl or tray and coat the cauliflower steaks with the mixture, making sure they are coated on all sides. Let them sit in the mixture for 30 minutes to absorb the flavors.

To roast: Heat the oven to 400°F (200°C). Line one or two baking sheets with parchment paper. Arrange the steaks in a single layer. Roast until tender and nicely browned around the edges, about 30 minutes.

To grill: Make sure the grill is clean. Heat it to high heat.

Carefully arrange the cauliflower steaks on the grill. Grill until they are nicely browned and tender but retain some bite, 3 to 4 minutes on each side.

Serve at once, with some chilled yogurt or tahini sauce alongside.

The Righteous Eggplant

Close your eyes and try to conjure up the flavor of an eggplant. Not so easy, right? Now think about garlicky baba ghanoush or umami-packed caramel-glazed fried Asian eggplants. Mouthwatering. While eggplant doesn't have much of a distinct flavor of its own, its unique spongy texture enables it to absorb any flavor you want to imbue it with, making it incredibly versatile. But that texture also makes eggplant a high-maintenance vegetable.

If you want to cook like an Israeli, you must get friendly with what many consider the king of local vegetables. True, eggplant has devotees around the world, from Italy to India, but nowhere is it more prominent than in the Levant. Fried, oven-roasted, or burnt; whole, cubed, sliced, mashed, or stuffed—eggplants are prepared in countless ways and find their way into salads, stews, spreads, soups, pastries, and pickling jars. They pair beautifully with other defining flavors of our local cooking—olive oil, garlic, lemon, tahini, tomatoes, peppers, and chiles—but they'll welcome almost any flavor you can think of.

As with all fresh produce, everything starts with choosing a good eggplant. Pick eggplants that are relatively light for their size because they contain fewer seeds, and fewer seeds means less bitterness and less water.

Another common bit of advice is to choose relatively small eggplants—supposedly younger and better tasting. In Israel, however, the best eggplants you can find are very large, round

specimens, going by the name *baladi* (page 101), which translates to "heirloom," "local," or "native."

The skins should be richly colored and glossy, whether they're the typical purple variety, lighter lavender ones, or even white like some Thai eggplant varieties. The skin of a globe (sometimes called Italian) eggplant should be very dark purple—almost black—unblemished, shiny, and very taut. Check the stem, which should be green and fresh looking and clinging snugly to the eggplant.

Use your eggplants promptly. If you must store them, wrap them tightly in plastic wrap and keep in a dark place at room temperature no more than two days.

Prepping Eggplant

Before you start to cook, you'll need to prep the eggplants for optimal performance:

PEELING

If you're going to fry or roast eggplants, you first need to cut them into rounds, chunks, or planks—whatever your recipe calls for. But before cutting, you'll have to figure out whether to peel them.

During frying or roasting, the skin gets a bit leathery, adding an appealing texture, but too much can be unpleasant. Our advice is to go for the middle ground: Using a vegetable peeler, peel the eggplant from top to bottom in zebra stripes; this way, you'll have some skin, but not too much.

SALT-CURING

Eggplants are 90 percent water. To ensure successful frying, you need to draw out as much moisture as possible. Cut them as directed in the recipe, put them in a colander, and coat liberally with kosher salt (or other coarse salt), making sure all the pieces are covered. Curing time is 30 minutes minimum, but longer is better. Once cured (you will see beads of moisture forming on the surface), quickly rinse the eggplants under running water to remove the salt, then thoroughly pat them dry with a paper towel. Don't soak them or get them too wet—you want to remove the excess salt but you don't want the eggplant to suck back all the moisture you've just coaxed out.

Cooking Eggplant

In Israeli cuisine, we use three main techniques to cook an eggplant–frying, roasting in the oven, and charring over an open flame (or, in a pinch, under the broiler).

FRYING

Properly fried eggplants are delicious–sweet, creamy-soft, with a bit of crunch around the edges. The problem is that these spongy vegetables drink up a lot of oil, which is why curing is a must; otherwise, they'll spatter and won't fry nicely. To fry eggplants, fill a wide, deep skillet with about 1 inch (2.5 cm) of oil and heat the oil over medium-high heat for about 3 minutes. Without crowding the pan (work in batches, if needed), add the eggplant and fry for 2 to 3 minutes on each side. Lift one eggplant chunk or slice and check the bottom: If it's deep golden brown, it's time to flip. Every now and then, give them a gentle stir and shake the pan so the slices don't stick together. Using a slotted spoon or spatula, transfer the fried eggplants to a plate lined with paper towels to absorb excess oil. Fried eggplants can be used at once or stored in an airtight container in the fridge for a couple of days.

ROASTING

This is a simple and lighter alternative to frying, with less oil and much less hassle. Cut or slice the eggplant as directed in the recipe, sprinkle with olive oil and kosher salt, scatter on a baking sheet, and roast in a hot oven for about 30 minutes, until the pieces are soft, golden, and a bit crispy around the edges. Whether the eggplant needs to be cured prior to roasting is debatable. Our advice is that if you were able to procure a nice eggplant that is young and taut, with only a few seeds, you can skip the curing.

Roasted eggplants keep well in an airtight

container in the fridge for up to 1 week–just make sure you let them cool before storing them. A stash of charred eggplant can come in handy for countless dishes: tomato-based pasta sauces, shakshuka, salads, sandwiches, and so much more.

CHARRING

This is the sexiest way to cook an eggplant, because even before you add any seasonings or mix it with other ingredients, the eggplant already has a lovely smoky aroma. The method is easy, just a bit messy.

- *Charring on a gas stovetop:* Line your cooktop with aluminum foil. Place a wire rack over one of the burners and put an eggplant or two on the rack. Turn the heat to medium and char the eggplants over the flame, turning them as needed with tongs, until the skin is blackened and blistered on all sides. During roasting, the flesh should collapse, making the eggplant very soft. If you sense tougher spots, position the eggplant so the tougher spots get direct heat and leave to char for a few more minutes.

  Often the skin bursts during charring and some of the liquid oozes out–no need to worry, this is all part of the process (but aren't you glad you lined your cooktop?). Total cooking time for a typical large globe eggplant is 25 to 35 minutes; smaller varieties may cook faster. And in case you are wondering, there's absolutely no need to prick eggplants before putting them on the stove.

- *Charring under the broiler:* Line a baking sheet with aluminum foil, arrange the eggplant on the pan, and place it as close to the broiler as you can without actually touching the element to the eggplant. As one surface blackens, turn the eggplant until all surfaces are nicely charred and the eggplant is fully softened. With this broiler method, they'll soften up nicely but won't have as much of that heady aroma we like so much.

- *Charring on a grill:* If you have an outdoor grill going, use it! A charcoal or, ideally, hardwood grill fire will produce sublime results. (A gas grill will work too, though it won't give you that kiss of wood smoke.) Whenever you're having a barbecue, toss an eggplant or two on the grill and let them roast while you're grilling the rest of the menu.

Once properly charred, remove the eggplants from the heat source and transfer to a colander to cool a bit and drain some moisture. When cool enough to handle, peel them or slit them open and scoop out the flesh using a large spoon.

Drizzle the eggplant flesh with a bit of fresh lemon juice, which will keep it nicely light colored. Some cooks like to season the eggplant while still warm, feeling that it will absorb flavors better. Others prefer to put the peeled eggplant flesh in a colander for about an hour to let it drain even more moisture.

Charred eggplant flesh is extremely versatile. You can use it to make dips and salads (see some ideas on pages 98-100), fillings for pastry, soups (see page 230), or topping for shakshuka (see page 149), or you can serve it whole, with all kinds of goodies on top (see opposite).

WHOLE CHARRED EGGPLANT

At least four famous Israeli chefs claim they were the first to come up with this brilliant idea: Rather than chopping up eggplant flesh and mashing it with other ingredients to make a dip or a salad, you slit the whole charred eggplant open and pour the ingredients on top of its warm, soft flesh. In the midnineties, this was the "it" dish in the new wave of Israeli restaurants, so much so that at some point it became a cliché and almost disappeared from menus.

Which is a pity, because it's a great way to serve a charred eggplant–simple, delicious, visually stunning, and easy to do at home. You can pour some creamy tahini on top (and call it a deconstructed baba ghanoush); yogurt or tzatziki work great as well. Another option is to drizzle the eggplant with extra-virgin olive oil, squeeze on some fresh tomato pulp, and season with Maldon or other flaky, crunchy salt and freshly ground black pepper.

If serving whole unpeeled eggplant sounds messy or you're worried that some of the charred skin will make its way into your mouth, you can use a more elegant (but a bit more time-consuming) method: Carefully peel the eggplant, but leave it whole. If possible, leave the stem attached to the flesh. Put the peeled eggplant on a plate, then spoon the toppings right on top of or next to the eggplant.

Quick Charred Eggplant Spreads, Salads, and Dips

Peek into the display of a typical market deli and you'll see at least a dozen varieties of creamy spreads and dips (in Israel, we insist on calling them salads) based on charred eggplants. At one of the Balkan delis at the Levinsky shuk in Tel Aviv, we actually counted twenty! This is the best proof of how versatile eggplants are and why they are such a big part of local cooking.

To make any of these preparations, coarsely chop the charred eggplant flesh on a cutting board, transfer it to a bowl, and mash it with the other ingredients. The amounts given here are for 2 medium eggplants with a total weight of about 1½ pounds (680 g), which should yield about 1½ cups/340 g charred flesh, but do regard them only as guidelines.

Taste as you go, and play with seasonings according to what is most delicious to you. Serve the salads or dips as part of a meze table or on bruschetta or nice crusty sourdough bread.

Charred Eggplant with Garlic, Lemon, and Olive Oil. In Israel, we call this salad or dip *hatzil tev'i*–"natural eggplant." If you were lucky enough to find a perfect eggplant–sweet and with very few seeds–this simple salad is the perfect showcase for it. Mash the eggplant with 3 tablespoons delicate olive oil (or a mixture of olive oil and neutral-tasting vegetable oil), 2 to 3 tablespoons fresh lemon juice, 2 minced or grated garlic cloves, and kosher salt and freshly ground black pepper to taste.

Charred Eggplant with Tahini (Baba Ghanoush). This Levantine classic is perhaps the most famous eggplant salad in the world. Mash the eggplants with ½ cup (120 ml) raw tahini, 3 tablespoons fresh lemon juice, 2 minced or grated garlic cloves, and kosher salt and freshly ground black pepper to taste. If the mixture is too thick, add a bit of water, 1 to 2 tablespoons at a time, and mix until you have nice creamy texture. Garnish with toasted pine nuts and chopped fresh parsley before serving.

Charred Eggplant with Yogurt. Follow the procedure for Charred Eggplant with Tahini above, but instead of tahini, use 3 to 4 heaping tablespoons plain Greek-style yogurt. Because yogurt is quite acidic, go easy on the lemon juice or skip it altogether.

Charred Eggplant with Mayonnaise. It may not sound authentically Middle Eastern, but this is one of the most popular (and delicious) eggplant dips in Israel. Mash the eggplant flesh with 2 to 3 tablespoons of your favorite mayonnaise (homemade would be ideal), 2 minced or grated small garlic cloves, 2 tablespoons fresh lemon juice, a tiny drizzle of honey, and of course kosher salt to taste.

Charred Eggplant and Peppers (Kyopolou). This Balkan classic brings together two of the most beloved vegetables in the region. Roast a couple of red bell peppers along with the eggplants. Cool, peel, core, seed, and finely dice the peppers. Mix with the eggplants and add about ⅓ cup (80 ml) extra-virgin olive oil, 2 minced or grated garlic cloves, and kosher salt to taste. You can also add a grated tomato (see page 50), which will add a touch of acidity and bright color. If you want to spice it up, add a bit of harissa (see page 26), a pinch of cayenne, or a roasted, cored, seeded, and finely chopped small fresh chile.

Charred Eggplant and Pomegranate Salad. Mix chopped eggplant flesh with 2 tablespoons extra-virgin olive oil, 2 to 3 tablespoons chopped fresh parsley, 2 tablespoons fresh lemon juice, and kosher salt and freshly ground black pepper to taste. You can also add 1 to 2 tablespoons raw tahini to make the salad creamier. Just before serving, toss with ⅔ cup (120 g) pomegranate seeds and garnish with more parsley.

TIP *If the eggplant flesh is bitter, add a bit of honey. Start with about ½ teaspoon, taste, and see if you need more; you don't want it to taste sweet, you just want to balance out the bitterness.*

WHAT IS BALADI?

As you walk around Israeli markets, you'll hear vendors lauding their produce as *baladi*. The exact meaning of the word in Arabic is "from the country" or "from the village," and the closest equivalent in English would be "heirloom." True *baladi* produce comes from ancient local varieties, is cultivated by traditional methods, and is always seasonal.

The most famous representative of the *baladi* family is the eggplant. *Baladi* eggplants are large, usually round, and have deep rounded grooves that make them look like three-dimensional fans. These are hands-down the best eggplants you have ever tasted—without a trace of bitterness and very few seeds, but whether they are really "from the village" is another matter. Once a sought-after seasonal rarity, they are now grown commercially and are available all year—you can even buy *baladi* eggplant seeds on Amazon! Still, they are called *baladi*, and the name was even extended to one of the most iconic Israeli dishes—a whole charred eggplant, slit and drizzled with tahini (see page 97). In fact, more and more dishes and ingredients are now described (and promoted) as *baladi*, which has become a buzzword for anything local, traditional, and authentic.

Freekeh with Crunchy Seeds, Charred Eggplant, and Yogurt-Tahini Sauce

1 cup (155 g) freekeh

2 quarts (2 L) boiling water

1 teaspoon kosher salt, plus more as needed

3 tablespoons extra-virgin olive oil

3 tablespoons hulled pumpkin seeds (pepitas)

2 tablespoons pine nuts

2 tablespoons hulled sunflower seeds

2 tablespoons dried barberries or coarsely chopped unsweetened dried cranberries

4 tablespoons fresh lemon juice

1 large or 2 small eggplants, charred (see page 97)

1 jalapeño chile, roasted, cored, peeled, seeded, and chopped (see page 155)

½ cup (120 ml) Yogurt-Tahini Sauce (page 114)

Cilantro leaves

This dish matches the smoky aroma of charred eggplant with the equally smoky notes of freekeh (page 252), creating a harmonious balance of flavors. Its texture, however, offers an intriguing contrast between the creamy eggplant and the crunchy nuts and seeds. To me, it's the healthy upgrade to baba ghanoush.

Rinse the freekeh a few times in a bowl of cool water until the water runs clear. Transfer to a medium pot, pour in the boiling water, and add the salt. Bring the water back to a rapid boil and cook until the grains are tender but still have a little bit of bite, 20 to 25 minutes. Transfer to a colander and rinse under cold water to stop the cooking. Set aside.

Line a plate with paper towels. Heat about 1½ tablespoons of the oil in a small skillet over medium heat. Add the pumpkin seeds, reduce the heat to medium-low, and fry, shaking the skillet and stirring frequently, for 2 minutes. Add the pine nuts and sunflower seeds and fry for another minute. Remove from the heat as soon as the pine nuts start to change their color to golden. Spread the contents of the skillet over the paper towels to drain. Strain the oil and set aside.

Combine the freekeh with the nuts and seeds in a large bowl. Pour in the remaining 1½ tablespoons oil and the oil reserved from frying the seeds. Add the barberries and 3 tablespoons of the lemon juice, season with salt, and toss to combine. Taste again and adjust the seasoning.

Peel the eggplant or slit it open and scoop out the flesh. Coarsely chop the flesh and pile it into a large bowl. Sprinkle with the remaining 1 tablespoon lemon juice (this will make the color lighter) and add the jalapeño and sauce. Mix thoroughly.

Spread the eggplant on a serving plate, leaving a well in the center. Mound the freekeh salad in the well, and scatter on some cilantro leaves. Serve right away.

My Mom's Sweet-and-Sour Baked Eggplant

2 medium globe or 4 smaller Asian eggplants

Kosher salt

Vegetable oil, for frying

1 medium onion, thinly sliced

½ cup (120 ml) tomato paste

1½ cups (360 ml) water

1 tablespoon sugar

2 to 3 tablespoons fresh lemon juice

¼ teaspoon chile flakes

The Shabbat oven in an observant household like my mother's is always filled to capacity. An overnight main dish like Iraqi *tbit* (see page 190) takes up most of the space, with a pot of overnight bread like *kubaneh* (see page 315) filling much of the rest. Into any remaining space, my mom would tuck a couple of vegetarian sides, such as this sweet-and-sour melt-in-your-mouth delicacy.

You'll be frying the eggplant before baking it; for notes on frying eggplant, see page 95.

Slice the eggplants into ½-inch-thick (1.5 cm) rounds and transfer to a colander set in the sink or over a bowl. Cover the eggplants generously with salt and let sit for 30 to 45 minutes to draw out the water.

Preheat the oven to 210°F (100°C) if you want to bake the dish overnight, or to 250°F (120°C) for a 3-hour bake.

Rinse the eggplants thoroughly and pat dry with paper towels.

Line a plate or tray with paper towels. Fill a wide deep skillet with vegetable oil to a depth of about 1 inch (2.5 cm) and heat over medium-high heat for about 3 minutes, or until it reaches 350°F (175°C) on a deep-fry thermometer. Depending on the size of your pan, add about half the eggplant slices; they should be in one layer with some space between them. Fry for 2 to 3 minutes, then lift one eggplant slice and check the bottom—if it's deep golden brown, it's time to flip. Fry for 2 minutes on the second side, shaking the pan occasionally so they don't stick together and will fry evenly. Using a slotted spoon or a spatula, transfer the fried eggplant to the paper towels to drain excess oil. Repeat with the rest of the eggplant. Let the eggplant cool; don't wash the pan yet.

Add the onion slices to the remaining oil in the pan and fry gently over medium heat until soft, fragrant, and slightly golden, about 10 minutes. Drain on more paper towels to remove excess oil.

Line the bottom of a medium gratin or casserole dish with the onion. Sprinkle with salt. Layer the fried eggplant slices on top of the onion.

Whisk together the tomato paste, water, sugar, lemon juice, chile flakes, and salt to taste in a small bowl and pour the mixture over the eggplant. Cover the dish with a lid or aluminum foil and bake for at least 3 hours at 250°F (120°C) or overnight at 210°F (100°C).

Serve warm or at room temperature. Store in an airtight container in the fridge for up to 4 days.

Sabich Salad

1 large or 2 small globe eggplants

Kosher salt

4 large eggs

Vegetable oil, for frying

½ cup (120 ml) Amba Aioli (recipe follows)

1 cup (160 g) drained and rinsed canned chickpeas

½ pint (8 ounces/225 g) cherry tomatoes, halved

1 teaspoon fresh lemon juice

Fresh parsley or cilantro leaves, for garnish

This salad is my riff on the *sabich* sandwich, created by Iraqi Jews and madly popular in Israel (see page 109). The original *sabich* kiosk was right near my childhood home, and I grew up on the sandwiches. I introduced my American restaurant customers to *sabich* over a decade ago, and they're still one of my most popular dishes.

The salad has all you need for a well-balanced meal, and quite a filling one at that, but it does require a few steps: frying eggplants, boiling eggs, and whisking *amba* aioli. You can make everything in advance and toss the salad at the last moment. Just be sure to bring all the ingredients to room temperature; this will wake up the flavors that tend to dull in the fridge.

Eggplants fried to sweetness are the key ingredient in this otherwise straightforward salad. See tips for the perfect fried eggplant on page 95, and read more about *sabich*'s origins and tips for making *sabich* sandwiches on page 109.

Using a vegetable peeler, peel the eggplant from top to bottom to make zebra stripes. Cut it into ½-inch-thick (1.5 cm) rounds and transfer to a colander set in the sink or over a bowl. Cover the eggplant generously with salt and let sit for 30 to 45 minutes to draw out the water. Rinse thoroughly and pat dry with paper towels.

Meanwhile, follow the instructions for cooking soft-boiled eggs on page 158.

Line a plate with paper towels. Fill a wide deep skillet with vegetable oil to a depth of about 1 inch (2.5 cm) and heat over medium-high heat for about 3 minutes, or until it reaches 350°F (175°C) on a deep-fry thermometer. Depending on the size of your pan, add half or one-third of the eggplant slices; they should be in one layer with some space between them. Fry for 2 to 3 minutes, then lift one eggplant slice and check the bottom—if it's deep golden brown, it's time to flip. Fry for 2 minutes on the second side, occasionally shaking the pan so they don't stick together and will fry evenly. Using a slotted spoon or a spatula, transfer the fried eggplant to the paper towels to drain excess oil. Repeat with the rest of the eggplant. Let cool.

To assemble the salad: Spread a thin layer of the aioli over a serving platter. Layer the fried eggplant rounds on top of the aioli, then scatter the chickpeas and tomatoes on top. Drizzle with the lemon juice. Quarter the soft-boiled eggs lengthwise and arrange them on top of the vegetables. The yolks will be a bit jammy, and this is exactly what you want. Drizzle generously with the remaining aioli, garnish with parsley or cilantro, and serve.

Recipe continues

Sabich on Challah with Amba Aioli:
Ashkenazi Shabbat bread meets Iraqi
Shabbat breakfast sandwich, and
the result is delicious and great for
entertaining. Lightly toast thick slices
of challah to give them a nice crunch.
You can use whichever toasting method
you prefer: in a pan with some oil,
in the oven, or in a toaster. Spread
a thin layer of Amba Aioli on each
slice. Layer with 2 or 3 slices of fried
eggplant, followed by one egg (cut into
quarters), and a generous drizzle of the
aioli. Garnish with flaky salt and fresh
parsley or cilantro, and serve at once.

Amba Aioli

Use this brightly colored, slightly spicy
aioli as you would mayo: in sandwiches,
with french fries, or on roasted vegetables.
MAKES ABOUT 1¼ CUPS (300 ML)

2 tablespoons water or fresh orange juice,
plus more as needed

1 tablespoon honey

1 tablespoon amba powder (see page 71)

1 cup (240 ml) mayonnaise

¼ teaspoon ground turmeric

1 small garlic clove, minced or grated

Whisk together the water or orange juice,
honey, and amba powder until smooth.
Whisk in the mayonnaise, turmeric, and
garlic until fully combined. If you would
like to make it a bit thinner, whisk in more
water or orange juice, 1 tablespoon at
a time. Store in an airtight container in
the fridge for up to 5 days. If you skip the
garlic, you can store it even longer, up to
2 weeks. The aioli will get considerably
thicker in the fridge; just add a couple of
tablespoons of water or orange juice to
dilute it before using.

Sabich

The New Israeli Street Food

Found all over Israel and included in the lineup of iconic street foods, *sabich* was first created to feed some hungry bus drivers. It was called *sabich* after its inventor–an Iraqi Jew named Sabich Halabi. Mr. Halabi opened his first kiosk in the sixties, and as it was next to the final stop of a major bus route in the town of Ramat Gan, it catered to bus drivers. Prodded by the busmen's requests to add "something to eat" to the basic menu of coffee, sodas, and snacks, Mr. Halabi came up with the concept for a pita sandwich based on what his wife used to serve for Saturday breakfasts.

In Iraqi families, Shabbat breakfast consists of golden slices of fried eggplant, hard-boiled eggs, pickles, vegetables, hummus, tahini, pita, and the spicy bright yellow relish called *amba* (more on page 71). This colorful spread would await the family as they returned from morning prayers, so everybody could make their own Shabbat sandwich.

As years went by, the fame of the *sabich* sandwich spread–first in Ramat Gan (home to a large Jewish Iraqi community), then to the neighboring town of Givatayim, and eventually to almost every city across the country. Today *sabich* is mentioned in one breath with falafel, *bourekas*, or shawarma as the leading Israeli street food. Many cafés and restaurants feature elevated versions of *sabich*, from eggplant and eggs on a slice of sourdough bruschetta to deconstructed *sabich* salad.

Here are tips for making an authentic and delicious *sabich* sandwich:

- Pry open a fresh pita with a small knife, creating a pocket with a large opening. Hold it flat in one hand, squishing the sides to widen the opening.

- Smear the insides of the pita with a thin layer of hummus (see page 121).

- Add a slice of fried eggplant (see page 95) and push it down to the bottom.

- Add a couple of tablespoons of Israeli Salad (page 42). Then layer on two or three more slices of eggplant, taking care to distribute them evenly inside the pita.

- Slice a hard-boiled egg using an egg slicer, trying to keep the egg intact on one end, and open it up like a fan. Layer the sliced egg on top of the eggplant, flattening it a bit and pushing it slightly toward the bottom.

- Depending on your appetite (and the size of the pita) you can add another spoonful of salad and/or another slice of eggplant.

- Finally, drizzle everything generously with tahini (see pages 114–117) and sparingly with *amba* (see page 71), and add a sprinkle of chopped fresh parsley.

A good sabich sandwich is overstuffed and will probably drip as you eat it–make sure you have lots of napkins on hand.

If you are entertaining, it is best to adopt the Jewish Iraqi breakfast routine: Arrange all the ingredients on the table and let your guests make their own sandwiches. Make sure your pitas are fresh and warm–homemade is best (see page 312)!

The making of a sabich sandwich at Aricha Sabich near Mahane Yehuda Market in Jerusalem.

CHAPTER 4

Tahini and Chickpeas: Our National Obsession

We can't imagine our kitchen without these Levantine treasures. Tahini—a nutty, creamy sesame paste—is our key special ingredient, used in countless ways to make spreads, dressings, glazes, and sweets. Make a jar of good tahini a permanent fixture in your pantry.

Deliciously earthy chickpeas pop up in salads, soups, stews, and savory pastries. And tahini and chickpeas join forces in hummus, our ultimate cult food.

Great Tahini

A Very Simple Art

Almost everything tastes better with tahini. We literally can't imagine our cooking without this rich, velvety sesame paste, and once you invite it into your kitchen, there is a good chance you won't either. We pour tahini over salads and serve it with roasted vegetables, fish, or meat; we cook with it, use it to make salad dressings, and spread it on sandwiches (tastier and healthier than mayo); and we even use it to make pastries and desserts.

You can turn raw tahini into a delicious sauce or dip in just minutes, so there is absolutely no reason to use store-bought sauces or dips. They never have that pure, lovely taste of freshly made tahini sauce, and they're usually overseasoned and loaded with all sorts of mysterious-sounding additives.

The most important thing is working with only the best-quality raw tahini. Israel boasts a spectacular array of tahinis (the best ones come from the area of Nablus, a city on the West Bank, considered the world capital of tahini and halva). Luckily, some of them are now available outside the region. Excellent brands include Har Bracha, Al Arz, Yona (Dove), and American-made Soom. To make sure you're using good tahini, taste the paste straight from the jar—the flavor of the raw paste might be a bit overwhelming if you're not used to it, but you shouldn't sense any bitterness or unpleasant aftertaste. Check the texture, which should be silky-smooth, not grainy. It will be fine in the cupboard for several weeks. Make sure you shake the jar or stir the tahini before starting on a recipe, as the oil and the solids tend to separate.

FRESH HERB AND PISTACHIO
TAHINI SAUCE

CLASSIC
TAHINI SAUCE

RED PEPPER AND
CHILE TAHINI SAUCE

HONEY-SOY
TAHINI SAUCE

Classic Tahini Sauce

**MAKES ABOUT 1 CUP
(240 ML)**

1 cup (240 ml) best-quality
raw tahini

¼ cup (60 ml) fresh lemon
juice, plus more to taste

Ice water

½ teaspoon kosher salt,
plus more as needed

1 small garlic clove, grated
or minced

Good-quality raw tahini can be used straight from the jar, but to elevate it into a sauce, you need only salt, lemon, and a touch of garlic. If I know I'm going to use the sauce over the course of the next few days, I won't add any garlic to the main batch; I'll stir in some fresh to order.

Pour the raw tahini into a medium bowl and add the lemon juice. Mix with a fork or a whisk until the color turns a shade lighter. The texture may become weird and lumpy; don't worry, this is part of the process.

Gradually whisk in about ½ cup (120 ml) ice water. The sauce should turn smooth, velvety, and almost white. The ½ cup (120 ml) water will make a thick dip; whisk in another ¼ cup (60 ml) or so to make a thinner sauce, if you'd like. Keep tinkering with water, lemon juice, and tahini until you get a consistency and flavor you like.

Whisk in the salt and garlic; taste and adjust your seasonings.

TIP *If you're making a large batch, use a food processor or blender to get a lovely, fluffy tahini spread. In this case, instead of ice water, use a couple of ice cubes to keep the temperature down while the motor is running, which will improve the color and the texture.*

Yogurt-Tahini Sauce

**MAKES ABOUT 1 CUP
(240 ML)**

⅓ cup (80 ml) thick yogurt

⅓ cup (80 ml) best-quality
raw tahini

¼ cup (60 ml) water

1 tablespoon fresh lemon
juice

½ teaspoon kosher salt,
plus more as needed

½ garlic clove, minced or
grated

Pinch of freshly ground
black pepper

The preparation couldn't be easier, and the result is brilliant. The color is light ivory, and the texture is creamy with a slight tang from the yogurt and a subtle nuttiness from tahini. You can just mix raw tahini with yogurt and add a bit of salt to taste. The ratio is up to you—mostly yogurt with some tahini, or vice versa. If the yogurt is thick, you may want to add some water; if it is mild tasting, lemon juice will brighten up the flavor. The following version has both, but you can balance the flavors any way you like. Use it just the way you would use tahini dip or yogurt, for that matter—it is very versatile.

Pour the yogurt into a small bowl. Add the tahini, water, lemon juice, salt, garlic, and black pepper and whisk to combine. Taste and adjust the seasoning to your liking.

Red Pepper and Chile Tahini Sauce

2 large red bell peppers,
  roasted, cored, seeded,
  and peeled (see page 155)

1 medium Fresno or other
  medium-hot fresh red
  chile, roasted, cored,
  seeded, and peeled
  (see page 155)

1 cup (240 ml) best-quality
  raw tahini

¼ cup (60 ml) fresh lemon
  juice, plus more as needed

1 medium garlic clove, finely
  grated or minced

1 teaspoon honey

1 tablespoon sweet paprika

1½ teaspoons kosher salt,
  plus more as needed

½ cup (120 ml) ice water

Roasted red peppers add bright color and a sweet flavor to this tahini. I serve it with savory pastry, roasted vegetables, or grilled lamb, and it makes a brilliant sandwich spread.

Put the bell peppers and the chile in a food processor or a blender, add the tahini, lemon juice, and garlic, and puree until completely smooth. Add the honey, paprika, and salt and pulse again to blend. With the motor running, slowly stream in the ice water and process until smooth. Taste and adjust the seasoning. Store in an airtight container in the refrigerator for up to 3 days.

Honey-Soy Tahini Sauce

1 cup (240 ml) best-quality
  raw tahini

1 medium garlic clove

1½ teaspoons kosher salt,
  plus more as needed

2 tablespoons fresh lemon
  juice

2 tablespoons rice vinegar

3 tablespoons honey

2 tablespoons soy sauce

2 teaspoons toasted
  sesame oil (optional)

¼ cup plus 2 tablespoons
  (90 ml) ice water

Consider this recipe proof of tahini's versatility. Add some soy sauce and rice vinegar, and it immediately tastes more Asian than Middle Eastern. This is a true go-to sauce for me, which I use as a dressing for crunchy vegetable salads or drizzle over roasted squash and eggplant.

Put the tahini, garlic, salt, lemon juice, vinegar, honey, soy sauce, and sesame oil (if using) in a food processor and process briefly to combine. With the motor running, slowly stream in the ice water until the spread turns thick, velvety, and smooth. Taste and adjust the seasoning. If not using at once, store in an airtight container in the fridge for up to 2 days.

Fresh Herb and Pistachio Tahini Sauce

1½ teaspoons chopped fresh rosemary

1½ teaspoons chopped fresh thyme

2 medium garlic cloves

1 jalapeño chile, cored, seeded, and chopped

¼ cup (30 g) shelled pistachios, toasted

¼ cup plus 2 tablespoons (90 ml) fresh lemon juice, plus more as needed

1 teaspoon kosher salt, plus more as needed

Freshly ground black pepper

1 cup (240 ml) best-quality raw tahini

¾ cup (180 ml) ice water

½ cup (25 g) fresh parsley leaves

½ cup (20 g) fresh cilantro leaves

Tahini mixed with finely chopped fresh parsley is one of its most popular variations. This version adds more nuances of flavor, with several kinds of herbs and toasted pistachios to enhance tahini's natural nuttiness.

Put the rosemary, thyme, garlic, jalapeño, pistachios, lemon juice, salt, several twists of pepper, and the tahini in a food processor and puree until completely smooth. With the motor running, slowly stream in the ice water and process until smooth. Add the parsley and cilantro and pulse again a few times until they are broken down into green flecks. Taste and adjust the seasoning. If not serving at once, store in an airtight container in the fridge for up to 2 days.

TAHINI, BANANA, AND DATE SHAKE

Craving something sweet and super nutritious? Make this delicious shake. Put 2 ripe bananas in a blender, add a couple of pitted dates, 2 to 3 tablespoons raw tahini, and 1 cup (240 ml) cold almond milk (you may want to add a few ice cubes too). If you like your shake a bit sweeter, add more dates or 1 tablespoon honey or silan. Blend until smooth. SERVES 2

Peanut Tahini Sauce

½ to ⅔ cup (120 to 180 ml) ice water

1 teaspoon finely grated lemon zest

¼ cup (60 ml) fresh lemon juice

1 medium garlic clove, finely grated or minced

1 teaspoon kosher salt, plus more as needed

½ cup (120 ml) best-quality raw tahini

¼ cup (35 g) chopped unsalted peanuts

3 tablespoons chopped fresh parsley

Peanuts and sesame have a delicious affinity, so the combination is a natural. And, of course, peanuts do here what they do so well—add crunch!

Whisk together ½ cup (120 ml) of the ice water, the lemon zest, lemon juice, garlic, and salt in a medium bowl. Add the tahini and whisk until smooth and creamy, with the consistency of mayonnaise. The mixture may look curdled at first, but keep whisking! Add the remaining ice water, 1 tablespoon at a time, if you need to. Stir in the peanuts and parsley. Taste and adjust the seasoning. If not using at once, store in an airtight container in the fridge for up to 2 days.

SWEET TAHINI SPREAD

Every tahini lover knows about this quick fix to satisfy your sweet tooth. Grab some good-quality raw tahini and mix it with honey, silan, or maple syrup. It will turn into a thick, sweet paste similar in texture to peanut butter. As with peanut butter, you can spread it on bread, waffles, or pancakes. For every 1 cup (240 ml) tahini, add between ¼ and ½ cup (60 to 120 ml) maple syrup, honey, or silan, depending on how sweet you want it.

Hummus for Beginners

If you're an Israeli, you must love hummus, and we know very few Israelis who do not. While no Israeli in his right mind would claim that hummus is anything but a Levantine classic and one of the hallmarks of Palestinian cooking, the status it has in Israel is unprecedented anywhere in the region. In Israel, it is the ultimate cult food, a religion of sorts. There are guides for best places to "mop up" hummus, and blogs extolling the virtues of mousselike Jerusalem hummus versus chunky Galilean ones. There is hummus aristocracy—half a dozen nationally acclaimed places worthy of a special trip and hundreds of "secret" spots known only to locals.

A typical *hummusiya* ("hummus joint" in Hebrew) is usually nothing more than a hole-in-the-wall swimming with the heady aroma of cooking chickpeas, which has a Pavlovian effect on hummus addicts. Another sign of an authentic

hummusiya is that freshly made hummus, with a few traditional add-ins, is the only dish on offer.

Tradition is the name of the game here. In a food culture where chefs are expected to invent new dishes on a daily basis, hummus is off-limits to innovation. There are certain, very specific ways to prepare, serve, and eat hummus, and you don't want to mess with them!

One of those ways is with pita. Eating hummus with a fork or dipping vegetable crudités into the chickpea mash is for weaklings and calorie-counters. True hummus buffs attack a plate of hummus with gusto and a thick slab of warm pita. You can ask for a hard-boiled egg, which will make your hummus meal even more substantial. A side of pickles, cracked bitter olives, and wedges of raw onion (the latter may sound extreme, but its clean, sharp taste goes beautifully with hummus) will show up without your even asking.

In spite of their passionate love affair with hummus, Israelis rarely make it at home. Not because making hummus is complicated (it is not), but because it does require a few steps that call for planning, and the shelf life of homemade hummus is short. So unless we're cooking for a crowd, we tend to outsource from our favorite hummus joint, which is usually just a short drive away. Obviously, this is not the case for those who don't reside in Israel, so roll up your sleeves and get to work.

Here are the basics you need to know to make delicious fresh hummus in your kitchen.

The Chickpeas

The flavor and texture of your hummus is dependent on the quality and freshness of the chickpeas. In Israel, a smaller variety (known as Spanish) is considered the most suitable for hummus (large ones are used for salads and stews). If you can find smaller chickpeas, go for them. But far more important than their size is their freshness. Stale chickpeas have a dusty flavor, won't cook evenly, and may never reach the creamy softness that we're after. It's almost impossible to tell whether your chickpeas are fresh until you cook them, by which time it is too late. Your best bet is to check the expiry date on the package, if there is one, and buy at places with a fast turnover.

SOAKING

Like most pulses (dried beans or peas), chickpeas require long soaking in a large amount of cold water. Twelve hours is the minimum; twenty-four is even better. Many hummus buffs change the water once or twice during soaking, which allegedly eliminates unpleasant aftertastes. Adding a pinch of baking soda is a common practice that speeds up the soaking process, though some cooks believe that it harms the chickpeas' nutrients (others claim the opposite). From our experience, adding a pinch of baking soda during both soaking and cooking is a good policy to ensure that chickpeas soften properly.

BOILING

Once soaked, rinse the chickpeas again and boil them in a large amount of water. How long depends primarily on the quality and variety of the chickpeas. The average time is about 1½ hours, but don't be discouraged if your batch takes longer. Keep cooking until they are so soft they almost fall apart and a chickpea squeezed lightly between your fingertips oozes creamy paste, but not

so long that they have a porridge-y consistency. That would mean the chickpeas are waterlogged (this would dilute the flavor and texture of your hummus).

REMOVING THE SKINS

Skins are another source of heated arguments, which, as you may have noticed by now, are a major part of hummus culture. In a nutshell: Getting rid of the skins will make your hummus smooth and "airy as a cloud" (say the supporters), but it will also weaken the flavor and make the hummus less nutritious (say the opponents). One thing all parties agree on is that peeling the tiny beans takes forever.

Don't stress about the skins. If you've cooked the chickpeas properly, the skins will be tender enough to be processed smoothly. Go ahead and skim off the easy targets that float to the surface during cooking, but otherwise, skins are just fine.

MAKING AHEAD

It takes a long time to soak and cook chickpeas, but fortunately, cooked chickpeas freeze nicely; make a large batch and freeze some in zip-top bags.

CHILLING

Now that your chickpeas are cooked to perfection, can you finally mash them to make hummus? Not just yet–you must chill them first. This is really important: Chickpeas are extremely sensitive to spoilage. The motor and the blades of the food processor heat them even more. Chill them completely before proceeding by placing them in a bowl set in a larger bowl filled with ice and water or by refrigerating them.

The Tahini

The second most important ingredient in hummus is tahini–your hummus will only be as good as the tahini you use to make it. Luckily some very good tahinis are now available outside of the Middle East (see page 112). The chickpea-tahini ratio is a matter of taste: More tahini will yield a creamier, richer hummus; less means your hummus will have a more pronounced chickpea flavor and fewer calories (most of the calories in hummus come from the tahini).

Seasoning

An acidic element is crucial to offsetting the earthy flavors of both chickpeas and tahini. Commercial hummus makers use citric acid, because it is cheap and prolongs the shelf life, but in terms of flavor, there is no substitute for fresh lemon juice.

Salt is mandatory, and some people add cumin and a touch of garlic. If you do, make sure you serve your hummus promptly. Garlic can become overpowering during storage. Olive oil is not a must for the texture (tahini is oily enough), but it does add a nice touch. Go for a fruity extra-virgin olive oil with a lot of personality.

Method

For centuries, hummus was mashed in a large wooden mortar and pestle (which is why you can hear a percussive beat at some authentic hummus places).

Nowadays, most hummus makers use a food processor. You can mash all the ingredients together, or you can start with just a small amount of tahini, lemon, and salt, then taste and add more as you go. It's worth remembering that not all tahinis and chickpeas taste the same. If, for example, you were lucky enough to stumble upon exceptionally tasty chickpeas, you may want to let their flavor take the lead and go easy on tahini. Usually a small amount of water is added to the mix. Some people use chickpea cooking liquid, but we prefer fresh water.

Storage, Uses, and Serving

Now that your hummus is ready, you can either serve it promptly or store it in an airtight container in the fridge–but for no more than two days!

In Israeli home kitchens, hummus is a dish in itself but also a go-to sandwich spread. Pita slathered with a generous dollop of hummus with a sliced pickle is a favorite kindergarten snack; pita with hummus and schnitzel is another local favorite, and street-food vendors will offer to line the inside of your pita with hummus before stuffing it with falafel or shawarma.

You can serve hummus on its own in a bowl, but adding some warm cooked chickpeas will make it so much better and compensate for the fact that the actual puree is cold. Other traditional toppings include *ful* (slow-cooked fava bean stew), tahini spread, and fried ground meat (see Hummus im Bassar, page 124).

Proper hummus is not spicy, but the finished dish can definitely use some heat, in the form of small fresh or pickled chiles, a dollop of a spicy condiment like *s'chug* (see page 25), or *tatbila*–a quick dressing made from chiles, cumin, garlic, and lemon juice. Chermoula (page 33), which is moderately spicy and lemony, is a really good match for hummus. Whichever spicy element you choose, top your hummus with it at the last moment before serving.

Perfectly Balanced Hummus

Simmering soaked dried chickpeas with a little baking soda helps soften them, resulting in smooth, silky hummus, especially if you take the time to skim off any chickpea skins that rise to the surface.

2½ cups (460 g) dried chickpeas, preferably small ones

1 teaspoon baking soda

¾ cup (180 ml) best-quality raw tahini

½ cup plus 2 tablespoons (150 ml) fresh lemon juice

2¼ teaspoons kosher salt

Freshly ground black pepper

1 teaspoon ground cumin

2 garlic cloves, smashed

3 tablespoons extra-virgin olive oil, plus more for drizzling

6 tablespoons (90 ml) ice water

Chopped fresh parsley (optional), for garnish

Sweet paprika (optional), for garnish

Classic Tahini Sauce (page 114; optional), for serving

Harissa, store-bought or homemade (page 26; optional), for serving

Pick through the chickpeas and discard any little stones (yes, that can happen) or peas that look very irregular in color or in shape. Rinse the chickpeas thoroughly under cold water. Transfer the chickpeas to a large bowl and add cold water to cover them by 3 to 4 inches (7.5 to 10 cm). Add ½ teaspoon of the baking soda. Soak for at least 12 hours and up to 24 hours.

Drain and rinse the soaked chickpeas under cold water until the water runs clear. Transfer the chickpeas to a large pot, pour in 3 quarts (3 L) cold water, and add the remaining ½ teaspoon baking soda. Bring to a boil over high heat, reduce the heat to medium, and cook at a lively simmer, uncovered, for 1 to 1½ hours. Use a slotted spoon to skim off any skins on the surface (the more skins you are able to remove, the smoother your hummus will be).

When the chickpeas are fully tender, but not yet getting at all mushy, scoop out about 1 cup (160 g) and set aside to use as a garnish. Cook the rest of the chickpeas until they are completely soft, slightly broken down, and can easily be smooshed with your fingers, another 20 minutes.

Fill a large bowl halfway with ice and water and set another large bowl on top. Drain the chickpeas and transfer them to the bowl. You should have about 5 cups (800 g, plus the reserved 1 cup/160 g). Let the chickpeas cool completely. Or, if you are not in a hurry, transfer the chickpeas to the fridge and chill them for a few hours or up to overnight. If you're so inclined, you can pick off more skins at this point.

Put the chilled chickpeas in a food processor and add the tahini, lemon juice, salt, a few twists of pepper, the cumin, garlic, olive oil, and 2 tablespoons of the ice water. Puree until smooth. If the hummus seems too thick, add the remaining ice water a bit at a time and puree until smooth. Taste and adjust the seasoning. (If not serving at once, transfer to an airtight container and refrigerate for up to 2 days.)

To serve, gently reheat the reserved 1 cup (160 g) cooked chickpeas. Spoon the hummus into shallow serving bowls (you may plate your hummus individually or serve it family-style), spreading it around the rim of the bowls, leaving a crater in the center. Add the warm cooked chickpeas to the crater (2 tablespoons for an individual serving or up to the full 1 cup/160 g for a large plate). Sprinkle with parsley, drizzle with oil, and very lightly dust with paprika. Serve at once with optional tahini and harissa.

PERFECTLY BALANCED
HUMMUS WITH WARM
CHICKPEAS, HARISSA, AND
CLASSIC TAHINI SAUCE

HUMMUS IM PITRIYOT

HUMMUS IM BASSAR

Hummus im Bassar

Hummus with Spiced Beef

2 tablespoons extra-virgin olive oil

1 medium yellow onion, finely diced

¼ teaspoon ground turmeric

½ teaspoon sweet paprika

1 teaspoon baharat, store-bought or homemade (see page 22)

1 teaspoon ground cumin

¼ teaspoon ground cinnamon

1 teaspoon kosher salt, plus more as needed

Freshly ground black pepper

1 pound (455 g) ground beef

3 tablespoons chopped fresh parsley

3 tablespoons pine nuts, fried or toasted (see page 69; optional)

2 to 3 cups (480 to 720 ml) Perfectly Balanced Hummus (page 121)

This is one of the most popular hummus dishes, so much so that at some point it even made its way to bars and pubs. I love the hummus paired with juicy, hot, robustly spiced meat, and I use this meat mixture in a lot of dishes, especially stuffed squash.

Heat the oil in a large skillet over high heat. Add the onion and cook until lightly browned, about 2 minutes. Reduce the heat to medium-low and sauté until golden brown, 7 to 8 minutes. Add the turmeric, paprika, baharat, cumin, cinnamon, salt, and a few twists of pepper and sauté for another 1 to 2 minutes. Increase the heat to medium and add the beef. Cook, stirring and crumbling the meat with a fork, for 3 to 4 minutes. Reduce the heat to medium and cook, stirring occasionally, until the meat is nicely browned, about another 5 minutes. Stir in the parsley and pine nuts (if using). Taste and add more salt or pepper to make it lively.

Spread the hummus on individual plates or a large serving plate and make a crater in the center. Spoon the warm meat topping into the crater and serve at once.

Hummus im Pitriyot

Hummus with Savory Mushrooms

2 tablespoons extra-virgin olive oil

1 large yellow onion, halved and thinly sliced

6 ounces (170 g) button or wild mushrooms, wiped clean with a paper towel, trimmed, and quartered

½ teaspoon kosher salt

Freshly ground black pepper

1 large garlic clove, minced or finely grated

½ teaspoon chopped fresh rosemary

½ teaspoon chopped fresh thyme

¼ teaspoon ground cumin

2 to 3 cups (480 to 720 ml) Perfectly Balanced Hummus (page 121)

Though not part of the authentic hummus set, this Israeli recipe was all the rage in the 1970s, even though fresh mushrooms were something Israelis read about in children's books and canned mushrooms were the sad reality. Luckily, fresh, locally grown mushrooms are available everywhere today, and I like to include some "wild" varieties such as chanterelles and oyster mushrooms, which bring even more personality to the dish.

Heat the oil in a large skillet over high heat. Add the onion and cook for a minute or two to brown a bit (but take care that the slices don't burn and turn bitter). Reduce the heat to medium-low and sauté until soft and golden, 7 to 8 minutes. Increase the heat to medium-high, add the mushrooms, and season with the salt and several twists of pepper. Sauté until the mushrooms are soft and golden brown, 8 to 10 minutes. Add the garlic, rosemary, thyme, and cumin and sauté until fragrant, another 1 to 2 minutes.

Spread the hummus on individual plates or on a large serving plate and make a crater in the center. Spoon the warm mushrooms into the crater and serve at once.

Masabacha

Whole Chickpeas in Warm, Spicy Tahini Sauce

2 cups (370 g) dried chickpeas

½ teaspoon baking soda

¼ cup (60 ml) boiling water

¾ cup (180 ml) best-quality raw tahini

1 teaspoon kosher salt

DRESSING

¼ cup (60 ml) extra-virgin olive oil

3 medium garlic cloves, minced or grated

½ jalapeño chile, cored, seeded, and finely chopped

¼ cup (60 ml) fresh lemon juice

1 teaspoon ground cumin

Kosher salt and freshly ground black pepper

FOR GARNISH

Chopped fresh parsley

Extra-virgin olive oil

Here, the same ingredients used in hummus yield a much different result. Instead of mashing cooked chickpeas and tahini into a smooth paste, they are briefly warmed together and served with a tangy cumin dressing. Those who prefer their hummus warm and spicy will love this version.

Pick through the dried chickpeas and discard any little stones (yes, that can happen) or peas that look very irregular in color or in shape. Rinse the chickpeas thoroughly under cold water. Transfer the chickpeas to a large bowl and add cold water to cover them by 3 to 4 inches (7.5 to 10 cm). Add ¼ teaspoon of the baking soda. Soak for at least 12 and up to 24 hours.

Drain and rinse the soaked chickpeas under cold water until the water runs clear. Transfer the chickpeas to a large pot, pour in 3 quarts (3 L) cold water, and add the remaining ¼ teaspoon baking soda. Bring to a boil over high heat, reduce the heat to medium, and cook at a lively simmer, uncovered, for 1 to 1½ hours. Use a slotted spoon to skim off any skins that float to the surface. The chickpeas are ready when they are completely soft, slightly broken down, and can easily be smooshed with your fingers. Drain the chickpeas thoroughly and return them to the pot.

Add the boiling water, tahini, and salt. Cook over medium heat for a couple of minutes, just until the chickpeas are warmed through.

Meanwhile, make the dressing: Whisk together the oil, garlic, jalapeño, lemon juice, and cumin in a small bowl and season with salt and pepper.

Ladle the warm chickpea mixture into a large serving bowl or individual plates and pour the dressing over the top. Garnish with chopped parsley and a generous drizzle of oil and serve at once.

TIP Masabacha *is delicious only when it is really warm, so many hummus makers keep the cooked chickpeas and tahini over a double boiler until serving and add the dressing at the last moment.*

Fatteh

Chickpeas with Toasted Pita in Warm Yogurt Sauce

2 cups (370 g) dried chickpeas

½ teaspoon baking soda

3 medium garlic cloves

2 pitas

1 teaspoon ground cumin

1 teaspoon kosher salt

¼ teaspoon freshly ground black pepper

2 cups (480 ml) whole-milk Greek yogurt (we like Fage)

3 tablespoons extra-virgin olive oil

¼ cup (35 g) pine nuts, toasted

Fresh lemon juice

¼ cup (13 g) coarsely chopped fresh parsley, for garnish

If *masabacha* (see page 126) is the sister recipe of hummus, *fatteh* is its distant cousin. Toasted pita chunks are layered with soft chickpeas and topped with warm yogurt laced with olive oil. The result is an unexpectedly delicious mishmash of flavors and textures. Part of the charm of this dish is that it evolves during the meal. When you bring a plate of *fatteh* to the table, the pita chunks start out very crunchy, but they gradually soften as they absorb the warm yogurt mixture (though they still retain some of their crisp).

Pick through the dried chickpeas and discard any little stones (yes, that can happen) or peas that look very irregular in color or in shape. Rinse the chickpeas thoroughly under cold water. Transfer the chickpeas to a large bowl and add cold water to cover them by 3 to 4 inches (7.5 to 10 cm). Add ¼ teaspoon of the baking soda. Soak for at least 12 and up to 24 hours.

Drain and rinse the soaked chickpeas under cold water until the water runs clear. Transfer the chickpeas to a large pot, pour in 3 quarts (3 L) cold water, and add 2 garlic cloves and the remaining ¼ teaspoon baking soda. Bring to a boil over high heat, reduce the heat to medium, and cook at a lively simmer, uncovered, for about 1 hour, until the chickpeas are soft but not mushy.

While the chickpeas are cooking, preheat the oven to 350°F (175°C). Line a baking sheet with parchment paper.

Split each pita into two discs and slice the discs into 1½-inch-wide (4 cm) strips. Arrange them on the prepared baking sheet and toast in the oven until very crunchy and deep golden brown, 15 to 20 minutes.

Reserve about 3 tablespoons of the chickpea cooking liquid, drain the chickpeas, and transfer to a large bowl. Pick out and discard the garlic. Add the cumin, salt, and pepper and toss to combine.

Warm the yogurt in a small pan, but don't bring it to a boil! (That would curdle it.) Remove from the heat and whisk in 2 tablespoons of the oil and the reserved chickpea cooking liquid.

Toss the pita chunks with the chickpeas and yogurt mixture and pile into a bowl. Drizzle with the remaining 1 tablespoon oil and grate the remaining garlic clove over the top. Sprinkle with the pine nuts, squeeze over some fresh lemon juice, and garnish with the parsley. Serve promptly.

Crispy Za'atar-Spiced Chickpeas

Vegetable oil,
  for deep-frying

Two 15-ounce (425 g) cans
  chickpeas

1 cup (160 g) rice flour

4 teaspoons za'atar, store-
  bought or homemade
  (page 24)

¾ teaspoon kosher salt

Crunchy on the outside and tender inside, these deep-fried chickpeas are a fantastic snack. Delicious freshly fried, they also make a great pantry item, which I like to toss in salads and soups as an alternative to croutons. Although canned chickpeas don't taste as good as the ones you soak and cook at home, they work just fine for this recipe and save a lot of time. If you want to use dried, cook them as directed on page 119, but remember to skip the baking soda and shorten the cooking time to about 1 hour so they're tender but not mushy.

Line a plate with paper towels. Fill a wide medium pot with vegetable oil to a depth of about 1 inch (2.5 cm) and heat over medium-high heat for 4 to 5 minutes, until it registers 375°F (190°C) on a deep-fry thermometer.

While the oil is heating, drain and thoroughly rinse the canned chickpeas; drain again and pat dry.

Put the rice flour in a medium bowl and add half the chickpeas. Toss until well coated, then use a slotted spoon to transfer them into a strainer and tap the strainer to remove excess flour.

To test if the oil is hot enough, drop a chickpea into the oil; if you see plenty of rapid bubbles around it, you're good to go. Using the slotted spoon, add the coated chickpeas to the hot oil and fry until just lightly golden, 2 to 3 minutes. Be careful not to overcook them—the chickpeas should remain tender but retain their shape. Use the slotted spoon to transfer the chickpeas to the paper towels. Coat and fry the remaining chickpeas in the same manner (be sure to let the oil return to temperature between batches).

Transfer all the fried chickpeas to a large bowl and toss with the za'atar and salt. Serve at once, or let cool and store in an airtight container in the fridge for up to 3 days. To bring them back to life, spread them on a parchment-lined baking sheet and warm them in the oven at 350°F (175°C) for a few minutes. They will be almost as good as new.

Shuk HaTikva/HaTikva Market

The story

Every time we come to this friendly market, we feel sorry we don't live closer. Shuk HaTikva may be the best food market in Tel Aviv and is definitely the most underrated one. Located in Schunat HaTikva–a working-class quarter in southeast Tel Aviv–it's sometimes called the poor man's version of the famous Carmel Market. This is a true neighborhood market, and the eclectic customer mix reflects the changes the quarter has undergone in recent years. Yemenite, North African, and Iraqi Jews, who have been living in the neighborhood for decades, were joined by new immigrants from Russia and Ethiopia, migrant workers, and African refugees. They all come here to do their regular shopping, and the market has everything they need at prices they can afford. If they have a few extra shekels and some time on their hands, they might sit down for a quick bowl of soup or a plate of hummus.

The vibe

One of the nicest things here is the feeling of community. The shopkeepers, who know many of their regular customers by name, are friendly, chatty, and very welcoming to visitors. They feel flattered that you took the trouble to come to their neighborhood market and will go out of their way to make sure you will come back.

But even this neighborhood market is catching on in popularity. New, trendier eateries have opened up recently. On our last visit, there was a band playing Mizrahi music right in the middle of the market, and we spotted quite a few "tourists" (mostly Israeli) who came to enjoy the preweekend hustle and bustle with a little bit less madness than at Carmel Market.

When to come

The market is open all week except Shabbat, but is at its best on Fridays.

Pickled olives and vats of Iraqi amba *and North African pickled lemons at Amiga Deli* **(ABOVE)**; *When the stalls close for Shabbat, the party at Saluf & Sons Bakery spills out onto the street* **(LEFT)**

Our Favorite Spots

SALUF & SONS BAKERY

1 HaTikva Street

During the week, the bakery does a brisk business selling traditional Yemenite pastries, and many regulars stop by for a quick breakfast of *lachuch* (a spongy Yemenite pancake; see page 320) served with salad, hummus, or shakshuka. On Fridays the place reinvents itself as a social club–and everybody is invited. On the menu: beer, arak, singing, and often dancing. In the afternoon when the shops close down, the party spills onto the street and the merriment continues until sunset, when Shabbat sets in.

AMIGA DELI

8 Nuriel Street

In 1950, Yizhak Amiga opened a small grocery that evolved into one of the best Mediterranean delis in the neighborhood (if not in Tel Aviv). There's a tempting–and strictly kosher–array of pickles, olives, cheeses, cured and smoked fish, and sausages, but the main draw is homemade Iraqi *amba*. Sold out of open tubs, it fills the air with the overpowering smell of mango and fenugreek (for more about *amba*, see page 71).

Saluf & Sons Bakery: freshly fried lachuch *flatbreads all week* (**ABOVE**) *and a party every Friday* (**RIGHT**). *The pre-weekend rush at the shuk's main drag; live music in the middle of the market; freshly made salad at one of the trendy recently opened eateries* (**OPPOSITE FROM TOP TO BOTTOM**)

Over the years, some of the more popular places evolved into generic nationwide chains and lost much of their original appeal. These two restaurants, however, located next to each other in a small cul-de-sac, retain some of their former glory and jointly share the title of best *shipudiya*, in the neighborhood that invented the genre. For some mysterious reason, they are both closed on Fridays.

BUKHARIAN BAKERY

52 Hanoch Street

Most of the space in this miniature bakery is taken up by a *tandyr*, a Bukharian clay oven that is worth peeking into (ask the shopkeeper nicely first). The dough is slapped on the inner walls of the oven and falls to its floor when ready. Two traditional Bukharian flatbreads are baked on the premises: soft, doughy *lepyoshka* with a dimple in the center; and huge, thin, crusty *töki*, which are often used as edible plates at festive gatherings.

SHAUL MUZEFI

15 Hamevaser Street

SHEMESH

13 HaTikva Street

The grill houses of HaTikva Quarter were all the rage in the 1970s and '80s and are credited with inventing what is locally called a *shipudiya* (literally, "skewer house")—a popularly priced restaurant that offers meze salads and skewered chargrilled meats, including a typically irreverent Israeli invention: skewered foie gras.

CHAPTER 5

Dairy and Eggs, for Breakfast and for Dinner

Open any typical Israeli refrigerator and you'll see an array of creamy dairy products—yogurt, labneh, feta, kefir, soft *gvina levana*, and our famous Israeli cottage cheese, arguably the best in the world. Except for Shabbat dinner on Friday nights, lunch is the main meal of the day and is usually meat-based. Breakfasts and dinners are light and mostly meatless. Since mornings are too hectic to cook a proper breakfast, we are happy to enjoy our beloved trifecta of eggs, dairy, and salad in the evening. On weekends they reappear on a brunch table, which is naturally more lavish and features at least three salads, a shakshuka (or other interesting egg dish), a plate of labneh, freshly made tahini, savory pastries, and of course delicious bread. With such a feast, who needs meat, anyway?

The Israeli Love of Dairy

Israelis are very proud of their dairy, and rightly so. Fresh, soft, spreadable cheeses, especially cottage cheese, are utterly delicious and so are all kinds of yogurts, labneh, and our beloved *gvina levana* ("white cheese"). The latter—a fresh-tasting low-fat and mildly tart cheese—is a legacy of the Templers, members of a German Christian society that settled in Palestine in the late-nineteenth century. The simple cheese they made was similar to the German quark and quickly became a local staple. Templers left the country shortly before World War II, but the cheese, which, by that time, was produced by local dairies, remained our favorite snack—next to a salad or spread on a slice of bread. Similar to *gvina levana* in texture but even creamier and certainly more tart is labneh—strained yogurt cheese. Used in numerous ways, this traditional Levantine staple is the current darling of Israeli chefs. It is also the easiest cheese to make at home (see recipe on page 140).

Another important family of local cheeses is collectively known as *gvina melucha* ("salty cheese") and was brought to Israel by immigrants from the Balkans (that's why it is also called *gvina bulgarit*–"Bulgarian cheese"). Even neighborhood groceries carry scores of this semi-hard, savory, snow-white slab akin to Greek feta or Turkish brinza and differing in fat content, the kind of milk used to make them (cow, sheep, or goat), and the texture that ranges from crumbly to velvety; Bulgarian feta is also less salty than many other fetas.

The most famous salty cheese is *gvina tzfatit*, named after the ancient Galilean town of Safed (Tzfat). Mild-tasting, with a silky, slightly rubbery texture, it matures into a rock-hard umami-packed cheese that is perfect for grating–a local equivalent of Parmesan, if you wish. It was first produced by Hameiri dairy. Founded in 1968, this is the oldest commercial dairy

farm in Israel, and the cheese, currently produced by the fifth generation of the founders, is considered the best in Israel.

Hard, ripened, moldy cheeses are relative newcomers to the local food scene. For many decades, we made do with a basic selection of industrial processed cheeses. Even the name given to these cheeses sounds a bit silly: *gvina tzehuba* ("yellow cheese"). Yellow cheese is still a big hit, especially for toasts and sandwiches, but boutique dairies that started to pop up around the country about thirty years ago educated local palates. Today there are over two hundred boutique cheese farms around the country, and even though they account for only a small percentage of the total cheese production, they are the pride and joy of local foodies. Locally produced goat's- and sheep's-milk cheeses are especially good.

Homemade Labneh

1 quart (960 ml) whole-milk
  plain yogurt

1 tablespoon kosher salt
  (optional)

1 tablespoon lemon juice
  (optional)

I've eaten labneh all my life, and it makes me so happy to see this simple cheese become more widely popular. I've shared it with several of my New York chef friends, who adore the creamy, glossy stuff. Labneh is basically yogurt strained through cheesecloth, and the longer you strain it, the thicker it will be. As the whey drains out, the fat content rises and the flavors concentrate, creating a soft cheese that's at once creamy and refreshingly tart. The classic way to enjoy labneh is to spread it on a plate, as you would hummus, drizzle it generously with fragrant extra-virgin olive oil, sprinkle it with za'atar, and swipe it up with warm pita.

But I use labneh as I would sour cream, crème fraîche, or cream cheese. For example, I'll add a dollop of cool labneh to hot steamed or roasted vegetables or even soup, spread it on a plate and top it with salads (see the recipe for Israeli Ceviche on page 47), spread it on bread and drizzle it with some honey and nuts for a light morning snack, or use it to make a cheesecake (see page 343).

Traditional labneh is made from goat's- or sheep's-milk yogurt, which has a more complex aroma than cow's-milk yogurt, but good-quality full-fat cow's-milk yogurt will do nicely. **PICTURED ON PAGE 139**

If you plan to use the labneh for desserts, like the cheesecake on page 343, don't add anything to the yogurt. For savory uses, stir the salt into the yogurt. If you'd like to make your labneh tangier (or if your yogurt was a bit bland in the first place), stir in the lemon juice, a little bit at a time, tasting as you go.

Take a long piece of cheesecloth and double or triple fold it so it will be denser. Arrange the cheesecloth in a strainer, leaving a generous overhang, and then set the strainer over the bowl. Pour the yogurt into the center of the cheesecloth–the idea is to weigh the cheesecloth down with the yogurt, to encourage dripping. Set the bowl in the fridge (you can cover the top of the strainer with plastic wrap if you'd like) and leave it there until the labneh reaches the desired consistency:

8 hours should be enough for soft labneh; a full 24 hours will get you a cream cheese-like texture. Store the finished labneh in the refrigerator for up to 1 week. You can use the whey left in your bowl in smoothies.

Another fun method for straining yogurt (especially if you want to make it really thick) is to gather up the overhanging cheesecloth into a bundle, tie it with a string, and hang it from the tap over your kitchen sink. If the temperature is cool, you can safely leave it there overnight (and up to 24 hours, if you can spare the sink). Otherwise, improvise some kind of hanging setup in the fridge (don't forget to put a bowl underneath to catch the whey). When the dripping becomes slow and almost stops, it's time to unwrap the bundle and reveal a ball of cheese almost as thick as feta, but malleable.

Marinated Labneh Balls

MAKES 16 TO 24 BALLS

With a jar of these beauties in your fridge, you're ready for an impromptu cocktail party any time.

2 cups (480 g) very firm labneh, ideally strained for 3 days

Extra-virgin olive oil

Za'atar, chopped fresh thyme and mint, finely chopped pistachios or hazelnuts, or dukkah, for garnish

Scoop out about 2 tablespoons labneh and roll it into a ball. Gently arrange the balls in a wide-mouth sterile jar or other sterile container with a tight-fitting lid. Once all the balls are in the jar, pour in enough oil to cover by about an inch. Tap the jar gently to dislodge any air pockets. Store the labneh balls in the refrigerator for up to 4 months.

To serve the labneh balls, remove them from the oil using a clean utensil (not your fingers) and arrange them on a plate. To dress them up, roll them in one or more of the suggested garnishes before serving.

MORE DELICIOUS DESTINATIONS FOR YOGURT

For Americans, yogurt is primarily a breakfast dish served with granola or fruit, or a healthy between-meals snack. Sometimes it also finds its way into cake batters, shakes, or salad dressings. In Israeli food culture, yogurt has much wider uses, as evidenced by the dizzying array of yogurts you can find in any supermarket: There are thin drinking yogurts, creamy yogurts that are handy for snacking and making dressings, and thick yogurts that can be used as a topping or a spread—just like tahini. Labneh, which is basically strained yogurt, is even thicker and creamier and has plenty of creative uses (see page 140). In Levantine cuisine, goat's-milk yogurt is also used for cooking meat (especially lamb) and vegetables (especially zucchini). One of the most famous yogurt-based dishes is Palestinian *shish barak*—tiny ravioli-like dumplings cooked in a spiced yogurt soup. Last but not least are chilled yogurt soups, which arrived in Israel from the Balkans and became one of our favorite summer treats (see page 243).

Here are some tips and ideas to enhance your yogurt experience:

- Make sure you buy plain yogurt. We know it sounds obvious, but since an average yogurt case is dominated by sweetened and/or flavored varieties, it is worth double-checking.

- Avoid fat-free yogurt. By its very nature, yogurt is a healthy low-fat product. Full-fat yogurt has about 7 percent fat, as opposed to 20 percent in sour cream and a whopping 34 percent in cream cheese. That 7 percent goes a long way to giving yogurt rich creaminess and a pleasing round taste.

- Yogurt is terrific for balancing out starchy, earthy foods. Your rice dish feels a bit dry? Top it with a dollop of yogurt. Your lentil or bean salad is a bit on the heavy side? A glug of yogurt will take care of that.

- Think about yogurt as a cooler. Is the dish or the sauce too spicy? A tablespoon or two of nice yogurt will quench the fire a bit.

- Serve yogurt with soups. It is a well-known fact that soups taste better a day or two after they are cooked, as they sour slightly in the fridge, which cuts through the earthiness of starchy vegetables and legumes. Yogurt has the same effect, while adding a pleasant creamy touch.

- And our most important advice: Be creative. Yogurt can be mixed with fresh and dried herbs, grated tomatoes, ground pistachios, all kinds of relishes (from *amba* to harissa), olive oil, preserved lemon, tahini—the list is practically endless, and once you start playing with it, you will come up with more ideas. Do be aware that if you boil yogurt, it may separate, so keep your temperatures moderate.

COTTAGE
CHEESE

FETA

GVINA
LEVANA

TAHINI

LABNEH

Israeli Breakfast

Israeli breakfast was born in the 1930s in a kibbutz communal dining hall. True to their ethos of living frugally and eating what they grow, kibbutzniks would eat a simple meal of eggs, some bread, fresh soft cheese, a warm porridge in winter, and of course a salad. A couple of decades later, when the first luxury hotels opened in Israel, this simple, wholesome meal morphed into the famous Israeli hotel breakfast. This breakfast had to be strictly kosher, so to compensate for the lack of meat, hoteliers offered an extravagant buffet with all manner of cheeses, yogurts, and other dairy goodies; cured fish; egg dishes; savory pastries; cakes; and more. Today, you can enjoy this feast not just in hotels but in cafés, restaurants, and rural inns, and, of course, at home–especially on weekends.

Shakshuka
Cinderella in a Skillet

Shakshuka came out of total obscurity and, in a couple of decades, evolved into one of the symbols of the local food renaissance. It then went on to conquer the world. If asked to name the top iconic Israeli dishes, most people would mention shakshuka next to hummus, falafel, and chopped salad.

So what is it about this simple eggs-in-sauce dish that makes it so appealing to so many people? In its homelands, Libya and Tunisia, shakshuka is a humble midweek breakfast or lunch fix, often made from the leftover sauce from some meat or fish stew. It arrived in Israel with North African immigrants and for many years remained almost unnoticed by the majority of Israelis. It did pop up here and there—sometimes stuffed in a pita at a roadside eatery or served out of huge trays at army canteens. Made in advance, messy looking, and overcooked, the shakshukas of the past were definitely not dishes to rave about.

It took one chef to change all that. In 1993, chef Bino Gabso opened up a place in Jaffa. Cavernous and decorated with knickknacks from a nearby flea market, the restaurant offered a selection of North African specialties, including hand-rolled couscous, *mafroum*, and *chraime*, but the star of the menu was shakshuka. Made to order, it was brought to the table in a cute little iron skillet, along with soft white bread to mop up the spicy sauce.

The public was smitten, and the restaurant—aptly named Doctor Shakshuka—became a destination for locals and tourists alike. Other chefs were quick to hop on the shakshuka bandwagon. In those days, many upscale restaurants started to serve elaborate breakfasts, and shakshuka was a perfect fit—egg-based and open for creative riffs.

And we mean creative. Not only tomato shakshuka, but also shakshuka based on mixed greens, mushroom ragout, seafood, goose liver, and more. In short, anything in a skillet with a couple of cracked eggs on top was labeled "shakshuka."

In the late nineties, a little-known neighborhood hummus joint in Ra'anana came up with *humshuka*–hummus topped with shakshuka–fusing two local food icons into one tasty, messy dish that was widely imitated.

Almost a quarter of a century later, Doctor Shakshuka is still going strong, and shakshukas are still served everywhere–from neighborhood cafés to fancy restaurants.

The three shakshukas in this chapter represent different faces of this beloved dish–classic tomato shakshuka, followed by a totally unorthodox bright yellow shakshuka scented with Yemenite spices, and a green shakshuka with roots in North Africa.

By nature, shakshuka is forgiving–follow these recipes the first time you make the dish, then feel free to play with spices and ingredients to come up with your own shakshuka. The most important rule is that once you add the eggs, you have 7 to 8 minutes before you serve the dish–plus, you can't stir the sauce or adjust the seasoning after the eggs have been added. So give your sauce the time it needs to get thick and packed with flavor, taste it, spice it to your liking, and only *then* crack some eggs on top.

Spicy Red Shakshuka with Charred Eggplant

2 tablespoons extra-virgin olive oil, plus more for finishing

2 medium yellow onions, finely diced

1 large red bell pepper, cored, seeded, and finely diced

2 tablespoons tomato paste

1 to 2 tablespoons Filfel Chuma (page 27)

8 large ripe tomatoes, finely diced, or one 28-ounce (795 g) can best-quality crushed tomatoes

1 teaspoon sugar

1 teaspoon sweet paprika

1 teaspoon ground cumin

½ teaspoon ground caraway

2 teaspoons kosher salt, plus more as needed

6 to 8 large eggs

1 eggplant, charred, drained, and peeled (see page 96)

Ground sumac

Crusty bread or challah, for serving

This is the real-deal North African tomato-based shakshuka, made extra authentic with the addition of *filfel chuma*, a traditional Tripolitan condiment heavy on chile and garlic. You can find the recipe on page 27, or use a combination of fresh chiles and garlic instead (see the variations). The charred eggplant topping adds a smoky aroma and soft texture that work deliciously with the spicy sauce; if you can't manage the charred eggplant, your shakshuka will still be delicious.

Heat the oil in a large skillet (10 inches/25 cm will be ideal) over medium heat. Add the onions and sauté until soft and translucent, about 6 minutes. Add the bell pepper and sauté until just softened, 3 to 4 minutes. Stir in the tomato paste and 1 tablespoon of the filfel chuma and sauté for another 2 minutes.

Stir in the diced tomatoes, sugar, paprika, cumin, caraway, and salt. Bring the mixture to a boil, reduce the heat to low, and simmer uncovered until the sauce is thick and shiny, about 20 minutes. Taste and adjust the seasoning, adding more salt or the remaining filfel chuma, if you like it spicier.

Use a large spoon to create little wells in the sauce. Carefully break 1 egg into a cup or ramekin, then slip it into one of the wells; repeat with the remaining eggs. (Cracking the egg into a cup first lets you inspect it for any runaway bits of shell.) Cover and simmer until the egg whites are set but the yolks are still a little runny, about 7 minutes.

Tear the eggplant flesh into large pieces and arrange them on top of the shakshuka, between the eggs. If the eggplant was roasted in advance, let it warm through on top of the shakshuka for a minute. Sprinkle with a big pinch of sumac and drizzle with more oil.

Serve the shakshuka directly from the skillet, with plenty of crusty bread or challah.

VARIATIONS

- Use harissa (store-bought, or see page 26) instead of *filfel chuma*, and add 1 cored, seeded, and sliced jalapeño chile to the skillet with the bell pepper and 3 minced garlic cloves with the tomato paste.

- Just before adding the eggs, layer 1 cup (30 g) coarsely chopped Swiss chard leaves (skip the stems here) or spinach on top of the sauce.

- Skip the eggplant and sprinkle some sliced goat cheese or crumbled feta cheese on top of the shakshuka just before serving—the cheese will melt a bit from the heat.

Yemenite Curry Shakshuka with Yellow Peppers, Preserved Lemons, and Coconut

2 tablespoons extra-virgin olive oil

1 medium onion, sliced

4 medium garlic cloves, chopped

2 large yellow bell peppers, cored, seeded, and thinly sliced

¼ cup (40 g) sliced preserved lemons (see page 30), seeded

1½ teaspoons Soup Hawaij (page 23)

½ teaspoon ground turmeric

1 teaspoon kosher salt

One 13½-ounce (380 g) can coconut milk

6 to 8 large eggs

TO SERVE

Classic Green S'chug (page 25)

Crusty bread or challah

Here's another example of how versatile the shakshuka formula can be: Put something delicious in a skillet, crack a few eggs, and bake.

This dish came from a happy accident. I had leftover coconut and seafood curry in the fridge. I decided to heat it up and crack some eggs into it, and the result was fantastic. I've since ditched the seafood and added preserved lemons and *hawaij*—both are flavors of my childhood.

Heat the oil in a large skillet over medium-high heat. Add the onion, garlic, and bell peppers and sauté until the peppers are soft, 5 to 7 minutes. Stir in the preserved lemons, hawaij, turmeric, salt, and coconut milk and cook for another 3 to 4 minutes. The mixture should be thick but not stiff; if it's too thick, stir in up to ½ cup (120 ml) water. Taste and adjust the seasoning.

Use a large spoon to create little wells in the sauce. Carefully break 1 egg into a cup or ramekin, then slip it into one of the wells; repeat with the remaining eggs. (Cracking the egg into a cup first lets you inspect it for any runaway bits of shell.) Cover and simmer until the egg whites are set but the yolks are still a little runny, about 7 minutes.

Serve directly from the skillet with s'chug and plenty of crusty bread or challah.

Green Shakshuka with Chard, Kale, Spinach, and Feta

¼ cup (60 ml) extra-virgin olive oil

2 leeks, white parts chopped and green tops very thinly sliced

3 medium garlic cloves, thinly sliced

1 small jalapeño chile, cored, seeded, and thinly sliced

5 or 6 Swiss chard leaves, leaves coarsely chopped, stems thinly sliced

1 small bunch Tuscan kale (also called lacinato or dinosaur), stemmed, leaves coarsely chopped

3 cups baby spinach or trimmed and coarsely chopped regular spinach

1 teaspoon ground caraway

1 teaspoon ground cumin

Kosher salt and freshly ground black pepper

½ cup (120 ml) homemade or low-sodium store-bought chicken stock or vegetable stock or water

1 tablespoon fresh lemon juice

6 to 8 large eggs

TO SERVE

5 ounces (140 g) feta cheese, coarsely crumbled

Extra-virgin olive oil

Za'atar

Crusty bread or challah

In Israel, the best time to make this shakshuka is in the winter when spinach, chard, and other leafy greens are at their sweetest. Thick, slightly tart stews made from slow-cooked greens are one of the hallmarks of both Tunisian and Libyan (Tripolitan) cuisine (see the recipe for Tripolitan T'Becha B'Salik on page 278). So if red shakshukas were made with leftover tomato stews, it's entirely possible that leftover stews of simmered greens were repurposed as green shakshukas. In Israel, green shakshukas are almost as popular as red ones, and they come in many versions. This one, relatively slowly cooked and seasoned with cumin and caraway, has some of the stewy texture typical of North African dishes, with the feta adding a Balkan note in the true Israeli spirit of culinary mash-up.

Heat the oil in a large skillet over medium heat. Add the leeks, garlic, jalapeño, and chard stems and sauté until softened and lightly caramelized, 10 to 12 minutes (take care not to brown the garlic). Add the kale, spinach, and the chard leaves and cook, stirring often, until wilted and soft, 3 to 4 minutes. Add the caraway and cumin, and season very lightly with salt (the feta is quite salty) and several twists of pepper.

Add the stock and the lemon juice and cook for 5 to 7 minutes, then reduce the heat to low and cook for another few minutes, until the greens meld into a thick, dark green, stewy sauce. Taste and adjust the seasoning.

Use a large spoon to create little wells in the greens mixture. Carefully break 1 egg into a cup or ramekin, then slip it into one of the wells; repeat with the remaining eggs. (Cracking the egg into a cup first lets you inspect it for any runaway bits of shell.) Cover and simmer until the egg whites are set but the yolks are still a little runny, about 7 minutes. Remove the skillet from the heat.

Sprinkle the shakshuka with the feta, drizzle with oil, and sprinkle generously with za'atar. Serve the shakshuka directly from the skillet, with plenty of crusty bread or challah.

Balkan-Style Scrambled Eggs with Roasted Peppers, Olives, and Feta

6 to 8 large eggs

Kosher salt and freshly ground black pepper

2 tablespoons extra-virgin olive oil or vegetable oil

½ cup (100 g) halved and pitted Kalamata olives

2 red bell peppers, cored, seeded, and roasted, thoroughly drained or blotted with a paper towel, and coarsely chopped (see opposite)

½ cup (75 g) crumbled feta cheese

Pinch of chile flakes, for garnish

Chopped fresh parsley, for garnish

Roasted peppers, feta cheese, and black olives form the very essence of Balkan cooking. All three will appear as separate small dishes on a typical meze table, or they'll join forces in a salad or a pastry. Or they can redefine something as everyday as scrambled eggs, as they have in this recipe. Just be sure to drain the peppers thoroughly or the eggs will be soggy.

Crack the eggs into a medium bowl, season with ¼ teaspoon salt (go very light on the salt–the feta and olives are salty) and several twists of black pepper, and whisk until nicely foamy.

Heat the oil in a large nonstick pan over medium heat. Add the olives and roasted peppers and sauté until they are warmed through, about 2 minutes. Reduce the heat to low, add the eggs, and cook, stirring and folding continuously, until fluffy curds form and the eggs are set, 2 to 3 minutes. If you prefer your eggs less runny, cook them a bit longer.

Add the feta, stir briefly, and remove from the heat. Garnish with the chile flakes and chopped parsley. Serve at once.

THE EASY WAY TO ROAST PEPPERS

The traditional way to roast whole peppers—on an open flame or a charcoal grill—is a messy business. By the time the skin is properly charred, the flesh almost falls apart, and when you pry the peppers open to remove their seeds and membranes, you end up with mushy shreds. The following method is clean and easy and produces perfectly roasted peppers. Use it for both sweet (bell) peppers and chiles of all varieties.

Preheat the broiler to very high. Line a baking sheet with parchment paper. If you like, place a rack on top.

Stem the peppers and halve them lengthwise; remove the seeds and membranes.

Arrange the halved peppers skin-side up on the prepared baking sheet and drizzle with a little olive oil. Position the tray close to the broiler and broil until the skin is charred and the flesh feels completely soft, 20 to 25 minutes (small chiles will need less time).

Transfer the peppers to a zip-top plastic bag or lidded container, seal or cover, and let cool (this will create a steaming effect that will loosen the skins). Peel the peppers and use as directed in a recipe. If not using at once, transfer them to an airtight container, add olive oil to cover, and store in the fridge for up to 3 days.

Sficha

Yemenite Malawach with Spicy Ground Beef, Spinach, and Poached Egg

MEAT TOPPING

2 tablespoons extra-virgin olive oil

1 large yellow onion, finely chopped

1 or 2 small jalapeño chiles, cored, seeded, and finely chopped

1 pound (455 g) ground beef

2 tablespoons chopped fresh parsley

¾ teaspoon ground cinnamon

1 tablespoon sweet paprika

1 teaspoon ground turmeric

1 tablespoon ground cumin

1 bay leaf

1 tablespoon kosher salt

¾ teaspoon freshly ground black pepper

¼ cup (35 g) pine nuts, toasted

¼ cup (35 g) currants

SPINACH AND EGGS

2 teaspoons extra-virgin olive oil

8 ounces (225 g) baby spinach

Kosher salt

4 large eggs

MALAWACH

Vegetable oil, for frying

4 discs frozen malawach

Best described as panfried puff pastry, and quite similar to Indian paratha, *malawach* is a unique, complicated Yemenite bread that, thankfully, comes in frozen form. You can even find it in the kosher sections of supermarkets in the States (or order it online). Delicious on its own or with some grated tomatoes and *s'chug* (which is how we ate it growing up and how it's traditionally served in little eateries at shuks all over the country), *malawach* becomes downright irresistible when topped with meat and spinach and crowned with a poached egg. Fold it over like a slice of pizza and dig in, letting the warm, runny egg mix with the meat and the spinach and drip down your chin—yes, it gets drippy! If poached eggs sound intimidating, see the variations for easier options.

Make the meat topping: Heat the oil in a large skillet over medium heat. Add the onion and jalapeños and sauté until the onion is soft and translucent, 5 to 7 minutes. Add the ground beef, parsley, cinnamon, paprika, turmeric, cumin, bay leaf, salt, and pepper and cook, crumbling the meat with a fork, until the meat is broken down and nicely browned, 8 to 9 minutes.

Turn off the heat, discard the bay leaf, and stir in the pine nuts and currants. Cover the skillet to keep the filling warm.

Cook the spinach: Heat the oil in another large skillet over medium heat. Add the spinach, season with a pinch of salt, and sauté until the spinach just starts to wilt but is still bright green, 2 to 3 minutes. Turn off the heat and cover the skillet to keep the spinach warm.

Poach the eggs: Line a large plate with paper towels. Fill a wide medium saucepan three-quarters full with water and bring it to a very low simmer—you should just barely see a bubble here and there. Any roiling bubbles mean the water is too hot, so reduce the heat and let it cool a bit if you see them.

Crack one egg into a small bowl. Using a wooden spoon, give the simmering water a swirl to create a "tornado" (which will help corral the egg white so it doesn't spread too much) and carefully slide the egg into the tornado. Cook, undisturbed, for 2 to 3 minutes, until the egg white has just firmed up but the yolk is still runny. Carefully remove the egg with a slotted spoon and transfer it to the paper towels to absorb excess water. Repeat to cook the remaining eggs, one at a time.

Recipe continues

Fry the malawach: Five minutes before you're ready to cook the malawach discs, transfer them from the freezer to the fridge.

Heat 1 teaspoon vegetable oil in a medium nonstick skillet over medium-high heat. Add one disc of malawach (keep the others in the fridge so they don't become sticky and the wrapper becomes hard to peel) and fry until crispy and golden, 2 to 3 minutes on each side. Transfer to a serving plate (if possible, heat the plate in advance to keep the malawach warm until serving). Repeat to cook the remaining malawach discs, adding a bit more oil to the pan between batches, if needed, and setting each fried malawach on a separate serving plate.

While the malawachs are frying, check on the meat and spinach—if they've cooled down, reheat them for a minute or two.

To serve: Divide the spinach evenly among the malawach discs, leaving about 1 inch (2.5 cm) exposed around the edges, top with the meat and a poached egg, and serve at once.

VARIATIONS

If you can't find *malawach*, use puff pastry instead: Remove it from the freezer and let sit for 10 to 15 minutes at room temperature, just until it thaws a bit so you can spread out the sheet. Roll out the pastry to make it a bit thinner and cut out four 7-inch (17.5 cm) discs. Poke each disc with a fork in several places (this will prevent the pastry from puffing up too much). Heat the oil and fry one disc of dough for 3 minutes on each side, or until golden. Transfer to a plate and repeat with the rest of the discs, adding a bit more oil between batches, if needed.

You can use fried eggs—sunny-side up—instead of poached, if you like. Fry each one individually and make sure it's not overcooked—the yolk should be runny, and the white should be cooked but not rubbery.

Or top the dish with soft-boiled eggs: Fill a bowl with ice and water. Fill a medium-small pot about three-quarters full with water and bring it to a boil. Once boiling, reduce the heat to medium and carefully slide in the eggs. Cook for 8 minutes exactly (use a timer). Remove the eggs with a slotted spoon and immediately transfer them to the ice bath to stop the cooking. Let the eggs cool completely before peeling.

Little Herb Omelets

5 medium eggs

2 teaspoons all-purpose flour

½ teaspoon ground turmeric

½ teaspoon ground cumin

½ teaspoon chile flakes

1 teaspoon kosher salt

1 cup (40 g) finely chopped parsley

1 cup (40 g) finely chopped cilantro

½ cup (50 g) thinly sliced scallions

½ cup (20 g) finely chopped dill

1 very small onion, finely chopped

2 tablespoons canola oil

1 tablespoon olive oil

In Hebrew we call them *havitot yerek*—herb omelets—but the name could be misleading. These are not omelets with herbs, but herbs with a bit of eggs to hold them together. They are popular across the Middle East, and there is a similar recipe in Persian cuisine (famous for its copious use of herbs). Moist and bright with every shade of green, these little fellows are a great way to put all those herbs routinely stored in an average Israeli fridge to a good use. Serve them as a part of a weekend breakfast spread with chopped salad, tahini spread, or thick yogurt. They are also delicious in a pita or in a sandwich, with some pickles, sliced tomatoes, and mayo or tahini.

Crack the eggs into a large bowl, add the flour, turmeric, cumin, chile flakes, and salt, and whisk until nicely foamy. Add the parsley, cilantro, scallions, dill, and onion, and mix thoroughly until fully combined.

Heat both oils in a large nonstick skillet over medium heat.

Pour about ⅓ cup of the mixture for each omelet into the hot pan. Don't crowd the skillet—once you pour the mixture, it tends to spread. Fry for 2 to 3 minutes on each side, until the patties are golden brown, and transfer to a plate lined with paper towels to drain the oil. Repeat with the rest of the herb and egg mixture. If the skillet gets dry, add another tablespoon of oil. Serve warm with a dollop of tahini.

Egg Salad with Caramelized Onions, Zucchini, and Preserved Lemon

8 large eggs

3 tablespoons extra-virgin olive oil

3 medium yellow onions, cut into ⅛-inch (3 mm) dice

2 medium zucchini, coarsely grated

1½ teaspoons kosher salt

1 medium garlic clove, minced

⅓ cup (80 ml) mayonnaise

2 tablespoons Preserved Lemon Paste (see page 31) or fresh lemon juice

¼ teaspoon chile flakes

1 teaspoon ground coriander

Pinch of freshly grated nutmeg

The curious Israeli invention of faux chopped liver dates back to the early fifties, a time of deep economic crisis and food rationing. Made with hard-boiled eggs, fried onions, and fried zucchini or eggplant (sometimes both), the dish somehow managed to have the look and taste of the classic Ashkenazi delicacy without even an ounce of real liver. It was the first dish I learned to make in cooking school, but here I infuse it with a healthy dose of shuk chic by adding chile flakes, preserved lemon paste, and ground coriander. If you can grind your own, all the better. Serve it on toasted challah or good sourdough bread.

Fill a bowl with ice and water. Fill a medium pot about three-quarters full with water and bring to a boil. Once boiling, reduce the heat to medium and carefully slide in the eggs. Cook for 12 minutes exactly (use a timer). Remove the eggs with a slotted spoon and immediately transfer them to the ice bath to stop the cooking. Let the eggs cool completely before peeling. If not using at once, refrigerate for up to 1 day.

While the eggs are cooking, heat the oil in a large skillet over medium heat. Add the onions and cook, stirring often, until deep golden brown, 12 to 15 minutes.

Add the zucchini and sauté for 5 to 6 minutes, then season with about ½ teaspoon of the salt (this will help to draw out moisture). Add the garlic and cook until all the liquid has evaporated and the contents of the skillet look golden brown and quite mushy, another 5 to 6 minutes. Transfer the mixture to a bowl or plate and let cool.

Whisk together the mayonnaise and the preserved lemon paste (or lemon juice) in a small bowl, season with the remaining 1 teaspoon salt, the chile flakes, coriander, and nutmeg. Set aside.

Peel the eggs and quarter them lengthwise. Transfer to a salad bowl, add the onion-zucchini mixture and the dressing, and toss gently, taking care not to mush up the eggs. Serve at once or store in an airtight container in the fridge for up to 3 days.

Shuk HaNamal/Tel Aviv Port Farmers' Market

The story

Tel Aviv Port was founded in 1936 and closed down thirty years later, when a bigger deep-water port was launched in the southern city of Ashdod. For decades it remained largely deserted and housed body shops and plumbing supply warehouses, but in the last decade, following a major overhaul, it became a sprawling leisure and shopping complex. One of its main attractions, certainly for a foodie, is the first local farmers' market.

Despite our deep tradition of shopping at shuks, actual farmers' markets are a relatively new phenomenon in Israel. With so many existing food markets offering fresh, local, and mostly seasonal produce, the feeling was that farmers' markets were redundant. But two young women entrepreneurs, Shir Halpern and Michal Ansky, started a small farmers' market in 2008 and are making a go of it.

The vibe

On our first visit, a couple of weeks after the market was officially launched, there were just ten plastic tables huddled under a tent in a parking lot, yet the tiny market was buzzing with activity.

The first thing that caught our eyes was a cornucopia of cherry tomatoes—red, yellow, pink, chocolate brown, and striped, some round, others shaped like tiny bottles and miniature plums. This was our first encounter with the famous tomatoes from the desert (see page 50), which we had heard so much about but never had a chance to taste because they were almost exclusively exported. We also remember our first encounter with buttery Ratte potatoes, extra-crunchy cucumbers the size of a pinkie finger, perfect green asparagus, and all kinds of berries we didn't even knew grew in Israel. Today, all these fruits and vegetables are available at mainstream markets, but they made their first appearance here. So we kept coming back, and every time, there were more farmers, more surprises, and many more shoppers. Despite the fact that growers sell their goods directly, with no go-betweens, don't expect bargains. The prices are high, but so is the quality. Seasonality is the name of the game, and much of the produce is organic or comes from small specialized farms. Michal and Shir have opened additional markets in other cities around the country, but the one in Tel Aviv remains the most attractive and bustling. In 2010, a small roofed market opened next door, with gourmet shops, a few restaurants, and permanent stalls hosting some of the leading farmers.

When to come

The roofed market is open all week (except Sunday) and is worth checking out if you're in the area, but for a taste of the real farmers' market, come on Friday. The market now is sixty stalls strong, and every time we come, we take home something new and delicious.

Dainty Tinkerbell peppers from the Negev desert (LEFT); Right next to the market is the "first Hebrew carousel," constructed in 1932 and recently renovated (BELOW LEFT); Even basic vegetables taste better when you buy them directly from the growers (BELOW RIGHT)

Freshly picked dates (TOP); *Rainbow carrots and cherry tomatoes* (RIGHT); *Apples from the Golan Heights* (OPPOSITE TOP); Baladi *produce stall* (OPPOSITE LEFT); *Hibiscus fruit for stuffing and pickling* (OPPOSITE RIGHT)

CHAPTER 6

Mad About Chicken

A whole chicken for roasting, chicken legs or drumsticks for braises and stews, boneless chicken thighs for grilling, ground chicken for patties and stuffing, chicken necks and carcasses for soup, chicken liver for chopped liver, and—last but not least—thinly sliced chicken breasts for schnitzel: If you look into a typical Israeli freezer at any given time, you'll likely find at least three of these options. If an average Israeli eats meat for lunch, there's about a 90 percent chance it will be chicken. At a *mangal* ("cookout"), most of the meat will be chicken, and even for Shabbat and holiday meals—which are supposed to be more lavish than daily fare—there will usually be a chicken dish on the table next to more prestigious meats.

Orange Blossom–Scented Roast Chicken and Potatoes

1 large (4-pound/1.8 kg) whole roasting chicken

2 garlic cloves, finely grated or minced

¼ cup (60 ml) fresh orange juice

4 tablespoons (60 ml) extra-virgin olive oil

2 teaspoons honey or silan

1 tablespoon sweet paprika

1 teaspoon ground cumin

4½ teaspoons kosher salt

1 medium orange

4 medium russet potatoes, peeled and cut lengthwise into 8 wedges each

1 tablespoon orange blossom water

A simple addition of orange blossom water makes this already delicious recipe even more intriguing. Just a tablespoon perfumes the entire bird with a subtle floral aroma.

Preheat the oven to 375°F (190°C).

Remove the chicken from the fridge about 30 minutes before cooking to bring it close to room temperature (this will encourage even cooking).

Combine the garlic, orange juice, 2 tablespoons of the oil, the honey, paprika, cumin, and 3 teaspoons of the salt in a bowl. Whisk to blend. Set aside.

Pat the chicken dry inside and out with paper towels. Stuff the orange inside the chicken's cavity (cut it in half if the cavity is small), then tie the end of the drumsticks together with kitchen twine so the orange stays put.

Put the potatoes in a deep rectangular baking dish that can easily accommodate the chicken (9 by 13 inches/23 by 33 cm or similar size) and toss them with the remaining 2 tablespoons oil and the remaining 1½ teaspoons salt. Spread the potatoes out in the baking dish, then place the chicken on top of the potatoes, breast-side down.

Put about one-third of the orange juice mixture in a small bowl for basting; set the remainder aside. Using a basting brush, brush the chicken's back and legs (i.e., the parts that are facing up) with the basting mixture.

Roast the chicken for 1 hour, then remove the dish from the oven and flip the chicken over. Give the reserved orange juice mixture a good stir and brush half of it over the breast. Return the pan to the oven and roast for another 20 minutes.

Stir the orange blossom water into the remaining orange juice mixture. Remove the chicken from the oven and brush the orange juice mixture all over. Return the pan to the oven and roast for another 8 to 10 minutes, until the chicken's skin is beautifully burnished and the potatoes are nicely browned, crispy on the outside, and cooked through inside. To check for doneness, make a small incision in the thickest part of one thigh and make sure the juices run clear. If they're still pink, roast for a few more minutes. If you have an instant-read thermometer, the chicken should be at 165°F (74°C) in the thickest part of the thigh.

Remove the pan from the oven, loosely tent it with aluminum foil, and let the chicken rest for 7 to 8 minutes.

Carve and serve with the potatoes and any juices in the baking dish. You can also remove the orange from the chicken, cut it up, and add it to the potatoes, or slice it and arrange it on top of the carved chicken on a platter.

Doro Wot

Ethiopian Chicken

6 bone-in, skin-on chicken legs, separated into thighs and drumsticks

1 tablespoon lemon juice

2 tablespoons kosher salt, plus more as needed

¼ cup canola oil

2 large onions, finely diced or chopped

3 garlic cloves, smashed

1 teaspoon ground cumin

1 teaspoon ground ginger

1 teaspoon ground cardamom

1 teaspoon ground turmeric

1 teaspoon paprika

1 teaspoon ground fenugreek seed or leaf

1 teaspoon freshly ground black pepper, plus more as needed

6 hard-boiled eggs, peeled

2¼ cups (500 ml) homemade or low-sodium store-bought chicken stock or water

Lachuch, for serving (page 320)

In Israel, there is a large Ethiopian Jewish community, but the majority of Israelis are not familiar with their unique cuisine. I, however, have always felt super connected with Ethiopian culture, partly because I had Ethiopian girlfriends when I was young, and partly because it reminds me of my Yemenite father's culture. The fragrance of this dish, the fenugreek in particular, transports me back to my childhood home. In an Ethiopian kitchen, this dish would be served with injera, a famous Ethiopian spongy flatbread that's perfect for mopping up sauce. But you can substitute with Yemenite *lachuch*, which is quite similar and very delicious; see page 320 for the recipe.

Rub the chicken with the lemon juice and 1 tablespoon salt and let it sit for 30 minutes.

Meanwhile, heat the oil in a heavy-based wide skillet or Dutch oven (large enough to hold the chicken in one snug layer) over medium heat, add the onions and the remaining tablespoon salt, and sauté gently until fragrant, golden brown, and sweet, about 20 minutes. Do not let the onions actually brown.

Add the garlic, cumin, ginger, cardamom, turmeric, paprika, fenugreek, and pepper and stir for a minute so the spices bloom in the oil. Nestle the chicken pieces and the eggs into the pan and pour in the broth.

Cover the pan and adjust the heat to a solid simmer. Cook for about 30 minutes. Then remove the lid (so the sauce will reduce and thicken a bit) and continue to simmer until the chicken is very tender when poked with a knife and the juices run clear (or until the thickest part of the thigh or drumstick reaches 165°F/74°C on an instant-read thermometer), 45 to 60 minutes.

Taste and adjust with more salt or pepper. Serve with lachuch to mop up the delicious sauce.

Mastering Schnitzel

Schnitzel is our guilty pleasure. Generously breaded and fried in a healthy amount of oil, who knows how many calories it costs us? We try not to think about them as we dip a piece of this crispy delight into ketchup or mayonnaise. Schnitzels are wildly popular in Israel, so much so that they've become synonymous with tedious everyday chores (as in, "I have better things to do than ironing shirts and frying schnitzels for the kids").

Austrian immigrants brought schnitzel to Israel in the 1930s, and for them, a proper schnitzel meant one made from thinly pounded veal—an expensive rarity in those days. So they settled for the chicken breast, and soon the rest of the Israelis fell in love with it. As with every popular home-cooked dish, variations abound, but one thing is beyond dispute: Schnitzel is only worth its reputation (and calories) if it's freshly fried.

THE CHICKEN

We like our schnitzels quite thin, about ¼ inch (6 mm) thick. Because schnitzels are so popular in Israel, thinly sliced chicken breast is sold in every supermarket, but this isn't necessarily the case in other parts of the world. Unless you have an obliging butcher, you'll have to do it yourself:

- Put a boneless, skinless chicken breast on a cutting board. Press it flat with your left hand (if you are left-handed, press it with your right hand).

- Using a large sharp knife held parallel to the cutting board, slice the breast horizontally into two even pieces. If you feel confident, or if the chicken breast is quite thick, you can try going for three slices.

- If the slices, or parts of them, are thicker than you want, lay them flat in a large zip-top bag and pound them lightly with the smooth side of a meat mallet (if you don't have a mallet, go over them

with a rolling pin or a smooth heavy object, such as a skillet). Chicken breast is very tender and tears easily, sometimes resulting in small, uneven pieces. No need to throw them away, though; small free-form schnitzels are just as tasty.

Speaking of smaller schnitzels, check out chicken tenders (in Israel, we call them chicken fillets), those small strips of flesh attached to the breast that are usually sold separately. They make great snack-sized schnitzels, and you don't need to slice or pound the meat.

THE SEASONINGS

A marinade is optional but recommended. Mild-tasting chicken breast is like a blank canvas that welcomes a wide range of flavorings: paprika, cumin, olive oil, pesto, soy sauce, orange juice, garlic, mustard, and more. A couple of hours are enough to marinate chicken breasts, but if it's more convenient, you can leave them in the marinade in the fridge overnight.

THE BREADING

You know the drill: flour, egg, bread crumbs. The flour dries the chicken pieces so the egg can coat them evenly, and the egg helps the crumbs stick to the meat.

Store-bought bread crumbs are fine (make sure they aren't seasoned), and panko (Japanese bread crumbs, available in most grocery stores) is even better. And if you have stale white bread (for example, challah leftovers from Shabbat), you can put it to good use by making homemade bread crumbs: Cut the bread into large chunks, scatter them over a parchment paper-lined baking sheet, and toast in the oven at 200°F (95°C) for a couple of hours, until they feel completely dry and hard to the touch. Crush the bread into fine crumbs in a food processor and store in an airtight container for up to 1 week.

A fun way to add extra crunch and flavor to your schnitzel coating is to mix the bread crumbs with crushed savory snacks. In Israel, a crunchy snack food called Bissli Grill became so popular for

breading schnitzels that the manufacturer came up with Bissli-flavored bread crumbs. If you want to try it, look for Bissli in the kosher section of any supermarket. Another great option is unsweetened cornflakes.

Put each breading ingredient (flour, egg, bread crumbs) in its own shallow bowl and arrange the bowls close to the stove with the ingredients in the order you use them: The bread crumbs should be closest to the stove, the eggs in the middle, and the flour on the other side. Set a large tray or plate next to the stove as well to hold the breaded chicken. Dip each piece of chicken first in the flour, shaking off any excess, then in the egg, letting any excess drip off, and finally in the bread crumbs; set the breaded chicken on the tray and repeat to coat the remaining pieces. The breading process is a bit messy. There are all kinds of tricks—like working with tongs or using one hand to dredge the chicken in the dry ingredients and the other hand to dip them in the eggs—but from our experience, they don't really work. When your fingers start looking like schnitzels, just rinse them.

THE FRYING

This is the make-or-break of a well-made schnitzel. The whole thing takes just a few minutes, so you need to be quick and precise and have everything ready so you don't lose momentum. Line a tray with a few paper towels and use it for the finished schnitzels. Choose a large, straight-sided skillet, and fill it with enough oil to equal the depth of the schnitzel (about ¼ inch/6 mm). Heat the oil over medium-high heat until it registers about 350°F (175°C) on a deep-fry thermometer, 2 to 3 minutes. To test the oil, toss in a few bread crumbs; if they sizzle, the oil is hot enough. (If they immediately go from light to dark brown, the oil is too hot—remove the skillet from the heat for a few moments to let it cool off and then test it again.)

Carefully add the schnitzels to the hot oil. To avoid crowding the skillet, don't fry more than two or three medium schnitzels at a time. Every additional piece will bring the oil temperature down, which means you'll have to fry them longer, and the breading will absorb more oil and turn soggy. Watch your schnitzels closely—you might need to raise or lower the heat as you go and move them around the skillet so they don't get brown spots. Once they're nicely golden on both sides, about 3 minutes on each side, immediately transfer them to the paper towels to drain and lightly blot them with another paper towel to absorb excess oil. Finish with a sprinkling of crunchy sea salt.

AND THE MOST IMPORTANT THING: SERVE YOUR SCHNITZELS RIGHT AWAY!

Schnitzels lose their beauty in a matter of minutes, and reheated schnitzels never taste the same. Our advice is to fry the amount you need for one meal, and if there are leftovers, eat them cold (cold schnitzels are not half bad on a slice of challah with some mayonnaise and a pickle). If you absolutely must prepare them ahead, we suggest breading the raw chicken slices and layering them in a plastic container or a large thick plastic zip-top bag, separating each slice with a piece of parchment paper or plastic wrap so they don't stick to one another. Store them in the freezer, and when ready to cook, let them thaw for 10 to 15 minutes at room temperature. Refresh the coating by dipping them briefly in bread crumbs and then sliding them into the hot oil.

Serve mustard and mayonnaise, and, if you're feeling fancy, spice up the mayo with harissa, *amba*, preserved lemon paste, wasabi, or Thai sweet chili sauce. And don't forget lemon wedges! A squeeze of fresh lemon juice cuts through the fattiness, making the schnitzels even more delicious. For lunch, we usually serve schnitzels with mashed potatoes (our favorite), french fries, or Israeli couscous. And of course chopped salad! Schnitzel is also delicious in a pita: Slather the insides with hummus, slide in a freshly fried schnitzel, add a couple of tablespoons of salad, and serve with a dip of your choice.

Extra-Crispy Israeli Schnitzel

A generous heap of parsley combines with some thyme, rosemary, garlic, and orange juice to become a flavor-packed marinade for chicken breasts. The juicy, herby flavor comes through in every bite, and crushed cornflakes in the breading add incomparable crunch. When mixed with mayo, harissa and preserved lemon paste make the best dipping sauces.

HERB AND CITRUS MARINADE

1 cup (50 g) coarsely chopped fresh parsley (include the stems)

Leaves from 1 fresh thyme sprig

Leaves from 1 fresh rosemary sprig

5 garlic cloves

½ cup (120 ml) fresh orange juice

2 tablespoons extra-virgin olive oil

SCHNITZEL

1 pound (455 g) chicken breasts, sliced and pounded ¼ inch (6 mm) thick (see page 172)

1 cup (125 g) all-purpose flour

3 large eggs

1 cup (30 g) unsweetened cornflakes

1½ cups (120 g) bread crumbs (preferably panko)

Kosher salt and freshly ground black pepper

Vegetable oil, for frying

TO SERVE

1 cup (240 ml) mayonnaise

1 to 2 tablespoons harissa (see page 26)

1 to 2 tablespoons Preserved Lemon Paste (page 31)

1 lemon, cut into wedges

Make the marinade: Put the parsley, thyme, rosemary, garlic, orange juice, and oil in a food processor and process until smooth.

Make the schnitzel: Put the chicken in a large shallow bowl or a Pyrex baking dish, pour over the marinade, and toss, making sure the pieces are evenly coated on both sides. Cover and refrigerate for 2 to 3 hours or up to overnight.

Remove the chicken from the fridge 30 minutes before frying to bring it close to room temperature (this will encourage even cooking). Set it in a colander over a large bowl to drain some of the marinade.

Set up a breading station: Put the flour in a shallow medium bowl. Lightly whisk the eggs in another bowl. Crush the cornflakes in a food processor or put them in a zip-top bag, flatten it slightly, and crush with a rolling pin or pound with a heavy skillet–you want the cornflakes finely crushed but not powdery. The crumbles don't have to be even. Transfer the crushed cornflakes to a third bowl and mix with the bread crumbs. Arrange the three bowls next to each other, close to the stove. Have two large platters nearby; line one of them with paper towels.

Take one chicken slice and season it with salt and pepper on both sides. Dip the chicken in the flour to get a thin, even coating and shake off the excess flour. Dip the chicken in the egg, lift it out, and let it drip for a second, then dredge it in the bread crumbs, making sure you have a nice even coating on both sides. Lay the breaded piece on the unlined platter, and repeat to bread the rest of the chicken.

Fill a large skillet with vegetable oil to a depth of about ¼ inch (6 mm) and heat the oil over medium-high heat for 2 to 3 minutes. Slide two or three pieces of the breaded chicken into the hot oil and fry until deep golden on the bottom, about 2 minutes. Using tongs or a couple of forks, flip the schnitzels and fry for 2 minutes on the second side. Transfer the schnitzels to the paper towel-lined platter and blot with another paper towel to remove excess oil. Repeat to cook the remaining chicken.

Make the dips: Divide the mayonnaise between two small serving bowls. Stir the harissa into one and the preserved lemon paste into the other. If the consistency of either is too thick, add a bit of water.

Serve the schnitzels right away, with the dips and the lemon wedges alongside.

Chicken Liver Schnitzel

SERVES 4

1 pound (455 g) whole chicken livers, trimmed, rinsed, and dried well

1 teaspoon kosher salt

½ teaspoon freshly ground black pepper

1 cup (125 g) all-purpose flour

3 large eggs

1 teaspoon Soup Hawaij (page 23) or baharat (see page 22)

1½ cups (120 g) bread crumbs (preferably panko)

Vegetable oil, for frying

Preserved Lemon and Mint Pesto (page 34), for serving (optional)

Crispy outside and buttery-soft inside, breaded chicken livers can win over the most reluctant liver eaters, especially when served with a bright Preserved Lemon and Mint Pesto (page 34). With a streamlined breading technique and no need to slice or pound, they're even easier to make than regular schnitzels. The plump livers take longer to cook and often splatter during frying, so use a splatter screen if you have one.

Line a plate with paper towels. Season the livers with the salt and pepper.

Whisk together the flour, eggs, and hawaij in a medium bowl to make a smooth batter. Put the bread crumbs in a shallow bowl next to the bowl of batter. Set an empty plate nearby. Dip the livers in the batter, then dredge them in the bread crumbs to coat and put them on the plate.

Fill a large deep skillet with vegetable oil to a depth of 1 inch (2.5 cm) and heat over medium-high heat for at least 3 minutes. Fry the coated livers in batches, 5 or 6 at a time, until they are just pink in the center, about 3 minutes on each side. Use a slotted spoon to transfer them to the paper towels and serve at once, with the pesto if desired.

Jerusalem Mixed Grill with Chicken and Merguez Sausages

2 tablespoons extra-virgin olive oil

2 large onions, thinly sliced

1½ pounds (680 g) boneless chicken thighs, trimmed and sliced crosswise into ⅓-inch-thick (9 mm) pieces

5 merguez sausages or other spicy lamb or beef sausage (about a total of 1 pound/455 g), chopped (about 1½ cups)

SPICE MIX

1 teaspoon ground cumin

1 teaspoon ground coriander

1 teaspoon sweet paprika

Scant 1 teaspoon ground turmeric

1 heaping teaspoon kosher salt

Freshly ground black pepper

TO SERVE

4 to 6 pitas

Amba Aioli (page 108) or Classic Tahini Sauce (page 114; optional)

Chopped fresh parsley, for garnish

Agrippas Street, the main drag leading to shuk Mahane Yehuda in Jerusalem, is lined with grill houses. Curiously, the dish that made these decades-old establishments famous isn't cooked on the grill. Legend has it, back in the 1970s, a group of hungry soldiers stopped by the now defunct Makam restaurant just as the place was about to close for the day. According to one version of the story, the chef had run out of charcoal. According to another, he ran out of meat. From the looks of it, he had run out of both, since the dish he whipped up was made from chicken and offal scraps that he stir-fried on the griddle with a heap of onions and spices. The soldiers went away happy, and a new Israeli food icon was born. Before long the dish gained a name, *meorav yerushalmi* (Jerusalem mix), and spread to other parts of the country. Israelis love grilled chicken offal, especially livers, hearts, and spleens. I felt these might be too "exotic" for the American palate, so I replaced them with *merguez* sausage. As for the chicken, use boneless thighs and not breasts; otherwise the dish will be dry. **ALSO PICTURED ON PAGE 166**

Heat the oil in a large skillet over medium heat. Add the onions, reduce the heat to medium-low, and cook, stirring every now and then, until they are soft and deep golden brown, about 20 minutes.

Add the chicken thighs and sausages to the skillet and give them a good stir. Cook, stirring frequently, for about 10 minutes, until the chicken is cooked through (cut into one slice and check inside).

Meanwhile, make the spice mix: Stir all the spice mix ingredients in a small bowl.

Add the spice mix to the skillet and sauté for another 2 to 3 minutes.

To serve, divide the mixture among the pitas, drizzle with amba aioli or tahini, and garnish with a sprinkle of fresh parsley.

Musahan

Chicken and Onion Confit on Flatbread

3 cups (720 ml) extra-virgin olive oil or vegetable oil, or a blend

4 chicken legs, thighs and drumsticks separated, patted dry

Kosher salt

3 large or 4 medium yellow onions, thinly sliced

1 tablespoon ground sumac

¼ teaspoon ground cardamom

½ teaspoon ground cinnamon

½ teaspoon allspice berries

TO SERVE

2 large (ideally 8-inch/20 cm) laffa flatbreads (see page 317) or Indian naan

1 small yellow onion, thinly sliced (optional)

Ground sumac

Toasted pine nuts (optional)

Handful of fresh parsley leaves

The credit for this brilliant recipe goes to Nof Atamna-Ismaeel, a microbiologist turned chef, and one of Israel's greatest experts on authentic Levantine cooking. Nof grew up eating *musahan*, a popular Palestinian *taboon*-baked flatbread topped with caramelized onions and roasted chicken and generously dusted with sumac. She loved everything about it except the perennially too-dry chicken. So she came up with a solution: Rather than cooking the onions and chicken separately, she uses the confit method to gently cook them together in a generous amount of spice-infused olive oil. The chicken turns out incredibly succulent and the onions tender and sweet. As for the flatbread (we call it *laffa* in Israel), you can use store-bought Indian naan or make your own *laffa* (for a fast-and-simple pan-toasted version, see page 317).

Preheat the oven to 350°F (175°C).

Heat 2 tablespoons of the oil in a large skillet over medium-high heat for a couple of minutes. Add half the chicken pieces, skin-side down, season lightly with salt, and sear until nicely browned, 4 to 5 minutes. Transfer the chicken to a deep roasting pan, skin-side up, and pour in any juices and rendered chicken fat from the pan. Sear the remaining chicken pieces in the same manner, adding a bit more oil, and add them to the roasting pan. If you see nice browned bits stuck to the bottom of the skillet, add a little water to the skillet and stir, scraping them up with a wooden spoon to dissolve them, then add to the roasting pan. Add the sliced onions to the roasting pan, covering the chicken pieces.

In a medium bowl, whisk together the remaining oil, 1 tablespoon salt, the sumac, cardamom, cinnamon, and allspice. Pour the mixture into the roasting pan over the onions and chicken—in the beginning they will peek slightly out of the liquid, but as they cook, they will shrink and become completely submerged. Wrap the pan tightly with aluminum foil. Bake for 2½ hours, or until the onions are soft and mushy and the chicken is almost falling off the bone. Remove the pan from the oven and let cool a bit before removing the foil.

Using a slotted spoon, scoop out the onions and transfer them to a strainer placed over a bowl to drain. Remove the chicken with tongs or the slotted spoon and set aside on a large plate. (If you'd like, strain the spice-infused oil through a fine-mesh sieve, transfer it to an airtight container, and store it in the fridge for up to 2 weeks to reuse in other dishes.) At this point, the chicken and the onions can be stored in two separate airtight containers in the fridge for up to one day before serving.

When ready to serve, preheat the oven to 450°F (230°C). Line a baking sheet with parchment paper.

Put the flatbreads on the prepared baking sheet. Divide the cooked onions between the two flatbreads and arrange them evenly to cover the bread, leaving about 1 inch (2.5 cm) exposed around the edges. Arrange 4 chicken pieces, skin-side up, over the onions on each flatbread. Roast until the chicken is warmed through and the skin is nicely browned, 7 to 8 minutes.

Combine the sliced raw onion (if using) with ½ teaspoon sumac and pile it on top of the chicken. Sprinkle with pine nuts, if desired, and the parsley. Give the dish another generous sprinkle of sumac and serve. The diners should take a piece of chicken and sort of pull apart the oniony bread–not the neatest dish to eat, but definitely one of the most glorious!

Sautéed Chicken Liver Toasts with Figs and Port

1½ tablespoons extra-virgin olive oil, plus more for the toasts

2 shallots, halved and sliced thin

2 garlic cloves, sliced thin

1½ pounds (680 g) chicken livers, trimmed

5 sun-dried tomatoes in oil, cut into thirds

1½ teaspoons kosher salt

Freshly ground black pepper

⅓ cup port

1 dried hot chile

5 fresh figs, quartered or halved if small

6 to 8 slices sourdough bread, grilled or toasted and brushed with olive oil

½ teaspoon ground sumac

Chicken livers love sweet flavors and here, the sweetness comes from fresh figs and port. To preserve their look and fruitiness, the figs join the skillet for just a few minutes. I like to serve the dish as an appetizer on slices of grilled bread, but it will be excellent as a main dish, especially with mashed potatoes.

Heat the oil in a large skillet over medium-high heat. Add the shallots and sauté until fragrant and lightly golden, about 4 minutes; don't let the shallots brown too much. Add the garlic and cook another minute until the garlic is soft but not browned.

Add the chicken livers and sun-dried tomatoes, season with the salt and several twists of black pepper, and sauté until they are cooked but still quite pink in the center, 3 to 4 minutes depending on the size.

Pour in the port, add the chile, adjust the heat to a simmer, and simmer until the port has reduced by about half. Add the figs and cook until the figs are soft and slightly broken down, another 3 to 4 minutes.

Adjust the seasoning with more salt and pepper if you like. Remove the chile, spoon the chicken livers and sauce over the grilled bread, sprinkle with the sumac, and serve right away.

FIGS: THE TRUE FRUIT OF PARADISE

Summer brings so many gorgeous fruits to Israeli markets that we get spoiled, yet one fruit in particular is always exciting: figs.

Figs start showing up at the market in late June, and the vendors, aware of their selling potential, take time to present them in the most fetching way—in neat rows, with their pointy stems facing straight up. We start salivating just by looking at this display, and even though figs are costly, especially early in the season, we can't resist taking these luscious beauties home. We place them carefully at the top of the shopping cart, so as not to mush their delicate flesh (plus this way it is more convenient to munch on them on the way home).

When we've had our fill of fresh figs, we start playing with them in the kitchen—cut them in half and toss them into a bowl of green salad, bake beautiful summer tarts, pair them with cheese, and, when the prices go down somewhat, make jams and preserves.

We also love adding figs to savory dishes. Figs are very high in sugar, which caramelizes during cooking to add tons of flavor and color to a variety of meat and chicken preparations.

CHAPTER 7

All About the Rice

So what's for lunch? Schnitzel *ve orez* (schnitzel "with rice"), *ktzitzot ve orez* ("meatballs with rice"), *orez im adashim* ("rice and lentils"), *marak sh'uit al orez* ("bean soup over rice"). . . . Sure, we love mashed potatoes, french fries, and pasta as much as anyone, but somehow rice has evolved into the most popular carb in the Israeli kitchen, be it a simple side of white rice or an exquisite layered pilaf that combines rice with meat, chicken, and vegetables. However you season or garnish the dish, the rice comes first and needs to be perfectly cooked.

Perfect Pilaf Rice

2 cups (370 g) jasmine rice (sometimes called Thai rice)

2 tablespoons vegetable oil

1 tablespoon kosher salt

3 cups boiling water

This method, in which rice grains are briefly sautéed in oil, giving them an additional layer of toasted flavor, is officially called pilaf. It yields fluffy, soft rice where each grain retains its independence. In Hebrew we call it *orez ehad-ehad*, "one-by-one rice." I usually use jasmine rice because I like the texture—the grains are relatively hefty—and it has a nice floral aroma. You can use basmati rice, but with a slightly different method, which I include in the recipe.

This perfectly plain rice is a joy on its own, but it's just the beginning. You can add vegetables, spices, herbs, and all kinds of crunchy toppings.

Rinse the rice in a colander until the water runs clear. Drain and let dry for a couple of minutes in a colander.

Pour the oil into a medium nonstick pan and heat for a minute over medium heat. Add the rice and sauté just until most of the grains turn opaque, 2 to 3 minutes. Add the salt and the boiling water, give it a good stir, reduce the heat to low, cover with a tight-fitting lid, and cook for 18 minutes (use a timer!). Do not stir or open the pot during cooking.

After 18 minutes, let the cooked rice sit in the covered pot for 5 more minutes. Fluff with a fork, transfer to a serving bowl, and serve at once. The rice is at its best if served shortly after cooking, but if you have some left over, the best way to reheat it is in the microwave.

For basmati rice: Put the uncooked rice in a bowl, cover with tap water, and soak for 10 minutes. Drain and cook as explained above, but use 1 cup of boiling water for each cup of rice.

VARIATIONS

These add-ons are not mutually exclusive; you can mix and match with whatever sounds good and complements the rest of your meal.

- Toss in a cinnamon stick with the rice grains.

- Add 1 teaspoon whole cumin seeds with the rice.

- Stir in ½ teaspoon ground turmeric with the boiling water.

- Before adding the rice, heat the oil and sauté 1 small finely diced onion and/or 1 finely diced carrot until the onion is soft and the carrot is slightly golden, 4 to 5 minutes. Then add the rice and continue as explained above.

- Add 1 cup peas (fresh or frozen and thawed) with the boiling water.

- Add up to 2 cups finely chopped dill and/or cilantro with the boiling water.

- If you have nice homemade broth (chicken, beef, or vegetable), use it instead of water. In this case you should consider using less salt.

- Goodies you can add to the prepared rice:

  ⅓ cup slivered toasted almonds

  ⅓ cup toasted pine nuts

  ¼ cup dried currants or dried barberries

¼ cup golden raisins (sauté them briefly in a bit of oil before adding to the rice)

⅓ cup finely chopped fresh herbs (parsley, dill, cilantro, mint)

¼ cup caramelized onions (page 316) or crispy shallots (see below)

Crispy Shallots

Soups, salads, grilled meats, mashed potatoes—I can't think of a dish (except maybe desserts) that this addictively crunchy, oniony garnish wouldn't complement. I give the shallots a light dusting of rice flour, which makes them even crispier than if you used all-purpose flour and has the added benefit of being gluten-free. But in a pinch, regular all-purpose wheat flour will do fine. **MAKES ABOUT 2 CUPS (220 G)**

2 cups (480 ml) vegetable oil

12 medium shallots, very thinly sliced

½ cup (80 g) rice flour

Kosher salt

Line a plate with paper towels. Heat the vegetable oil in a small saucepan over medium-high heat until it reaches 325°F (165°C) on a deep-fry thermometer.

While the oil is heating, gently separate the sliced shallots into rings. Put the rice flour in a bowl, add the shallots, and toss to coat with the rice flour. Transfer the shallots to a strainer and tap to dust off any excess flour.

To check that the oil is hot enough, drop a shallot ring into the oil. If you see a lot of rapid bubbles around it, you're good to

go. Reduce the heat to medium-low and add about half the shallots to the hot oil. Fry, stirring the shallot rings gently to keep them separated, until they turn golden brown, about 10 minutes. If they're browning too fast, reduce the heat (they'll taste bitter if they cook too fast or get too dark). Using a slotted spoon, transfer the shallots to the paper towels. Sprinkle lightly with salt while they're still warm. Repeat to fry the remaining shallots.

If not using at once, store the shallots in an airtight container on the counter for up to 3 days . . . if you can resist snacking on them, that is.

Persian Tahdig Rice

4 cups (740 g) jasmine rice

4 teaspoons kosher salt

¼ cup plus 2 tablespoons (90 ml) vegetable oil

Small pinch saffron (optional)

Toppings (optional):

½ cup (55 g) dried barberries

¼ cup (25 g) chopped, toasted pistachio nuts

2 to 3 tablespoons Candied Orange Zest (recipe follows)

Rice, water, oil, salt, and a pinch of saffron if you're feeling fancy—this is all you need to produce the crown jewel of Persian rice dishes: perfectly cooked, delicately perfumed rice crowned with tahdig, the scrumptious golden crust that everybody at the table will be fighting for. The three-step method requires some attention and may take a few tries to perfect, but the result is stunning.

Tahdig rice is a perfect companion for another Persian classic, Ghormeh Sabzi (page 197), but it will be beautiful with any stew or braise that has a lot of sauce.

To make tahdig rice, you'll need a colander, a bowl, a large pot (like the one you use for cooking pasta), and another pot to finish the dish. The latter has to be relatively wide (so you will have a lot of surface for the crust), nonstick, and equipped with a snugly fitting lid. You will also need a clean, odorless kitchen towel—no fabric softener, please!

Put the rice in a colander and rinse it thoroughly under running water until the water runs clear.

Transfer to a bowl, cover with water, and stir in 1 teaspoon of the salt. Let stand for half an hour. Transfer the rice back to the colander, rinse briefly, and drain.

Meanwhile, bring about 4 quarts of water to a boil in a large (pasta) pot, add 1½ teaspoons of the salt and the drained rice, and cook uncovered at a lively simmer until the rice is slightly tender but not completely cooked, 4 to 5 minutes; when you bite into a grain, you'll feel a slight resistance in the center. While cooking, give your rice a few good stirs to collect the grains that stick to the walls or the bottom.

Once the rice is ready, pour it into the colander and rinse again with cold water to stop the cooking.

Transfer the cooled rice to a bowl. Stir in the remaining 1½ teaspoons salt and 2 tablespoons of the oil.

Now it's time to use the nonstick pan. Pour the ¼ cup (60 ml) oil into the pan, add a pinch of saffron (if using), and heat for 1 to 2 minutes on medium heat until fragrant. Add enough rice to form a 1-inch layer, and cook uncovered for about 5 minutes without stirring. Adjust the heat so you can hear a gentle sizzle.

Now carefully add the remaining rice, making sure you don't disturb the bottom layer. Cover the pot first with a damp towel and then with the lid (this will create a steaming effect without adding water). Reduce the heat to low and cook for 40 minutes. If you're not serving the rice at once, you can leave it in the covered pot for 3 to 4 hours in a warm place.

Shortly before serving, increase the heat to medium and cook for another 5 minutes to brown the crust.

When ready to serve, remove the towel and the lid. Run a spatula around the walls of the pan, to release the rice. Cover the pot with a platter or a large round tray, and holding the tray and the pot, flip it. Lift the pot carefully and uncover a molded rice cake crowned with golden tahdig. If you like, sprinkle on some barberries, pistachios, and/or candied orange peels. Bring to the table and make sure every guest gets a bit of the crunchy crust along with the rice.

Candied Orange Zest

1 or 2 oranges

½ cup (125 ml) water

¾ cup (150 g) sugar

1 teaspoon orange blossom water or rose water

Using a vegetable peeler, remove the zest (just the orange part, without the white pith). Each orange should yield five or six 2-inch-wide (2.5 cm) ribbons. Slice each ribbon crosswise into very fine strips.

Transfer the zest to a medium pan, cover with water, bring to a boil, and blanch for 2 minutes—this will help to drive away the bitterness. Drain the strips on a paper towel.

Mix the water and sugar in a small pan and bring to a boil. Add the orange blossom water and the blanched zest, return to a boil, reduce the heat to low, and cook for 5 minutes. Pour the zest and the syrup into a small jar and let cool. Store in the fridge.

When you want to use the zest, remove the desired amount with a slotted spoon and drain on paper towels.

Tbit

Iraqi Chicken and Rice Casserole

4 cups (740 g) jasmine rice

3½ tablespoons kosher salt

1 large (4-pound/1.8 kg) whole roasting chicken

Freshly ground black pepper

¼ cup (60 ml) vegetable oil, plus more for greasing

1 medium yellow onion, finely diced

3 tablespoons tomato paste

½ teaspoon sugar

½ teaspoon ground cardamom

2 teaspoons sweet paprika

½ teaspoon ground cinnamon

4 cups (960 ml) boiling water

How can you make your best meal of the week on the day when you can't cook? This paradox of Jewish cooking has led to some unique casseroles, placed in the oven before Shabbat starts and left to cook slowly until Saturday noon. This Iraqi *tbit* is one of those dishes. The rice is perfumed with sweet spices and juices from the slowly roasting chicken, and the final texture of the rice is slightly pudding-like—with a crisp crust and falling-off-the-bone-tender chicken. I learned to make *tbit* from my mother's friend Silvy Keshet, who has cooked it this way for sixty years. Note: You'll need a heavy pot or Dutch oven with at least a 5-quart capacity.

Put the rice in a large bowl, add 3 cups (720 ml) water and 2 teaspoons of the salt, and set aside to soak for 2 hours. Rinse several times under running water and drain well. Transfer to a bowl and set aside.

Remove the chicken from the fridge about 30 minutes before roasting to bring it close to room temperature (this will encourage even cooking).

Pat the chicken dry. Remove the fatty white flap from the chicken cavity and chop it finely. Set aside. Season the chicken inside and out with several generous twists of pepper and about 1½ teaspoons of the salt.

Heat the vegetable oil in a large heavy ovenproof pot or Dutch oven over medium-high heat. Add the chicken and brown until its skin turns golden brown, 5 to 7 minutes on each side. (If it's easier, you can brown the chicken in a large skillet.) Remove from the pot and set aside.

Reduce the heat to medium, add the onion and chopped chicken fat, and sauté, stirring often, until the chicken fat melts and the onion is soft and golden, 7 to 8 minutes. Add the tomato paste and sugar and cook, stirring, for another minute or so. Remove from the heat and transfer the onion mixture to the bowl with the rice. Season with the cardamom, paprika, cinnamon, and 2 tablespoons of the salt and mix until well combined. If you like, tie the chicken's legs together at the end of the drumsticks with kitchen twine to help keep its shape.

Preheat the oven to 315°F (160°C).

Wipe out the pot and lightly slick it with oil. Add a layer of the rice mixture to the bottom of the pot just to cover it (it should be about ½ inch/1.5 cm thick). Place the chicken on the rice, breast-side up, and spread the rest of the rice mixture around and over the chicken; the chicken should be mostly buried in rice, with its breast peeking out. Gently pour in the boiling water.

Bring the water back to a boil over high heat. Cover the pan with a tight-fitting lid and transfer to the hot oven. Bake for 2½ hours. By this time, the chicken will be very tender and the rice will be soft and kind of mushy, which is part of its charm.

VARIATIONS

If you want crisp chicken skin and an appetizing brown crust on the rice, remove the lid and raise the temperature to 400°F (205°C) for the last 15 minutes of cooking.

If you want to cook the dish in the Shabbat oven, preheat the oven to 200°F (95°C) and cook overnight (8 to 10 hours).

Chicken Maqloubeh

Palestinian Rice, Vegetables, and Chicken Pilaf

1 large globe or 2 smaller
   Asian eggplants

Kosher salt

3 large or 4 small chicken
   legs, thighs and
   drumsticks separated

Freshly ground black pepper

4 tablespoons (60 ml)
   extra-virgin olive oil

1 large cauliflower, cored
   and cut into bite-sized
   florets

3 cups (555 g) jasmine rice

5½ cups (1.3 L) boiling water

1½ teaspoons baharat
   (see page 22)

1½ teaspoons ground
   turmeric

½ teaspoon ground
   cinnamon

Fresh pickles

Harissa, store-bought or
   homemade (see page 26)

There are many ways to prepare *maqloubeh* ("upside down" in Arabic). You can use beef, lamb, or chicken, or skip the meat altogether. You can substitute bulgur wheat for the rice or add vegetables such as potatoes and broccoli to the mandatory cauliflower and eggplant. As long as you layer the ingredients and flip the pan, preferably in front of the cheering guests, you can call it *maqloubeh*.

To keep the *maqloubeh* from sticking, it helps to use a nonstick pot and employ the trick detailed in the method to cool the crust before flipping.

Using a vegetable peeler, peel the eggplant from top to bottom in zebra stripes. Slice it lengthwise into ½-inch-thick (1.5 cm) planks, then halve each plank horizontally and transfer to a colander set in the sink or over a bowl. Cover the eggplant generously with salt and let sit for 30 to 45 minutes to draw out the water.

Preheat the oven to 350°F (175°C). Line two baking sheets with parchment paper.

Season the chicken thighs and drumsticks with a generous pinch each of salt and pepper and let sit at room temperature while you work on everything else.

Rinse the eggplant thoroughly and pat dry with paper towels. Put the eggplant in a bowl, drizzle with 1 tablespoon of the oil, season lightly with salt and pepper, and toss to coat. Spread the eggplant over one of the prepared baking sheets. Put the cauliflower in the same bowl, add

1 tablespoon of the oil, season lightly with salt and pepper, and toss to coat. Spread the cauliflower over the second prepared baking sheet. Roast the vegetables until tender and golden, 20 to 25 minutes for the eggplant and 30 to 35 minutes for the cauliflower.

While the veggies are in the oven, put the rice in a medium bowl, add 2 cups (480 ml) water, and set aside to soak for 20 to 30 minutes. Drain and rinse several times under running water (this will make the rice less starchy).

Heat the remaining 2 tablespoons oil in a large heavy nonstick pot or a Dutch oven over medium-high heat for 1 to 2 minutes. Add the chicken pieces in one layer, skin-side down, and sear, without flipping the pieces, until the skin is crispy and golden brown, about 5 minutes—you only want to brown the skin, not cook the chicken through.

Arrange three-quarters of the rice over the chicken in the pot, making sure the rice is tucked between the chicken

Recipe continues

pieces (during cooking, the rice will trickle down between them). Add a layer of the eggplant, followed by a layer of the cauliflower. Top with the remaining rice and smooth it into an even layer.

Whisk together the boiling water, baharat, turmeric, cinnamon, and 1 tablespoon salt and slowly pour the mixture over the rice, taking care not to disrupt the layers. Cover with a tight-fitting lid and cook over low heat for 1 hour, or until the rice is cooked through. Increase the heat to medium-high and cook for another 5 minutes; if you're lucky, this will brown the bottom part of the rice and form a crust.

Wet a large kitchen towel with cold water and place it on a heatproof surface on the counter. Place the pot on the towel and let it sit, covered,

for 3 minutes to cool the bottom and prevent the rice from sticking (this is the unstick trick!).

Remove the lid and run a spatula around the walls of the pot to release the rice. Place a large flat serving plate over the top of the pot and, holding the pot and the plate together, flip them over in one swift, decisive move. Lift off the pot carefully to reveal the gorgeous rice and chicken "cake." Serve at once, with fresh pickles and harissa alongside.

You can make the dish a few hours ahead. Once assembled, cook the maqloubeh for 50 minutes over low heat. When ready to serve, cook for another 10 minutes over low heat and then 10 minutes over high heat, then let cool and unmold as directed.

TIPS *Make sure the serving plate is considerably wider than the pot (ideally an 11-inch/28 cm platter for a 9-inch/23 cm pan).*

If you are using a smaller pot, you may need to repeat the layers. Your maqloubeh *will be taller and even more stunning, but perhaps less stable.*

Don't be discouraged if the maqloubeh *collapses when you lift the pan–just mix everything together and serve.*

VARIATION
Garnish with toasted pistachio nuts and/or parsley.

MAQLOUBEH: DRAMA AT THE TABLE

The scene: A festive dinner in a famous Jerusalem restaurant. The guests have just finished their first course and are looking forward to the main event. The chef comes out of the kitchen carrying a massive pot covered with an even bigger copper tray. With a visible effort, he flips over the pot and tray together, places them on the table, and ceremoniously drums on the bottom of the pot with a large wooden spoon. A hush falls over the room as he slowly raises the pot and reveals a tall mound of golden rice studded with vegetables and crowned with juicy morsels of meat. *Oohs, aahs*, a round of applause . . . and all this before anybody has had their first taste, which is exactly the effect the chef was aiming for. This is *maqloubeh* ("upside down" in Arabic), a famous Palestinian pilaf—and a fantastic party dish.

Ghormeh Sabzi

Persian Lamb and Herb Stew with Rice

3 pounds (1.4 kg) lamb shoulder, trimmed and cut into 1½-inch (4 cm) chunks

2 tablespoons vegetable oil

5 teaspoons kosher salt and freshly ground black pepper

1 medium yellow onion, thinly sliced

2 garlic cloves, smashed

1½ tablespoons dried fenugreek leaves

1 teaspoon ground cumin

½ teaspoon ground turmeric

One 14-ounce (400 g) can chickpeas, drained and rinsed

5 ounces (140 g) baby spinach (about 3 cups)

1¼ cups (50 g) coarsely chopped fresh cilantro

1 cup (50 g) coarsely chopped fresh parsley

1 cup (50 g) coarsely chopped fresh dill

¼ cup (13 g) coarsely chopped fresh mint

2 dried Persian limes, cracked

1 teaspoon sugar

¼ cup (60 ml) fresh lemon juice

4 cups (960 ml) homemade or low-sodium store-bought chicken stock

Perfect Pilaf Rice (page 186) or Persian Tahdig Rice (page 188)

Persian cooks are famous for their stews (collectively known as *ghormeh*), as well as their profuse use of herbs. Both traditions feature prominently in this slow-cooked, exotically fragrant casserole that is one of my mom's greatest hits. It's so iconic that Iranian expats initiated an International Ghormeh Sabzi day, celebrated two days after Thanksgiving. A proper *sabzi* contains meat (lamb or beef), herbs, and usually kidney beans or split peas, but here chickpeas play that role. Serve with plain rice, or better still, with crusty tahdig rice (see page 188).

Remove the lamb from the fridge about 30 minutes before cooking to bring it close to room temperature (this will encourage even cooking).

Preheat the oven to 325°F (165°C).

Heat the vegetable oil in a large Dutch oven or a heavy ovenproof pan over medium-high heat for 2 to 3 minutes. Toss the lamb with ½ teaspoon of the salt and a few twists of pepper. Working in batches so you don't crowd the pan (which would steam the meat rather than sear it), add the lamb chunks and sear until the meat is nicely browned on all sides, 4 to 5 minutes total. Transfer the lamb to a platter and repeat to brown the remaining lamb.

Return all the lamb to the pan, add the onion, and sauté until soft and translucent, another 5 minutes or so. Add the garlic, fenugreek leaves, cumin, and turmeric and sauté until fragrant, another 1 to 2 minutes.

Add the chickpeas, spinach, cilantro, parsley, dill, mint, dried limes, and sugar and sauté for about 2 minutes. Add the lemon juice, stock, and the remaining 4½ teaspoons salt. Bring to a simmer, then cover the pot with a tight-fitting lid or cover well with aluminum foil. Transfer to the oven and cook until the lamb is very tender and the herbs turn very dark green and mushy, 2 to 2½ hours. Serve over rice.

Bakhsh

Bukharian Rice Pilaf with Mixed Meats and Fresh Herb Salad

3 cups (555 g) jasmine rice

3 tablespoons extra-virgin olive oil

1 large yellow onion, finely chopped

1 leek, white and light green parts only, finely chopped

2 medium garlic cloves, minced or grated

2 merguez sausages (about 8 ounces/225 g total weight), cut into ½-inch (1.5 cm) chunks

4 ounces (115 g) ground beef

2 boneless, skinless chicken thighs, cut into ½-inch (1.5 cm) chunks

4 chicken livers, trimmed and cut into ½-inch (1.5 cm) chunks

5 scallions, coarsely chopped

1½ cups (60 g) finely chopped fresh cilantro

1 cup (50 g) finely chopped fresh dill

½ cup (25 g) finely chopped fresh mint

1 cup (50 g) finely chopped fresh parsley

1½ tablespoons kosher salt

Freshly ground black pepper

4 cups (960 ml) boiling water

Fresh Herb Salad (page 56)

This fragrant pilaf is loaded with fresh herbs, typical of its Bukharian origins. The Bukhari Jews originated in central Asia—in what is modern-day Uzbekistan. Most of the population now lives in Israel and New York.

My aunt Tzippi was Bukhari, and her cooking was similar to that of my mother, who is Persian. In the old country, they cooked this dish in a cloth bag immersed in boiling water, and Tzippi used to talk about using an old pillowcase for the task. But don't worry—forget the linens, use a Dutch oven on the stove! It's just as authentic.

Put the rice in a bowl, add cool water to cover, and set aside to soak for 2 hours. Drain and rinse several times under running water (this will make the cooked rice less starchy).

Heat the oil in a large wide pot over medium-high heat. Add the onion and leek and sauté until both are soft and translucent, 5 to 7 minutes. Add the garlic, sausages, and ground beef and sauté until the sausages are crumbly and golden, another 3 minutes. Add the chicken thighs and livers and sauté until the livers turn a lighter shade and the thighs are light golden, about another 5 minutes.

Add the rice and sauté until the grains are coated in oil and turn opaque, about 2 minutes.

Add the scallions, cilantro, dill, mint, parsley, and salt and several twists of pepper. Pour in the boiling water and bring back to a boil over high heat. Reduce the heat to low, cover with a tight-fitting lid, and cook until the rice and meats are cooked through, 40 to 50 minutes. Turn off the heat and let sit, covered, for 10 to 15 minutes before serving. Serve with Fresh Herb Salad as an accompaniment.

Shuk Mahane Yehuda/ Mahane Yehuda Market

The story

If you only visit one market in Israel, it has to be Mahane Yehuda or, as Jerusalemites refer to it, the Shuk. The incredible thing about this rambling, century-old market, which covers a whole neighborhood in downtown Jerusalem, is that it manages to be one of the main tourist attractions in a city packed with mind-blowing sights, as well as its hottest nightlife spot, yet it remains a place where locals of all ages, denominations, and income levels actually shop. In a city torn by conflict and extremism, Mahane Yehuda is an island of cheerful sanity, a place where we're somehow able to put our differences aside and enjoy its peculiar brand of magic together.

We haven't yet met a Jerusalemite who doesn't have a soft spot for the Shuk. Take our friend Renana, a food writer and university professor. She lives in Mevaseret Zion in the suburbs of Jerusalem and works at Hebrew University on Mount Scopus. To get to the Shuk, she must take a long, inconvenient detour, but this doesn't deter her from making it there at least once a week. For Renana, spending time at the Shuk is not just about buying fresh produce at good prices ("If you add the cost of gas and parking, it doesn't really make sense economically," she says). She loves coming here to reconnect with everything she admires about her hometown–the sense of tradition, the feeling of community, the contrast between old and new, religious and secular, and of course the smells and flavors of her childhood. Meeting friends and relatives, many of whom work at the market or live in the quarters around it, is an added perk. Like many Jerusalemites, Renana comes early to beat the crowds, follows a routine path to visit her preferred stalls and shops, and is done before nine o'clock, in time for a quick espresso before she gets on with her day.

The vibe

By the time she leaves, the Shuk is fully awake–Etz Hayyim Street, the impressive and most gentrified roofed main drag of the market, is abuzz with action, as are the smaller alleys crisscrossing it. The entire unbelievably diverse mosaic of people who live in or visit Jerusalem is represented here, and if you listen carefully, you'll hear Hebrew and Arabic, Yiddish, Russian, English, French, and possibly a few other languages. Hasidic families navigate baby strollers (which double as shopping carts) through the teeming alleys; elderly ladies haggle with vendors over prices; guides hold their umbrellas high to make sure the tourists on their roster don't wander away, lured by a stall of gourmet cheese or trays of honeyed baklava; Instagrammers take pictures of gorgeous-looking fruit, while vendors watch them with exasperation ("Stop admiring and buy something already"); Halva Kingdom salespeople with paper crowns on their heads push free tastes of halva; tattooed hipsters sip beers and cappuccinos at little cafés located on almost every corner; elderly gents gather in a small courtyard at the heart of the market for a game of backgammon and a round of gossip.

Come noon, there's a new influx of visitors who want to grab lunch–most go to one of the simple restaurants serving what became known as Jerusalem soul food: homey, stewy fare including (but not limited to) Kurdish Iraqi *kubbeh* soups, Sephardic *sofrito*, North African couscous, and more. There are also good hummus places, little cafés, and a great selection of street foods–local and foreign, traditional and innovative.

Thursday is the busiest day for serious shoppers who come to stock up for Shabbat. Most of the action is at the Iraqi market (aka "the small shuk"), a few narrow alleys at the northern tip of Mahane Yehuda. The feel here is different. The merchandise is more basic, everybody seems to be in a hurry, the vendors are the loudest, and the prices are the cheapest you'll find anywhere in the city. Many of the Thursday shoppers will return on Friday for some last-minute shopping, often just a pretext to hang out with friends and enjoy the cheery preweekend groove.

As the evening approaches, stall owners start pushing down the metal shutters of their shops, revealing stunning graffiti spray-painted by a local artist, Solomon Souza– some 150 portraits of famous personalities, from Albert Einstein to the Queen of Sheba. The shoppers hurry to

Huge pots of tavshilim *simmering on kerosene-fueled stoves at Azura restaurant* (ABOVE); *Next to the restaurant, elderly gents gather daily in a small courtyard for a game of backgammon and a round of gossip* (RIGHT)

finish their errands as the Shuk gets ready for the night shift. In the last decade, Mahane Yehuda has evolved into the hottest nightlife venue in Jerusalem, with literally dozens of bars that stay open until the wee hours and spill into one another, making the Shuk look like one huge nightclub. Live music, alcohol, and merriment are also evident on Friday afternoons, which are even busier than weekday nights. And then, quite suddenly, it is all over–everybody hurries home before Shabbat sets in, and the Shuk goes to sleep until Sunday.

When to come

Thursdays and Fridays offer the best Mahane Yehuda experience. And of course, try to stay late to enjoy the Shuk's night scene. On Friday afternoons, the Shuk closes down for Shabbat and reopens on Sunday, which is the slowest day of the week. Many of the nightspots are also open on Saturday nights.

"Bird's nest" baklava: honeyed pistachios nestled in crunchy kadayif *pastry* (TOP); *A cook chatting with customers at the famed Machneyuda restaurant* (LEFT); *a produce stall specializing in rare tropical fruits from small growers* (OPPOSITE TOP); *Jerusalem slow food at its best: a braise of* koftas, *potatoes, eggplants, and spinach from Azura* (OPPOSITE MIDDLE); knafe *skillets ready for frying at Knafeh Bar* (OPPOSITE BOTTOM)

Our Favorite Spots

MACHNEYUDA

10 Bet Ya'akov Street

When three well-established Jerusalem chefs first opened this restaurant in 2009, the local foodie crowd was placing bets on how soon it would close down. Nobody believed that three male chefs (complete with their big egos) would be able to share one kitchen. A decade later, Machneyuda is still hugely successful and maintains its reputation as one of the most acclaimed restaurants in Israel. The décor is deliberately shabby and quirky, with mismatched furniture and vegetable crates as the leading design elements; the menu–typewritten daily on an old-fashioned typewriter–is full of insiders' quips; the cooks in the small open kitchen may spontaneously break into song during a dinner service, accompanying themselves by drumming on pots and pans and making a lot of noise in the already very noisy establishment. But all this silliness stops when it comes to the food, which is taken very seriously, and is sensual, seasonal, and intimately connected to the neighboring Shuk.

The Machneyuda Group is now one of the power players in both local and international restaurant scenes, with four restaurants in Jerusalem, two in London, one in Paris, and counting. If you want to enjoy the food in a slightly less frenetic atmosphere, come for lunch; if you are not averse

to dancing on a table after a fantastic meal, come for dinner and book well in advance. Or pop into Yudaleh, a more casual but equally delicious bar from the same chefs.

AZURA

4 Ha'eshkol Street

Dating back to 1953, Azura is arguably the most famous eating institution at the Shuk. It started as a hole-in-the-wall, and over the years became famous for its delicious comfort food and brusque service. A few years ago, the restaurant, located in a small courtyard

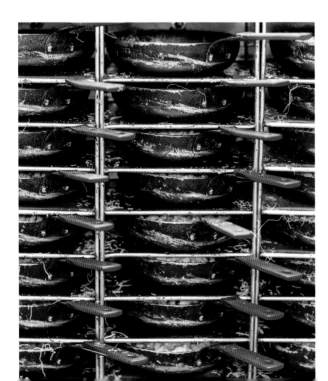

next to the Iraqi market, took over the adjacent shop and added more seating, making it a more pleasant place for lunch. In other words, the waiters won't urge you to finish up to make room for the next round of diners.

The extensive menu reads like a hit parade of Jerusalem classics: a selection of meze salads, a variety of *kubbeh* dumplings in soup, rice with beans, *mujaddara*, stuffed veggies, and awesome hummus. But for us, the best thing here are the *tavshilim*—a collective name for slow-cooked stews and braises—which simmer away in huge pots sitting on kerosene-fueled stoves. Among our favorites are braised beef cooked with green beans and bone marrow, deep-flavored oxtail stew, and Turkish-style eggplant stuffed with ground beef and perfumed with cinnamon.

MORDUCH

70 Agrippas Street

As opposed to Azura, which enjoys a prime location at the very heart of the Shuk, Morduch is tucked away on Agrippas Street, leading to the market, so it seems the owners are a bit more eager to please—the place is clean,

A tiny bar crammed between shops and produce stalls (TOP); *One of the 150 graffiti art works by Solomon Souza on metal shutters around the market* (ABOVE); *Hasidic families brush shoulders with hipsters and tourists at Etz Hayyim Street, the Shuk's main drag* (RIGHT)

The Iraqi market (aka "the small shuk") is where budget-conscious Jerusalemites shop for Shabbat (LEFT); A decadent Georgian cheesy pie freshly baked at Hachapuria (BELOW)

and the service is patient and cordial. In the early hours, when we make our way to the Shuk, we like peeking through the windows and watching the cooks deftly rolling *kubbeh* dumplings that will be served for lunch in a bowl of steaming broth. The Kurdish-style *kubbeh* soups served here are the best you can find at the Shuk.

JIMMY'S PARLIAMENT

5 Ha'eshkol Street

This tiny, friendly *hammarah* (Levantine-style watering hole) is the place where the Shuk's vendors and many of their veteran clientele get together to discuss current affairs and the latest gossip. Thirty-six kinds of home-brewed flavored arak are on offer here, served with simple meze plates and, on Thursdays, a fantastic *chraime* (North African fish stew).

HACHAPURIA

5 Ha'shikma Street, corner of Ha'eshkol

The food of Georgian Jews, most of whom immigrated to Israel in the 1970s, remained relatively unknown until recently, and this is one of the first places to make this exquisite cuisine popular in Israel. *Khacha* means "cheese," *puri* is "pastry," and this is what this small bakery-cum-eatery excels at. There is a classic boat-shaped *acharuli khachapuri* with cheese and an egg, *megrui khachapuri* with cheese and spinach (our favorite), or *achma khachapuri* with cheese and butter. All these decadent pies are baked to order, so prepare to wait for quite a few minutes, going weak with hunger as you watch and smell the pies that come out of the *taboon*.

CHAPTER 8

Ktzitzot: Patties, Latkes, and Meatballs

Ktzitzot ("minced ones" or "chopped ones" in Hebrew) refers to all manner of patties, meatballs, and burgers, but they are so much more. *Ktzitzot* are the epitome of Israeli home cooking. Inexpensive and designed to stretch a bit of protein to feed a family, they can be tiny or large, ball-shaped or flat; made from chicken, beef, lamb, fish, vegetables, or legumes; and fried, grilled, or—our favorite—cooked in a sauce. Every family has a selection of *ktzitzot* recipes. Here are some of our favorites.

Aruk

Iraqi Herb and Potato Patties

SERVES 4 TO 6 (MAKES ABOUT 24 PATTIES)

3 medium russet potatoes, (about 1½ pounds/680 g total)

1 large yellow onion

2 large eggs, lightly beaten

2 tablespoons all-purpose flour

¼ cup (25 g) chopped scallions

¾ cup (30 g) chopped fresh parsley

¾ cup (30 g) chopped fresh cilantro

1 teaspoon ground cumin

1 teaspoon sweet paprika

1½ teaspoons baharat, store-bought or homemade (see page 22)

1 tablespoon kosher salt

Freshly ground black pepper

Vegetable or olive oil, for frying

Red Pepper and Chile Tahini Sauce (page 115), for serving

Friday lunches in traditional Jewish households are light, easy to fix, and often meatless, to leave room for the substantial Shabbat meals that lie ahead. So in Jewish Iraqi homes, you'll often find these fragrant, golden-green latkes made with loads of fresh herbs, because they come together with minimal effort. Unlike the more familiar and labor-intensive Ashkenazi latkes, made with raw grated potato, these use mashed, precooked potatoes, resulting in crispy patties with a soft interior.

The first aruk I ever ate were cooked by Berta, the Iraqi mother of one of my army friends. I went to her house for lunch and was blown away by how delicious her aruk were.

I bake my potatoes, rather than boil them, because I like the richer, more potatoey flavor. The drier texture makes the latkes fluffier too.

Preheat the oven to 350°F (175°C). Bake the potatoes in their skins until completely soft when poked with a skewer or thin knife, about an hour. Let them cool on the counter.

Scoop out the cooled potato flesh and roughly mash in a large bowl. Grate the onion into another bowl. Squeeze out as much moisture as you can, and then add the onion to the potatoes. Add the eggs, flour, scallions, parsley, cilantro, cumin, paprika, baharat, salt, and several twists of pepper and mix thoroughly. If you have time, cover and refrigerate for 30 minutes (this will stabilize the texture).

Line a tray or plate with two layers of paper towels. Fill a large nonstick skillet with vegetable oil to a depth of ¼ inch (6 mm) and heat the oil over medium-high heat.

While the oil is heating, rub your hands with additional oil and shape the potato mixture into patties about 2½ inches (6 cm) across. Working in batches, add the patties to the hot oil and fry until they are deep golden-green and crispy, 2 to 3 minutes on each side. Transfer to the paper towels to drain. Repeat to cook the remaining patties.

Serve hot or warm, with red pepper tahini sauce. Aruk latkes are best fresh out of the skillet, but you can keep leftovers in an airtight container in the fridge for a day; reheat them at 350°F (175°C) for 5 to 7 minutes.

TIP *To speed things up, you can pulse the herbs and the onion in a food processor until they are finely chopped.*

Herbs by the Cupful

If you peek into an average Israeli fridge, there is a good chance you will find several bunches of fresh herbs sitting in the vegetable drawer waiting to be added to salads, soups, stews, patties, or omelets. Israelis love their herbs. They don't buy this or that herb only when they need it for a specific recipe, but casually add the word *asabim* (Hebrew for "herbs") to their shopping list. Most wouldn't even bother to be specific–every cook knows what she needs. For Yemenite, North African, or Georgian cooks, cilantro is the number one herb. Come to think of it, all three cuisines are very spicy, and cilantro has a lovely cooling effect on chiles. A Palestinian herb set consists of mint, parsley, and za'atar (wild oregano), while cilantro is almost never used. Dill, along with parsley and celery, are the herbs of choice for Ashkenazi cooks, but dill is also common in Persian cookery. Persians are the record-holders in herb consumption. They don't just cook with oodles of herbs–they also munch on them between courses to cleanse their palates and spike their appetites. A typical Persian herb platter contains cilantro, mint, basil, tarragon, watercress, and chives.

All of these herbs are on display at specialized herb stalls found at every food market. These are the prettiest stalls at any shuk, and definitely the best-smelling ones. Cilantro, parsley, mint, and dill take up most of the space, along with scallions and celery, but we like peeking at hidden corners where more exotic stuff is tucked away, such as lovage–used for the Romanian chorba soup–or fenugreek leaves favored by Persian and Indian cooks.

Fresh herbs are highly perishable, so it is always a good idea to use them as soon as possible. If you must store them, wash and dry whole stalks and discard any leaves that look dry or discolored. Moisten several sheets of paper towel and squeeze them out so they are barely damp. Wrap the herbs and store in a vegetable drawer for 3 to 4 days. This wouldn't work for mint and basil, though, because they tend to turn black very quickly if refrigerated.

When you're ready to cook, rinse the herbs in plenty of cool water, then dry them completely using a salad spinner. Wet herbs are a disaster unless you're adding them directly into a soup or stew. To chop, be sure your knife is sharp and chop through the herbs in just one pass. Chopping the same pile of herbs over and over will bruise them.

Beet Latkes with Preserved Lemon and Yogurt Dressing

1 medium russet potato (270 g), peeled

1 large or 2 small beets, peeled

1 medium yellow onion

1 large egg

1 tablespoon chopped fresh thyme

1 teaspoon chopped fresh rosemary

¼ cup (30 g) all-purpose flour

Freshly ground black pepper

Vegetable oil, for frying

1 tablespoon kosher salt

Preserved Lemon and Yogurt Dressing (see page 214) or plain yogurt, for serving

I'm a beet freak, so when I wanted to give an upgrade to the traditional Ashkenazi potato pancake, beets were my solution. Unlike potatoes, beets don't start turning black the moment you grate them, and they preserve their crispiness a bit longer, so it's easier to pace their preparation and serving. These crunchy-chewy latkes have just the right hint of sweetness to offset the bright dressing.

Grate the potato coarsely on the large holes of a box grater or in a food processor using the grating blade. Wrap the grated potatoes in a clean kitchen towel (no fabric softener, please!) and squeeze vigorously to get rid of any excess liquid. Transfer to a large bowl. Do the same with the onion. If you don't care about staining your dish towel, do the same with the beets. Otherwise, grate the beets and squeeze out the moisture by hand; add to the bowl with the potatoes and onion.

Add the egg, thyme, rosemary, flour, and several twists of pepper and mix thoroughly–your hands are good for this.

Line a plate or tray with paper towels. Fill a large nonstick skillet with vegetable oil to a depth of ¼ inch (6 mm) and heat the oil over medium-high heat. When the oil is hot, stir the salt into the latke mixture, pick up a small handful, and squeeze out even more liquid (depending on the potato and onion you use, you might have quite a lot of liquid). Shape the mixture into a round, flat patty about 3 inches (7.5 cm) in diameter and carefully add it to the hot oil. Repeat until you have a panful of patties, but with plenty of room between them to flip the latkes. Fry until the latkes are crunchy and slightly browned, about 3 minutes on each side. Transfer to the paper towels to drain. Repeat to form and fry the remaining potato mixture.

Serve at once, with the preserved lemon and yogurt dressing or plain yogurt alongside.

Preserved Lemon and Yogurt Dressing

8 wedges preserved lemon, store-bought or homemade (see page 30)

1 jalapeño chile, cored, seeded, and coarsely chopped (optional)

¼ cup (60 ml) fresh lemon juice

¼ cup (60 ml) water

2 tablespoons honey

1 teaspoon ground turmeric

2 teaspoons kosher salt

2 tablespoons extra-virgin olive oil

2 cups (480 ml) whole-milk Greek yogurt (we like Fage)

This vibrant yellow, citrusy dressing is a wonderful match to subtly sweet beet latkes, but that's just the beginning. Serve it on roasted vegetables or panfried or grilled fish, or as a dipping sauce for any deep-fried snack (the acidity cuts right through the fat). It can keep for up to two weeks in the fridge, though it will probably be gone sooner.

Rinse the preserved lemon wedges and remove the seeds. Combine the preserved lemon, jalapeño (if using), lemon juice, water, honey, turmeric, salt, and oil in a food processor and puree until you have a completely smooth mixture—this may take a couple of minutes, so be patient.

Add the yogurt and pulse a few times, until the sauce is smooth and lemony yellow.

If not using at once, store in an airtight container in the fridge for up to 1 week.

VARIATION
Keep the sauce chunky: Instead of mixing everything in a food processor, finely dice the preserved lemon and jalapeño and fold together with the rest of the ingredients.

A Guide to Making Ktzitzot

- All meat-based *ktzitzot* need some fat for flavor and succulence. For best results, combine two kinds of meat, aiming for a balance of 80% lean and 20% fat. If you are making chicken patties, dark meat is ideal because of its higher fat content. Some cooks combine ground chicken breast with ground beef.

- In addition to meat, practically all *ktzitzot* contain onions. We recommend grating them rather than chopping. It takes less time; plus, grated onion will meld into the mixture and give it an oniony flavor without unexpected and often unwanted bits of onion. Use a coarse grater. Another common add-in is bread. You can use bread crumbs (homemade or store-bought), but if you have some stale white bread or challah, do as frugal grandmothers do: Briefly dunk sliced bread in water, squeeze gently, crumble into small pieces, and add to the meat mixture.

- Take the time to knead the mixture thoroughly–this will melt the fat and incorporate the flavorings in the meat. How do you know you have kneaded enough? The color will turn a shade lighter, and the texture will be softer and smoother.

- If you have time, refrigerate the mixture for 15 to 30 minutes; this will stabilize the texture and allow the spices and aromatics to blend in. Briefly knead again before shaping.

- To make sure the meat mixture is seasoned to your liking, make one small test patty and fry it–take a bite, then adjust the seasoning if necessary before cooking the remaining mixture.

- When shaping the patties, rub your palms with vegetable oil (wetting them with water can cause the hot oil in the pan to spatter when you add the meatballs). Roll the patties between your palms, making sure the surface is smooth–this way, the patties will absorb less oil in the pan and retain their shape.

- Most *ktzitzot*, including those that are cooked in liquid, are first fried. Use a nonstick pan, but be generous with oil–this won't make your patties fattier, it just creates a delicious browned crust. Don't crowd the pan–work in batches, and as soon as the patties are ready, transfer them to paper towels to absorb excess oil.

Chicken Patties with Chard, Leeks, and Celery in Lemony Broth

BROTH

2 tablespoons extra-virgin olive oil

2 leeks, white and light green parts only, cut into large chunks

1 bunch Swiss chard, stems cut crosswise into thin slices and leaves coarsely chopped

4 or 5 celery ribs, with leaves (if possible), quartered crosswise

1 jalapeño chile, cored, seeded, and thinly sliced (optional)

½ teaspoon ground turmeric

1 bay leaf

1½ teaspoons sugar

½ cup (120 ml) fresh lemon juice

2 cups (480 ml) homemade or low-sodium store-bought chicken stock

1 teaspoon kosher salt

Freshly ground black pepper

These delicate, juicy *ktzitzot* are cooked in a light lemony broth, which is similar to so many Persian broths my mother made. The patties rely on ground dark-meat chicken for the juiciest texture, so if you can't find it, buy boneless thighs and grind them at home with a proper meat grinder, or look for ground dark-meat turkey.

PATTIES

1 pound (455 g) ground
  chicken (preferably dark
  meat)

1 medium onion, coarsely
  grated

2 garlic cloves, minced or
  grated

1 egg yolk

3 tablespoons bread
  crumbs, or 1 thick slice
  challah, soaked in water
  and squeezed

1½ teaspoons kosher salt

Pinch of ground white
  pepper

Vegetable or olive oil,
  for frying

Cooked white rice,
  couscous, or mashed
  potatoes, for serving

Make the broth: Heat the oil in a large wide saucepan over medium heat. Add the leeks and chard stems and sauté, stirring frequently, for 5 minutes, or until the vegetables are soft. Add the chard leaves, celery, and jalapeño (if using) and sauté for another 5 minutes. Add the turmeric, bay leaf, sugar, lemon juice, stock, salt, and several twists of black pepper. Simmer over low heat until the vegetables are tender, about 15 minutes. Taste and adjust the seasoning; the broth should have a deep, slightly tart flavor. Keep warm.

While the broth is cooking, make the patties: Put the chicken, onion, garlic, egg yolk, bread crumbs (or soaked bread), salt, and white pepper in a large bowl and knead until well mixed. Shape the mixture into golf ball-sized balls and flatten them slightly. The mixture will be fairly soft, so work gently.

Line a plate with paper towels. Coat the bottom of a large nonstick skillet with oil and heat the oil over medium-high heat. Working in batches, add the patties to the pan and fry until they turn golden, about 2 minutes on each side (they'll finish cooking in the broth). Don't crowd the pan; leave enough room to get your spatula under the patties without breaking them up. Use a slotted spoon or spatula to transfer the cooked patties to the paper towels. Repeat to cook the remaining patties; set aside.

Adjust the heat under the broth to bring it to a simmer. Slide the patties into the simmering broth, cover the pan, and cook over low heat until the patties are cooked through, 25 to 30 minutes.

Serve the patties over white rice, couscous, or mashed potatoes.

VARIATION
These chicken patties are also delicious served without the broth: Fry them for 4 to 5 minutes on each side and serve them as you would chicken burgers. We also like them at room temperature as a sandwich filling between two slices of challah.

Fassenjan Meatballs

Persian Beef and Duck Meatballs in Walnut-Pomegranate Sauce

MEATBALLS

1 pound (455 g) ground beef

1 pound (455 g) ground duck breast

1 yellow onion, coarsely grated

½ cup (25 g) finely chopped fresh parsley

1 teaspoon ground coriander

2 teaspoons kosher salt

Freshly ground black pepper

Vegetable oil, for frying

What this brownish and somewhat grainy sauce—called *fassenjan*—lacks in looks, it more than makes up for in rich, intense flavor, thanks to a powerful combo of walnuts, pomegranate juice, pomegranate molasses, and dried limes. The brown, rock-hard Persian limes won't win a beauty pageant either, but crack them in your hands and inhale the complex citrusy aroma with hints of smokiness, and you'll understand why cooks in Iran treasure them. You can find dried limes (or dried lemons) in Middle Eastern groceries or order them online. They're worth seeking out, and they keep indefinitely. Note: You can use all ground beef (2 pounds/910 g total) instead of the duck.

Prepare the patties: Put the beef and duck in a large bowl, add the onion and parsley, and season with the coriander, salt, and several twists of pepper. Knead thoroughly to blend the ingredients. If you have time, cover and refrigerate for 20 to 30 minutes to allow the flavors to blend.

Rub your hands with a bit of vegetable oil and shape the meat mixture into golf ball-sized meatballs; set them on a tray.

Line a plate or separate tray with paper towels. Coat the bottom of a large skillet with vegetable oil and heat over medium-high heat. Add the meatballs and fry quickly until they are just golden brown on all sides, 3 to 4 minutes total; shake the pan a few times to roll the meatballs in the oil and make sure they are browned evenly. For the best browning, don't crowd the pan; work in batches if you need to. Transfer the meatballs to the paper towels. Repeat to cook the remaining meatballs; set aside.

Prepare the sauce: Heat the oil in a wide saucepan over medium-high heat. Add the onion, garlic, and ginger and sauté until the onion is soft and translucent, about 3 minutes. Add the walnuts and sauté for another 3 minutes. Season with the cumin, ½ teaspoon salt, and several twists of black pepper. Pour in the pomegranate juice and molasses and add the dried limes. Bring to a simmer, stirring often. Taste and adjust the seasoning— once you add the meatballs, you won't be able to stir, so make sure the sauce is seasoned to your liking.

SAUCE

1 tablespoon extra-virgin olive oil

1 onion, coarsely grated

2 medium garlic cloves, grated or minced

1 teaspoon grated fresh ginger

1½ cups (180 g) very finely chopped walnuts

½ teaspoon ground cumin

½ teaspoon kosher salt, plus more if needed

Freshly ground black pepper

2 cups (480 ml) pure unsweetened pomegranate juice (we like POM Wonderful)

½ cup (120 ml) pomegranate molasses

2 dried Persian limes, cracked

Kosher salt and freshly ground black pepper

TO SERVE

Cooked white rice

Fresh pomegranate seeds, for garnish (optional)

Fresh cilantro leaves, for garnish

Gently slide the meatballs into the sauce in a single layer, making sure they are fully submerged in the sauce (shake the pan slightly to settle them). Cover the pan and simmer over low heat for 30 minutes. Remove the lid and cook until the sauce is thick and shiny, another 10 minutes or so. Serve hot over white rice, garnished with pomegranate seeds (if they are in season) and cilantro leaves. If not serving immediately, let cool and store in an airtight container in the fridge for up to 3 days; reheat gently.

Gondi Berenji

Meatballs Stuffed with Prunes in Spiced Chickpea Broth

BROTH

3 quarts (3 L) homemade or low-sodium store-bought chicken stock (or half stock and half water)

1 celery rib, with leaves, quartered

1 medium carrot, quartered

2 dried Persian limes, cracked

2½ cups (400 g) cooked chickpeas, or two 14-ounce (400 g) cans chickpeas, rinsed and drained

1 teaspoon ground turmeric

1 teaspoon ground cumin

Kosher salt and freshly ground black pepper

MEATBALLS

¾ cup (140 g) jasmine rice

2 teaspoons kosher salt

1 medium onion

1½ pounds (225 g) ground beef

½ cup (20 g) finely chopped fresh cilantro

½ cup (25 g) finely chopped fresh parsley

1 teaspoon ground cumin

½ teaspoon ground turmeric

Freshly ground black pepper

Vegetable oil

4 prunes, pitted and quartered

FOR GARNISH

Fresh parsley leaves

Fresh lemon juice

Until recently in Israel, Persian cuisine was familiar only to those who were lucky enough to be part of a Persian family (like me), or who married into one. It took a few good Persian restaurants to make local foodies pay attention to this exquisite cuisine. But, even today, many terrific dishes remain unknown outside the Persian community, like this unique dumpling made with beef and lots of fresh herbs that hides a sweet surprise inside.

Prepare the broth: Pour the stock into a large pot and add the celery, carrot, dried limes, chickpeas, turmeric, and cumin. Season generously with salt and pepper. Bring to a boil over medium-high heat. Reduce the heat to medium-low and simmer for about 30 minutes to reduce the stock and concentrate the flavors. Taste and adjust the seasoning to your liking.

While the broth is cooking, prepare the meatballs: Put the rice in a medium bowl and add 1 teaspoon of the salt and lukewarm water to cover. Soak for 15 minutes, then drain, rinse, drain again, and set aside.

Grate the onion coarsely over a small bowl, then squeeze out the liquid. Transfer the onion to a large bowl and add the soaked rice, ground beef, cilantro, and parsley. Season with the cumin, turmeric, several twists of pepper, and the remaining 1 teaspoon salt and knead thoroughly to blend.

Rub your hands with some oil and shape the meat mixture into 16 balls, each the size of an avocado pit.

Slightly flatten each ball in the palm of your hand and place a prune quarter in the center. Reshape the meat into a ball and roll it between your palms to smooth it.

Arrange the meatballs on a tray and refrigerate for 15 minutes; this will stabilize their texture and ensure they don't fall apart when added to the hot broth.

Bring the broth to a lively simmer and gently slide in the meatballs one by one. Cover and simmer until the rice is cooked through, 30 to 35 minutes. As the rice expands, it will poke out of the meatballs.

Place 2 or 3 meatballs in each soup bowl and ladle on some broth, including some of the chickpeas. Garnish with parsley leaves and a generous splash of fresh lemon juice.

Ktzitzot Abu Hatzerah

Braised Beef and Rice Patties in Semolina Crust

PATTIES

½ cup (90 g) jasmine rice

2 teaspoons kosher salt

1 large russet or Yukon Gold
potato, peeled

1 large onion

2 slices challah or other soft
white bread

1 pound (455 g) ground beef

½ cup (25 g) chopped fresh
parsley

½ cup (20 g) chopped fresh
cilantro

Freshly ground black pepper

COOKING LIQUID

4 cups (960 ml) homemade
or low-sodium store-
bought chicken stock

1 tablespoon sweet paprika

⅛ teaspoon ground
turmeric

1½ teaspoons kosher salt

Freshly ground black pepper

COATING

3 large eggs

1½ cups (280 g) coarse
semolina (farina or
Cream of Wheat)

Vegetable oil, for frying

When popular Israeli food blogger Yonit Tzukerman first published this recipe, it quickly went viral—no small feat in a country where every cook boasts a collection of signature *ktzitzot*.

In a perfect example of stretching a bit of meat to feed a large family, the ground beef gets bulked up with not only rice but also grated potatoes and a couple of slices of challah. Once formed, the patties get dredged in egg and semolina, briefly fried, then braised in a small amount of liquid. The patties absorb the liquid and swell considerably, resulting in a comforting and quite substantial meal. A couple of patties and a small salad are all you need for a filling dinner.

As for the name, the recipe was allegedly passed down to Yonit by members of the Abu Hatzerah clan, a famous rabbinic dynasty hailing from Morocco.

Make the patties: Put the rice in a medium bowl and add ½ teaspoon of the salt and lukewarm water to cover. Soak for 15 minutes, drain, rinse, and set aside.

Grate the potato on the large holes of a box grater over a small bowl and, using your hands, squeeze out the liquid. Transfer to a large bowl. Grate and squeeze the onion in the same way and add it to the bowl with the potatoes.

Fill a small bowl with water. Briefly dunk the bread in the bowl, squeeze out the excess liquid, and crumble the bread into tiny pieces. Add to the bowl with the potatoes and onions. Add the soaked rice, ground beef, parsley, and cilantro. Season with the remaining 1½ teaspoons salt and several twists of pepper. Knead thoroughly to combine. If you have time, cover and refrigerate for 15 to 20 minutes to allow the starchy ingredients to swell a bit.

Prepare the cooking liquid: Whisk together the stock, paprika, turmeric, salt, and a few twists of pepper in a medium bowl.

Coat the patties: Whisk the eggs in a medium bowl. Pour the semolina into a separate shallow bowl or plate.

Rub your hands with vegetable oil and form the meat mixture into large, plump, oblong patties (use about ½ cup/100 g of the meat mixture for each one). Dip each patty in the egg, letting any excess drip off, then dredge in the semolina until completely coated. Set the coated patty on a plate or rack and repeat to coat the remaining patties. Set aside.

Line a plate or tray with paper towels. Generously coat the bottom of a large skillet with vegetable oil and heat the oil over medium-high heat. Working in batches, if necessary, to avoid crowding the pan, add the patties to the oil, turn the heat down to medium, and fry until the patties have a golden shell-like crust, about 3 minutes on each side. Take care not to burn the coating. Use a slotted spoon to transfer the patties to the paper towels. Repeat to cook the remaining patties.

Arrange the patties in a single layer in a large saucepan or Dutch oven (12 inches/30 cm is ideal) and pour the cooking liquid over them (give it a whisk if it has separated). The patties should be almost submerged in the liquid.

Cover the pan with a tight-fitting lid and bring the liquid to a boil over medium-high heat. Reduce the heat to low and simmer until the patties drink up most of the liquid, about 40 minutes. Check every now and then to make sure the liquid in the pan doesn't dry out before the patties are fully cooked—add a little bit of stock or water if necessary.

Serve at once, or let cool, then store in an airtight container in the fridge for up to 3 days; reheat in the microwave. The patties actually taste better the next day.

Soups to Comfort and Refresh

The only reliable season in Israel is summer. Like an annoying relative, it always arrives too early and overstays its welcome. Winter plays hard to get—shows up for a week and disappears for a fortnight, leaving us wearing T-shirts and daydreaming about woolen sweaters and a bowl of piping-hot soup. So, when the skies finally cloud and the temperatures drop, we put a pot of soup on the stove, keeping our fingers crossed that the cold weather will stick around long enough to properly enjoy it. Here are some of our favorite winter soups followed by two chilled ones—perfect for our endless summer.

Saffron-Scented Chicken and Vegetable Soup with Fresh Herb Matzo Balls

SOUP

3 chicken legs, separated into thighs and drumsticks

Kosher salt and freshly ground black pepper

2 tablespoons vegetable oil

2 medium yellow onions, cut into ½-inch (1.5 cm) chunks

2 garlic cloves, minced

1 large carrot, cut into ½-inch (1.5 cm) chunks

1 celery rib, cut into ½-inch (1.5 cm) chunks

1 fennel bulb, sliced crosswise into ½-inch-thick (1.5 cm) pieces

1½ teaspoons finely chopped orange zest

½ teaspoon sugar

Scant 1 teaspoon saffron threads

½ teaspoon ground turmeric

1 teaspoon ground cumin

½ teaspoon fennel seed or aniseed

3½ quarts (3.5 L) cold water

1 tablespoon chopped fresh tarragon leaves

Festive meals in Israel are as diverse as the population, but some dishes pop up on almost every holiday table: honey cake for the Jewish New Year, jelly-filled doughnuts for Hanukkah, and chicken soup with matzo balls for Passover. This version is inspired by the flavors of southern France—saffron, fennel, and tarragon. The matzo balls (*kneidlach*) are laden with quantities of fresh herbs.

Make the soup: Remove the chicken from the fridge about 30 minutes before cooking. Pat it dry with paper towels and season with salt and pepper.

Heat the vegetable oil in a large soup pot over medium-high heat for 2 to 3 minutes. Add the chicken pieces, skin-side down, and sear, without flipping the pieces, until the skin is nicely browned, about 5 minutes. (You can brown the chicken pieces in batches if your pot isn't large enough to fit them all at once.) Transfer the chicken pieces to a plate and set aside.

Reduce the heat to medium, add the onions, and sauté until soft and golden, about 8 minutes. Add the garlic and sauté for another minute. Add the carrot, celery, and sliced fennel and cook until tender, about 12 minutes.

Add the orange zest, sugar, saffron, turmeric, cumin, fennel seed, a few twists of pepper, and 1 heaping teaspoon salt. Return the chicken to the pan and pour in the water. Add the tarragon. Bring to a boil, reduce the heat to low, cover the pot with the lid ajar, and simmer for about 1½ hours until the broth is deeply flavored. Toward the end of the cooking time, taste and season with salt, if needed.

While the soup is cooking, make the matzo balls: Put the matzo meal in a large bowl and stir in the boiling water. Break up the clumps with your fingers until the mixture looks like a coarse meal. Let sit for 15 to 20 minutes.

Meanwhile, combine the eggs, oil, salt, pepper, cilantro, parsley, and dill in a food processor and process until the mixture is smooth, foamy, and speckled with dots of green. Add the egg mixture to the matzo mixture, stir in the baking powder, and mix thoroughly. If the mixture feels liquidy, chill in the fridge for about 15 minutes.

Rub your palms with oil and form 1-inch (2.5 cm) balls (they will swell considerably during cooking), arranging them on a plate or a tray as you go.

MATZO BALLS

1½ cups (185 g) matzo meal (we like Streit's)

⅓ cup (80 ml) boiling water

5 large eggs

⅓ cup (80 ml) vegetable oil, plus more for greasing

1½ teaspoons kosher salt

⅛ teaspoon freshly ground black pepper

⅓ cup (15 g) coarsely chopped fresh cilantro

⅓ cup (17 g) coarsely chopped fresh parsley

⅓ cup (17 g) coarsely chopped fresh dill

¼ teaspoon baking powder

When all the balls are ready, slide them gently, one by one, into the simmering soup and cook over medium heat for about 10 minutes, or until cooked through (cut into one—it should be slightly fluffed up and have the same color all the way through).

Serve promptly. You can make the soup, without the matzo balls, a day or two in advance and store it in an airtight container in the fridge until ready to serve (the flavor will be even better); reheat before serving. Make the balls and add them to the soup shortly before serving.

Weeknight Lentil and Carrot Soup

3 tablespoons vegetable oil

1 large onion, chopped

1 large carrot, finely diced

2 garlic cloves, chopped

½ teaspoon chopped fresh thyme

1 teaspoon ground cumin

1 teaspoon ground turmeric

½ teaspoon ground coriander

Freshly ground black pepper

2 cups (400 g) dried brown or red lentils, rinsed

7 cups (1.7 L) water, plus more as needed

1 tablespoon kosher salt

TO SERVE

Extra-virgin olive oil

Lemon wedges

Classic Green S'chug (page 25; optional)

Lentils need no advance soaking and cook very quickly, which means you can have this thick, richly spiced soup on the table in around 30 minutes, start to finish. That's the good kind of fast food!

Heat the vegetable oil in a large pot over medium heat. Add the onion and sauté until it turns translucent, about 5 minutes. Add the carrot and sauté for another 5 minutes. Stir in the garlic, thyme, cumin, turmeric, coriander, and pepper to taste. Add the lentils, pour in the water, and bring to a boil. Reduce the heat to low, cover, and simmer until the lentils are soft but not mushy, about 25 minutes. If the soup is too thick, add up to 1 cup (240 ml) more water. Add the salt to taste.

Pour the soup into soup bowls, drizzle with oil, and squeeze some lemon juice over the top. For some welcome spiciness, add a tiny dollop of s'chug, if desired.

Creamy Charred Eggplant Soup

4 tablespoons (½ stick/ 55 g) unsalted butter

1 tablespoon olive oil

2 medium leeks, white and light green parts only, thinly sliced

1 medium yellow onion, chopped

2 small fresh sage sprigs

4 medium eggplants (about 3 pounds/1.4 kg), charred (see page 96)

1 tablespoon kosher salt, plus more as needed

Freshly ground white pepper

1½ quarts (1.5 L) water (or half water and half homemade or low-sodium store-bought chicken stock)

½ cup (120 ml) heavy cream or crème fraîche

3 tablespoons plain yogurt

TO GARNISH

1 large or 2 small tomatoes, halved

Za'atar

Finely chopped fresh chives

Extra-virgin olive oil

This minimalist soup, inspired by a recipe from noted Israeli chef Tomer Agai, is all about showcasing the lovely smoky flavor of "burnt" eggplants, achieved only through charring eggplants on an open fire or on a charcoal grill (see more about charring eggplants on page 96).

Melt the butter with the oil in a medium soup pot over low heat. Add the leeks and onion and cook, stirring occasionally, for about 20 minutes. You don't want to brown the vegetables, just cook until they are very soft and their oniony flavor gives way to buttery sweetness. Add the sage and simmer for another 3 to 4 minutes.

While the leeks and onion are cooking, peel the charred eggplants and let them sit in a colander in the sink to drain some of their liquid. It is not necessary to drain all the liquid—its smoky and slightly bitter flavor will add depth to the soup.

Transfer the drained eggplants to a cutting board and coarsely chop them, then add to the pot with the leeks and onion. Season with 1 tablespoon salt and a generous pinch of white pepper.

Cook over low heat, stirring often, until the mixture is smooth, about 5 minutes. Pour in the water (or water and stock) and adjust the heat to bring the mixture to a simmer. Reduce the heat to medium-low and cook for about 20 minutes so all the flavors develop and blend. Add the cream and cook for another 4 to 5 minutes to cook off the raw dairy flavor. Taste and add more salt and white pepper.

Carefully transfer the soup to a blender (work in batches, if needed) and thoroughly puree. Be patient—eggplants are fibrous and can take some time to break down properly.

Place a fine-mesh strainer over a clean pot or a large bowl, pour in the soup, and let it trickle through the strainer. Stir the soup with a ladle or a large wooden spoon, pressing it against the strainer to encourage the soup to pass through. If a lot of vegetable solids are left in the strainer, return them to the blender, add a bit of the strained soup to thin it out, and puree once again. Return to the strainer and repeat.

Stir in the yogurt, taste the strained soup, and adjust the seasoning.

Ladle the hot soup into serving bowls and squeeze the tomato halves over each bowl to coax out some fresh tomato pulp and juices—this will add a splash of color and fresh tanginess. You can also garnish the soup with a cluster of tomato seeds (or, as a famous and very poetic local chef calls them, "tomato ovaries"): Halve the tomatoes, remove the clusters with a teaspoon, and float them on the soup. Sprinkle with some za'atar and chopped chives, float a few drops of oil on top, and serve. If not serving at once, let cool, then store in an airtight container in the fridge for up to 3 days; reheat gently—don't bring to a boil. Creamy soups tend to thicken during storage—you may want to thin it with more water.

Hamud

Lemony Potato, Celery, and Chard Soup

3 tablespoons vegetable oil

1 pound (455 g) boneless beef chuck roast (preferably from the shoulder), cut into 1½-inch (4 cm) chunks

6 teaspoons kosher salt, plus more as needed

1 large yellow onion, cut into ½-inch (1.5 cm) chunks

1 large or 2 small carrots, cut into ½-inch (1.5 cm) chunks

2 celery ribs, cut into ½-inch (1.5 cm) chunks

5 garlic cloves, smashed

2 tablespoons dried mint

1 bunch Swiss chard (rainbow chard is nice for this dish), stems and leaves coarsely chopped

2½ quarts (2.5 L) homemade or low-sodium store-bought chicken or vegetable stock

2 medium russet potatoes, cut into 1-inch (2.5 cm) chunks

⅓ cup (80 ml) fresh lemon juice

1½ teaspoons sugar

Freshly ground black pepper

Many winter soups stray to the heavy side, but not this one. Hailing from Jewish Syrian cuisine, the tangy, brothy soup gets a refreshing, uplifting flavor from dried mint and fresh lemon juice. I sometimes make a vegetarian version by eliminating the beef and adding about a pound of butternut squash chunks when I add the broth. **PICTURED ON PAGE 224**

Heat the vegetable oil in a large soup pot over medium-high heat for 2 to 3 minutes. Add the beef, season lightly with salt, and sear until nicely browned on all sides, 6 to 7 minutes.

Add the onion, carrots, celery, garlic, and mint and sauté until the onion turns soft and translucent, 5 to 6 minutes. Add the chard stems and half the chard leaves and pour in the stock. Season with 4½ teaspoons of the salt. Bring to a boil, reduce the heat to medium-low, cover with the lid ajar, and simmer until the meat is tender, about 1 hour (possibly longer, depending on the meat you use).

Add the potatoes and cook until tender, another 15 to 20 minutes. Stir in the remaining chard leaves, the lemon juice, sugar, the remaining 1½ teaspoons salt, and several generous twists of pepper and cook for a couple of minutes, just until the chard leaves soften a bit—you want them to remain bright green. Taste and add more salt, if you like.

Serve hot. Like all soups, hamud can be stored for a few days and reheated.

CHARD REDISCOVERED

As you walk around Israeli markets in winter and spring, you can't ignore chard—eye-catching bunches of oversized veiny leaves. But its imposing looks are not the only reason to get friendly with chard; it can do anything spinach can do, but better and with less work. The flavor is slightly tarter than that of spinach, and the texture is more robust.

With chard you have two vegetables for the price of one. Juicy, muscular stems can survive lengthy cooking and are often used as a base for soups and stews. The green leaves are mostly added later in the cooking cycle. Just like spinach, the leaves wilt and shrink during cooking, so don't worry if it seems that the recipe calls for too much chard. If you ask us, there is no such thing as too much chard.

SERVES 8 TO 10

Yemenite White Bean Soup with Cilantro and Hawaij

- 1 pound (455 g) dried navy beans
- 2 tablespoons vegetable oil
- 1½ pounds (680 g) beef bones (with a little meat on them)
- 3 quarts (3 L) plus ½ cup (120 ml) water
- One 6-ounce (170 g) can tomato paste
- ½ bunch fresh cilantro
- 1 large yellow onion, cut into 1-inch (2.5 cm) chunks
- 1 whole head garlic, outer papery skin removed
- 2 teaspoons Soup Hawaij (page 23)
- 2½ teaspoons kosher salt

Thick, chunky, and robustly seasoned, Israeli bean soup isn't an elegant affair, but it's incredibly satisfying. In our family, we ate the Yemenite version of this soup with hawaij spice mix. My cousin Ronit's version was always better than mine—quite the irony for a chef.

Put the beans in a large bowl and add cold water to cover them by 3 to 4 inches (7.5 to 10 cm). Soak overnight (at least 8 hours, preferably longer). Drain and rinse.

Heat the vegetable oil in a large soup pot over medium-high heat for 2 to 3 minutes. Add the bones and sear until nicely browned, 6 to 7 minutes.

Pour in 3 quarts (3 L) of the water and bring to a boil. Reduce the heat to medium-low and simmer for about 1 hour, periodically skimming off any foam that rises to the top.

Whisk together the tomato paste and the remaining ½ cup (120 ml) water to thin it out and add it to the pot. Add the cilantro, onion, garlic head, hawaij, salt, and beans. Bring to a boil, then reduce the heat to maintain a gentle simmer, cover, and cook until the beans are soft and the soup is tasty, about 2 hours; if you are in no hurry, let it simmer away over very low heat for up to 4 hours, and it will be even better. Toward the end of cooking, remove the cilantro (it's fine if some has "escaped" into the soup), taste again, and add more salt if needed. Retrieve the garlic head, squeeze out the softened pulp, and stir into the soup.

Serve, or let cool and store in an airtight container in the fridge for a few days; reheat before serving. Like all legume soups, it will thicken during storage—add more water to thin it out.

SOUPS TO COMFORT AND REFRESH   235

Kubbeh Selek

Meat-Filled Dumplings in Beet Broth

Beet-stained to a vivid magenta, this Iraqi Kurdish delicacy looks like a cause for celebration and tastes like one too.

Traditional cooks will use semolina or thin bulgur wheat to make the dough, but those ingredients are tough to work with, so I use matzo meal and add eggs to make the dumplings far more forgiving to work with. It will still take you some time to shape the *kubbeh*, even this simplified version, but I promise that it's absolutely worth it. Read more about *kubbeh* soups on page 239.

SOUP

½ cup (120 ml) vegetable oil

2 medium yellow onions, finely chopped

2 leeks, white and light green parts only, chopped

4 celery ribs, sliced into ½-inch (1.5 cm) pieces

1 garlic clove, minced

4 medium beets, peeled and cut into ¾-inch (2 cm) chunks

1 teaspoon ground cumin

1 teaspoon baharat (see page 22), plus more as needed

¼ teaspoon chile flakes

¼ cup (50 g) sugar

½ cup (120 ml) fresh lemon juice

1 tablespoon kosher salt, plus more as needed

4 quarts (4 L) cold water

Make the soup: Heat the vegetable oil in a very large (about 8-quart/8 L) soup pot over medium heat. Add the onions and leeks and sauté until soft and golden, 10 to 15 minutes. Add the celery and cook, stirring occasionally, for 7 to 8 minutes. Add the garlic and sauté for another minute. Add the beets, cumin, baharat, chile flakes, sugar, lemon juice, and salt. Pour in the water and bring to a boil. Reduce the heat to low and simmer for 45 minutes. Taste and add more salt or baharat, if desired.

While the soup is cooking, start on the kubbeh dough: Put the matzo meal in a medium bowl and stir in the boiling water; cover and refrigerate until all the moisture has been absorbed and the mixture has cooled down.

Meanwhile, make the filling: Combine the ground beef, parsley, mint, onion, cumin, baharat, and salt in a large bowl. Knead thoroughly to blend, cover with plastic wrap, and refrigerate for 5 minutes; this will make it easier to shape the balls.

Rub your palms with some oil and, using a teaspoon, shape the meat mixture into ¾-inch (2 cm) balls, arranging them on a baking sheet as you go; you should end up with 25 to 30 balls.

Assemble the kubbeh: Lightly oil a baking sheet.

Stir the eggs, vegetable oil, salt, several twists of pepper, and the baking powder into the matzo mixture and mix thoroughly. Wet your hands or rub them with oil. Take a heaping tablespoon of the dough, shape it into a ball about 1 inch (2.5 cm) in diameter, and flatten it out to a disc–try to make it as thin as possible without tearing the dough; the dough is pliable, so it shouldn't be a problem. Place a meatball in the center and wrap the dough around it; pinch off any excess dough and return it to the bowl. Gently roll the dumpling between your palms to smooth out the surface, making sure there are no cracks or holes. Put the dumpling on the oiled baking sheet and repeat with the remaining dough and meatballs. If you can get the dough really thin, you

MATZO KUBBEH DOUGH

1 cup (125 g) matzo meal (we like Streit's)

¼ cup (60 ml) boiling water

3 large eggs

¼ cup (60 ml) vegetable oil

1 teaspoon kosher salt

Freshly ground black pepper

⅛ teaspoon baking powder

KUBBEH FILLING

½ pound (225 g) ground beef

2 tablespoons finely chopped fresh parsley

2 tablespoons finely chopped fresh mint

1 very small yellow onion, coarsely grated

½ teaspoon ground cumin

½ teaspoon baharat (see page 22)

1½ teaspoons kosher salt

Vegetable oil, for greasing

Fresh herb leaves (parsley, cilantro, dill), for garnish

should have enough for at least 25 of the meatballs. If you have a few meatballs left, just slide them into the soup along with the rest of the dumplings.

Make sure your soup is at a rapid simmer, then gently slide in the dumplings, one by one. Simmer for about 25 minutes—do not stir, as this may break the dumplings.

Using a slotted spoon, put 2 or 3 dumplings in each soup bowl and ladle over the soup and the vegetables. Garnish with fresh herbs and serve.

Kubbeh Soup
Jerusalem Soul Food

The second most common argument among the Israeli foodie crowd, after "Is there such a thing as Israeli cuisine?" would be "Is there such a thing as Jerusalem cuisine?" The jury is still out on both issues, but there is wide agreement that, yes, there is something you can call Jerusalem cuisine, and one of its icons is *kubbeh* soup.

Jerusalem cuisine was shaped by descendants of Spanish Jews, who arrived in the city from the Ottoman Empire in the seventeenth and eighteenth centuries. Slow-cooked meat stews, a variety of stuffed vegetables, and dainty savory pastries with mouthwatering names like *pastelikos*, *borekitas*, and *biscochos* are hallmarks of this cuisine. Jerusalem *kubbeh* soup is different. It arrived with Kurdish Jews–a relatively small and close-knit community, whose members immigrated to Israel over the course of the twentieth century and settled almost exclusively in Jerusalem. Kurdistan is a province of Iraq, but Kurdish Jews regard themselves as a separate group, certainly where food is concerned.

Historically, the Jewish Kurdish community was very poor, and so was their cuisine. Midweek meals consisted of bulgur wheat cooked with seasonal vegetables. *Kubbeh* dumplings, made from the same available ingredients plus a bit of inexpensive meat and fat, were a special treat served for Friday night dinners. Kurdish *kubbeh* dumplings are made from fine bulgur wheat (as opposed to Iraqi *kubbeh*, which are made from semolina). The stuffing is usually a mixture of ground beef and lamb fat, but authentic cooks pride themselves on stuffing the dumplings with finely shredded slow-roasted beef or lamb. As for the soup in which the dumplings are cooked and served, the most famous one is a tart and herby *hamousta* cooked with chard, celery, and zucchini and zinged with a lot of lemon juice; but there are also *kubbeh bamiah* (with okra), *kubbeh matfouniya* (with a mix of vegetables), *kubbeh masluhiah* (with turmeric and chickpeas) . . . the list goes on.

In Jerusalem, *kubbeh* remained a secret within the Kurdish community until the eighties, when a couple of eateries in and around Mahane Yehuda market added *kubbeh* soups to their menus next to meatballs, stuffed vegetables, and slow-cooked stews. Kurdish Jews, many of whom worked at the market or lived nearby, were delighted to find their favorite dish on the menu, and pretty soon Jerusalemites of other provenances joined the *kubbeh* fan club.

On Friday noon, especially in winter, it seems that everybody in Jerusalem is somehow involved with *kubbeh*–some are busy cooking it, others go back and forth carrying pots of it to friends and family, and many head to one of the little shuk eateries to have a piping-hot bowl of this ultimate Jerusalem comfort food.

Tomato, Strawberry, and Arak Gazpacho with Basil Bread Crumbs

5 or 6 ripe, sweet, fleshy tomatoes, coarsely chopped

1 large red bell pepper, cored, seeded, and cut into chunks

6 ripe large strawberries, hulled

1 medium garlic clove, coarsely chopped

1 tablespoon arak, ouzo, or pastis

2 tablespoons sherry vinegar or white wine vinegar

1 tablespoon kosher salt

1 cup (150 g) ice cubes

3 tablespoons extra-virgin olive oil

1 large fresh mint sprig

1 fresh tarragon sprig

1 celery rib, with leaves

Basil Bread Crumbs (recipe follows)

Israelis are mad about gazpacho, and no wonder—it tastes like a liquid version of an Israeli salad. Here the idea of adding strawberries comes from Israeli chef Guy Zarfati, and brings a layer of sweetness and tartness to this Spanish classic, making it taste brighter and juicier. A splash of arak (similar to ouzo or pastis) adds a subtle anise aroma.

Combine the tomatoes, bell pepper, strawberries, garlic, arak, vinegar, salt, and ice cubes in a blender and puree thoroughly until completely smooth. Once smooth, quickly blend in the oil. Transfer to a lidded container and add the mint, tarragon, and celery–they'll perfume the soup as it rests.

Transfer the soup to the fridge and chill for at least 2 hours or overnight, if possible–the longer the soup chills, the more the flavors can develop.

When ready to serve, remove the mint, tarragon, and celery and pour the chilled soup into cups, glasses, or soup bowls. Top each portion with 1 to 2 tablespoons basil bread crumbs and serve right away.

TIP *Because you are not peeling the vegetables, the texture will be a bit coarse, and many people like it just like that. But if you prefer a smoother, thinner gazpacho, place a fine-mesh strainer over a clean pot or a large bowl, pour in the chilled soup, and let it trickle through the strainer. Stir the soup with a ladle or a large wooden spoon, pressing it against the strainer to extract all the liquid–until all that is left in the strainer are bits of skin and seeds; discard those and serve the gazpacho as directed.*

Basil Bread Crumbs

An abundance of fresh basil turns these bread crumbs emerald green and infuses them with flavor. Keep them on hand to top soups (hot or chilled), grilled vegetables, and pasta. **MAKES A LITTLE OVER 1 CUP (240 G)**

3 thick slices sourdough or other hearth-style bread (it's best if the bread is slightly stale), crusts removed, coarsely chopped

¼ cup (25 g) coarsely grated or chopped Piave or Parmesan cheese

1 cup (40 g) lightly packed fresh basil leaves

1 medium garlic clove

2 tablespoons extra-virgin olive oil

Kosher salt and freshly ground black pepper

Preheat the oven to 250°F (120°C). Line a baking sheet with parchment paper.

Combine the bread, cheese, basil, garlic, and oil in a food processor and pulse until all the ingredients are finely chopped and the bread crumbs look like coarse sand.

Spread the bread crumbs over the prepared baking sheet and season lightly with salt and pepper. Bake for 12 to 15 minutes, until the bread crumbs are dry. The color should still be a vibrant green. Let cool. Store in an airtight container in your pantry for up to 1 week.

Chilled Yogurt Soup with Frozen Grapes

7 medium garlic cloves, unpeeled

2 cups (480 ml) plain whole-milk or low-fat yogurt

2 cups (480 ml) plain kefir

2 tablespoons extra-virgin olive oil

1 teaspoon honey

1 teaspoon kosher salt, plus more as needed

TO SERVE

1½ cups (225 g) seedless grapes (a mix of red, black, and green will look pretty), halved and frozen

½ small jalapeño or other medium-hot fresh chile, cored, seeded, and sliced paper-thin (optional)

1 small red onion, finely chopped (optional)

Extra-virgin olive oil

Tiny sprigs of fresh dill, tarragon, oregano, or mint, for garnish

Balkan-style garlicky yogurt soups with grated cucumbers and mint are very popular in Israel. But raw garlic tends to become overpowering during storage, and grated cucumbers dilute the soup and weaken its flavor. This recipe solves both problems. I blanch the garlic for an hour to give it a milder, sweeter flavor. And instead of grated cucumbers, I'll serve the soup with frozen grapes—a traditional summertime treat for kids in the sweltering Israel summer—for a juicy, refreshing crunch.

Put the garlic cloves in a small saucepan and add water to cover. Bring to a boil, reduce the heat to low, and simmer for about 1 hour, or until the cloves are completely soft. Drain and let cool.

Pour the yogurt and kefir into a blender. Add the oil, honey, and salt. Squeeze about 5 of the garlic cloves into a small bowl (discarding their skins), and add them to the blender. Blend until smooth. Taste and decide if the flavor is garlicky and salty enough. If not, squeeze out more garlic cloves and season with more salt. Give it another quick pulse, then pour into an airtight container and refrigerate for at least 3 hours or overnight.

When ready to serve, pour the chilled soup into small serving bowls and sprinkle with the frozen grapes and a few chile rings and a little bit of chopped onion (if using). Add a generous drizzle of oil and garnish with some fresh herb sprigs.

VARIATION

If you can't find kefir, use whole milk instead, in which case you may want to squeeze in a bit of lemon juice to add some tang.

Shuk Ha'ir Haatika/The Old City Bazaar

The story

"Jerusalem Syndrome" is a mental condition that afflicts deeply devout (and mentally fragile) individuals who visit the holy places of Jerusalem and become so overwhelmed that they suffer a nervous breakdown and delusions. Officially recorded in psychiatric literature, it affects Jews, Christians, and Muslims alike, and usually subsides within a few weeks after being removed from the area. But even without being diagnosed as a victim of the syndrome, it's impossible not to be affected by the intensity and proximity of these Old City monuments–the Church of the Holy Sepulchre, the Temple Mount, and the Western Wall–all of which are contained within a small walled area (about a third of a square mile) that, until the late nineteenth century, comprised the whole city of Jerusalem.

The vibe

And yet when you enter the Old City, usually via the main Jaffa gate, you'll find yourself in the middle of a gorgeous, winding, exotic tourist trap. There are myriad shops selling souvenirs, fake antiques, Oriental rugs, and belly-dancing attire; hustlers offering you anything from a tour of the city to illegal drugs; hordes of tourists everywhere; and terrible restaurants. The experience is surreal. You go down the steps of David Street, the market's main drag, trying to ward off pushy shop owners; then you take a quick left turn, and suddenly you're in front of the Church of the Holy Sepulchre. Go a few blocks down, turn right, and you are in the middle of the Jewish Quarter, just a few minutes away from the Wailing Wall, the most sacred and emotional place on Earth for the Jewish people.

Right next to it is the entrance to the Temple Mount–originally the site of the Jewish temple. Destroyed by the Romans, it's home to the Dome of the Rock and Al-Aqsa–two mosques second only to Mecca in their religious importance for Muslims.

Vintage sign at the entrance of a coffee roasting shop (RIGHT); *David Street, the market's main drag* (OPPOSITE)

The market covers the better part of the Christian and Muslim Quarters and goes back to the Roman Byzantine times. For centuries, the market catered mainly to pilgrims (the ancient form of tourism, if you like) and was described by travelers as dirty, cramped, and smelly; it was even nicknamed "the bad cooking market."

Today the market is clean and attractive, but finding good food is still a feat unless you know where to look; if you do, you'll discover gems. The rule is simple: If the restaurant is large and clean, and has a menu written in several languages and a waiter standing at the entrance, beckoning you in–stay away. If the place is small and tucked away down one of the side alleys, and the crowd looks local–it's worth peeking inside.

When to come

The market is open daily from early morning until about five p.m.

Our Favorite Spots

ZALATIMO SWEETS

Beit Habad Street, next to Station 7 of the Via Dolorosa

Zalatimo is a dynasty of pastry makers that have shops in Eastern Jerusalem, the West Bank, and even Amman, the capital of Jordan. They're famous for their delicious baklavas and individually wrapped *ma'amoul* cookies, but here, at their original location, next to the Holy Sepulchre, they only make *muttabak* ("folded" in Arabic)–a sheet of paper-thin dough filled with goat cheese or nuts, folded, briefly baked, and doused with syrup. The shop is nothing more than a small drab room with an oven and a few tables. The opening hours are erratic and the service is grumpy, but watching members of the Zalatimo clan rolling the pastry paper-thin with a small rolling pin, filling it, and folding it is almost as much fun as eating this crispy delight, which looks like a cross between baklava and crêpes Suzette.

ARAFAT/NIZMI HUMMUS

The Muslim Quarter, corner of David Street

The Old City is famous for its hummus, and justly so. There are quite a few really good hummus joints, including very famous ones such as Abu Shukri and Lina, but brave

Divine old-school hummus mashed with a wooden mortar and pestle at Arafat/Nizmi Hummus (TOP AND ABOVE)*; A boy takes care of business selling rugs to passersby while his father is out for lunch* (RIGHT)*; Muttabak, a crispy paper-thin pastry filled with cheese or nuts, is rolled out, filled, and baked to order at Zalatimo Sweets* (OPPOSITE)

KEBAB AL SHAAB
Perfumer Market, close to Beit Habad Street and Via Dolorosa

Here is another hole-in-the-wall with a reputation for selling the best kebab in the Old City (some even claim it's the best in the whole of Israel). Minced lamb is shaped into long slender patties, sometimes skewered with chunks of tomatoes and onions, and grilled to perfection on a small charcoal grill. You can have them stuffed in a pita or served on a plate, next to a bowl of chilled yogurt. There's no menu and no need for one, because that's all this tiny place offers. There's no sign, obviously, but the intoxicating smell of grilled meat will lead you here, and the small crowd of customers waiting for a free chair at one of the few tables will signal that you've arrived at the right place.

foodies deserve something a bit more adventurous. This place goes by two names: Nizmi Hummus, and Arafat (the name of the guy who runs the place). The name doesn't really matter, because the restaurant–composed of three little shops and a few tables scattered on the sidewalk between them–has no sign and no proper address. Luckily it's easy to find–just go down the steps of David Street until you hit a dead end, turn left toward the Muslim Quarter, and, within a minute or so, you will recognize it by the action around it. Arafat's hummus is old-school– freshly mashed by hand in small batches and served warm; it's relatively low in tahini and has a pronounced chickpea flavor. It's also very lemony, one of the hallmarks of Jerusalem-style hummus. In recent years, the place has expanded a bit, adding a few tables and a couple of non-hummus items to the menu. At noon it gets pretty full, with regulars waiting for the big moment–the flipping of a huge pot to reveal *maqloubeh*, a classic Palestinian rice-and-meat pilaf (see our recipe on page 192). Freshly cooked golden rice dotted with chunks of tender lamb and fried cauliflower, this is probably the best lunch you can buy in the Old City.

CHAPTER 10

Deliciously Stuffed

Seer memulayim (literally "a pot of stuffed ones"): These two words fill Israelis with longing for Shabbat meals and family gatherings. If *ktzitzot* (see page 207) are the essence of Israeli home cooking, *memulayim* are their special-occasion counterpart. And when it comes to grandmother's cooking, the difference between the two is not the cost of the ingredients but the time spent putting them together to create something that is far better than the sum of its humble parts. If you are looking for a quick lunch fix, you will find plenty of great options in other chapters. But if you are in the right mood and have some time on your hands, you will discover there is something soothing—therapeutic, even—in hollowing out beets, rolling onion skins, or otherwise stuffing delicious into more delicious!

Tahini-Crusted Stuffed Peppers with Lamb, Freekeh, and Prunes

8 to 10 large red bell peppers

FILLING

2 tablespoons vegetable oil

½ pound (225 g) ground lamb

½ pound (225 g) ground beef

1½ cups (240 g) freekeh, rinsed

2 medium yellow onions, coarsely grated or pulsed in a food processor

2 medium plum tomatoes, coarsely grated (discard the skins)

5 prunes, pitted and finely chopped

¼ cup (25 g) sliced blanched almonds

2½ teaspoons ras el hanout

¾ teaspoon ground cinnamon

2 teaspoons kosher salt

¼ teaspoon freshly ground black pepper

Bell peppers stuffed with meat and rice arrived in Israel with Bulgarian immigrants in the early 1950s and became a local classic. This version, however, is much closer in spirit to Middle Eastern cooking. Freekeh stands in for the usual rice, and toward the end of baking I cloak the peppers with tahini, which bakes into a golden crust. This technique is inspired by *sinaya*, a Palestinian casserole made of ground meat topped with tahini and baked in the oven. The addition of prunes is not rooted in any tradition; it just tastes delicious. **PICTURED ON PAGE 248**

Preheat the oven to 350°F (175°C).

Using a paring knife, cut off the top from each bell pepper and gently pull it off. Knock out the seeds from inside the pepper and remove the pithy membranes with your fingers or a paring knife. Shave a slice off the bottoms of the peppers so they stand upright, but be careful not to trim too much or there will be holes in your peppers and the filling will leak. Set aside.

Make the filling: Heat the vegetable oil in a large skillet over medium-high heat. Add the lamb and the beef and sauté, crumbling the meat with a fork, just until the meat starts to change color from red to light brown, 2 to 3 minutes. Transfer the meat to a large bowl. Add the freekeh, onions, tomatoes, prunes, almonds, ras el hanout, cinnamon, salt, and black pepper. Mix thoroughly.

Stuff the bell peppers with the mixture, filling each one about three-quarters of the way (the freekeh will swell during cooking). Arrange the peppers in a deep baking dish, just large enough to hold them snugly in one layer (a 9-by-13-inch/23-by-33 cm Pyrex dish works well; you could also use a large deep ovenproof skillet). If there is a gap left because the pan is too big, fill it with a whole tomato or onion; it will soften during cooking and add flavor to the cooking liquid.

Make the cooking liquid: Whisk together all the ingredients for the cooking liquid in a medium bowl, then pour it over and around the peppers—spoon some liquid directly onto the filling (the freekeh wants moisture in order to cook properly). Cover the baking dish tightly with aluminum foil and bake until the peppers are soft, the meat is cooked through, and the freekeh is tender, between 1 hour 20 minutes and 1 hour 45 minutes. You want the peppers to be very well cooked and soft.

COOKING LIQUID

½ cup (60 ml) tomato paste

2 cups (480 ml) water

¼ cup (60 ml) fresh lemon juice

¼ teaspoon ground cinnamon

Pinch of sugar

½ garlic clove, finely grated or minced

Kosher salt and freshly ground black pepper

TAHINI CRUST

½ garlic clove, grated or minced

3 tablespoons fresh lemon juice

½ cup (120 ml) best-quality raw tahini

6 tablespoons (90 ml) ice water

½ teaspoon kosher salt

Freshly ground black pepper

While the peppers are in the oven, make the tahini crust: Whisk together the garlic and lemon juice in a medium bowl, then whisk in the tahini. While whisking, add the ice water, a couple of tablespoons at a time, and whisk until the mixture is creamy and thick. Whisk in the salt and a few twists of black pepper. Set aside.

When the peppers are cooked, remove the baking dish from the oven and increase the oven temperature to 425°F (220°C). Uncover the dish and spoon the tahini mixture over the stuffing, dividing it evenly among the peppers so each one has a thin layer. Return the baking dish to the oven and bake, uncovered, until the tahini has formed a soft, golden brown crust, 10 to 15 minutes. Let the peppers cool for about 10 minutes before serving, so the juices have time to settle and thicken a bit.

Freekeh
Kissed by Fire

If you've ever lived in Israel, you've had a taste of what we call *hamsin* or *sharav*–extreme and oppressive heat waves, accompanied by hot sandy wind coming from the Egyptian desert. Even in modern-day Israel, these heat waves–which usually occur in spring–make farmers nervous, but in the ancient days, they were a farmer's worst nightmare.

In those times, wheat was the single most important crop in the area. Planted in the fall, it grew during the mild rainy winter, ripened in spring, and was ready for harvest in early summer. Once harvested, the grains could be stored safely for months, milled into flour and used to make bread–the mainstay of the ancient diet.

But what if something went wrong? What if one of those springtime heat waves was so harsh and lengthy that it destroyed tender young crops? The results could be catastrophic and lead to life-threatening famine. To insure themselves against such calamity, farmers would go into the fields in April or early May, harvest some of the young green wheat, toast the stalks on open fires, then hull and crack the grains. These greenish-brown grains–called *aviv* ("spring") or *aviv kaluy ba'esh* ("spring burnt by fire") in the Bible–could be stored for many months and cooked into gruels and stews, so even if there was no bread, the family would not go hungry.

The tradition of reaping and toasting green wheat remained part of the local agriculture and is still practiced today, but for completely different reasons. Currently known by its Arabic name, freekeh (or sometimes freekah), this toasted green wheat is highly prized for its unique smoky taste and interesting, slightly chewy texture. Many Palestinian farmers still reap, toast, and crack young wheat the old-fashioned way, and most wouldn't dream of selling it–they prefer to keep freekeh for important meals and festive gatherings.

During the last decades, commercially produced freekeh has gained popularity both in Israel and abroad. Apart from its taste, it's valued for its health benefits–green wheat has more protein and fiber and less gluten than regularly harvested wheat. Freekeh is sold as whole berries or cracked to a texture resembling bulgur wheat. Whole freekeh is less common, and we actually don't recommend it, because it needs to be soaked and cooked for a long time, resulting in a loss of flavor and aroma. In traditional cooking, freekeh is used to make pilafs and soups and to stuff vegetables, but it's also great for salads (see page 102).

Beets Stuffed with Quinoa in Lemon and Silan Sauce

8 small or 4 large equal-sized round beets

2 teaspoons kosher salt

STUFFING

1 cup (170 g) quinoa, rinsed and drained

1 cup (90 g) very finely chopped leeks (mostly the green parts, ideally saved from another recipe, such as the one on page 216)

2 teaspoons harissa, plus more as needed

1 tablespoon extra-virgin olive oil

2 teaspoons kosher salt

Freshly ground black pepper

COOKING LIQUID

½ cup (120 ml) fresh lemon juice

2 tablespoons silan or honey

1½ cups (360 ml) water

1 teaspoon kosher salt

Freshly ground black pepper

Chilled yogurt, sour cream, or freshly made Classic Tahini Sauce (page 114), for serving

Colorful beets make a pretty vehicle for stuffings, and their earthy flavor goes well with both meat-based and vegetarian fillings. Here the nutty, subtly bitter flavor of quinoa offers a particularly good match to the beets' natural sweetness, which is enhanced by the sweet-and-sour cooking sauce. Parcooking the beets makes them much easier to hollow out. Be sure to wear gloves if you're concerned about beet stains on your fingers.

Put the beets in a medium pot, add water to cover, add the salt, and boil until the beets are partially tender, 15 to 20 minutes. When you poke them with a fork, you should feel some resistance. Drain and set aside to cool for a few minutes.

If you don't want your hands to be magenta for a while, put on a pair of rubber gloves. When the beets are cool enough to handle, carefully peel them, without removing any flesh; a paring knife works well for this. Using a melon baller or a paring knife, hollow the beets to create a symmetrical cavity– you want to leave about ½ inch (1.5 cm) of flesh on all sides. Trim a thin slice from the bottom of each beet so it will sit flat on your work surface, but take care not to slice through into the cavity. Save the beet scraps for other recipes (see suggestions, page 255).

Preheat the oven to 350°F (175°C).

Make the stuffing: Stir together the quinoa, leeks, harissa, oil, salt, and several twists of pepper in a medium bowl.

Fill each beet with the stuffing, leaving a little room for the quinoa to swell when it cooks. Tap the beets gently on the counter to settle the stuffing. Arrange them side by side in a wide baking pan that can hold them all in a single layer. It's important that the beets fit snugly in the pan or they might roll over. If there's a gap left, squeeze in a whole peeled onion for support. As the beets cook, the onion will soften, drink up the cooking juices, and be a delicious bonus.

Make the cooking liquid: Whisk together the lemon juice, silan, and water in a small bowl and season with the salt and a few twists of pepper.

Recipe continues

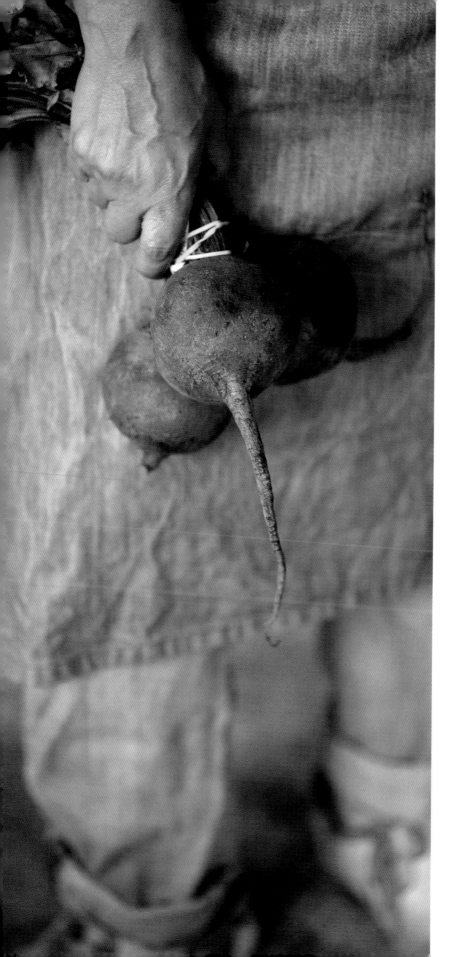

Set aside about ½ cup (120 ml) of the liquid and pour the rest around the beets; spoon some over the stuffing (the quinoa needs moisture to cook properly). Cover the pan with a tight-fitting lid or wrap it tightly with aluminum foil.

Bake for 30 minutes, then remove the pan from the oven, but don't turn the oven off. Spoon some of the reserved cooking liquid over the stuffing to keep it juicy. Cover the baking dish and bake until the quinoa is cooked through and looks swollen and the beets are completely soft, another 15 to 20 minutes.

Serve warm, with chilled yogurt, sour cream, or tahini sauce (if you want to keep the dish vegan).

TIP *Use the beet scraps to make a delicious Moroccan-style salad.*

If you used a melon baller to hollow the beets, the scraps look like cute little spheres. If you used a spoon, you may want to cut the scraps into even-sized bits. Toss them with fresh lemon juice, extra-virgin olive oil, a bit of honey, a pinch of ground cumin, kosher salt, and freshly ground black pepper. You can also add harissa or cayenne for some heat. Sprinkle with fresh cilantro and serve. The salad will keep in an airtight container in the fridge for a couple of days.

Delicata Squash Stuffed with Spiced Beef and Tahini

3 delicata squash, halved lengthwise

Extra-virgin olive oil

Kosher salt and freshly ground black pepper

STUFFING

2 tablespoons blended oil (half extra-virgin olive oil and half vegetable oil)

1 medium onion, finely chopped

1 small jalapeño chile, cored, seeded, and chopped

1 pound (455 g) ground beef

½ cup (25 g) chopped fresh parsley

¼ teaspoon ground cinnamon

1½ teaspoons sweet paprika

½ teaspoon ground turmeric

1½ teaspoons ground cumin

1 bay leaf

1½ teaspoons kosher salt, plus more as needed

½ teaspoon freshly ground black pepper

¼ cup (35 g) dried currants

¼ cup (35 g) pine nuts, fried or toasted (see page 69), plus more for garnish (optional)

½ cup freshly made Classic Tahini Sauce (page 114), for serving

Until ten years ago, the world of Israeli pumpkins and winter squashes boiled down to what is locally known as a Tunisian pumpkin. It's so huge you can hide a small child inside, so it's usually sold in large chunks. Though fancier varieties of winter squash have become trendy in recent years, the selection in Israel is still a far cry from what's available in the States. For example, we don't have delicata, one of my favorite winter squashes. It's pretty and flavorful, and the skin is thin enough to eat, so you don't need to peel it.

When you cut a delicata lengthwise, you get two boats perfect for filling with this mixture of spiced beef, currants, and pine nuts. Each one is just the right size for an individual serving, making it a great option for special dinners.

Preheat the oven to 400°F (205°C). Line a baking sheet with parchment paper.

Using a melon baller or a teaspoon, scrape out the seeds from each squash half to create a boatlike cavity. Trim a thin slice from the bottom of the squash so it will sit flat on your work surface. Arrange the squash boats cut-side up on the prepared baking sheet. Drizzle a bit of oil in the cavities, season generously with salt and pepper, and roast until the squash is fork-tender but still firm, about 20 minutes. Remove the baking sheet from the oven but keep the oven on.

While the squash is in the oven, make the stuffing: Heat the oil in a medium saucepan over medium heat. Add the onion and jalapeño and sauté for 3 to 4 minutes, until soft.

Add the ground beef and break it up with a spoon or spatula. Add the parsley, cinnamon, paprika, turmeric, cumin, bay leaf, salt, and ½ teaspoon pepper. Increase the heat to high and cook, stirring continuously and crumbling the meat with a fork, for 4 to 5 minutes, until the meat is browned.

Transfer the meat mixture to a strainer set over a bowl and let some of the fat drip out. Discard the bay leaf. Transfer to a medium bowl and stir in the currants and pine nuts. Taste and adjust the seasoning with salt and pepper, if needed.

Divide the stuffing among the boats and roast until the meat browns and crisps a bit on top, 8 to 10 minutes. Remove from the oven, arrange on a platter, drizzle with tahini sauce, garnish with more pine nuts, if desired, and serve warm.

Beef-Stuffed Onions in Pomegranate and Dried Mint Sauce

5 or 6 large yellow onions

COOKING LIQUID

½ cup (120 ml) pomegranate juice

½ cup (120 ml) homemade or low-sodium store-bought chicken stock or water

2 tablespoons pomegranate molasses

¼ teaspoon ground cinnamon

¼ teaspoon chile flakes

½ teaspoon sweet paprika

1 teaspoon sugar

2 teaspoons kosher salt

1 teaspoon dried mint

STUFFING

1 pound (455 g) ground beef

⅓ cup (17 g) chopped fresh parsley

¼ cup (20 g) chopped fresh cilantro

¼ cup (35 g) pine nuts, toasted (see page 69)

¼ cup (30 g) dried barberries or chopped unsweetened dried cranberries

1 medium onion, grated

½ teaspoon ground cinnamon

1 teaspoon sweet paprika

1 teaspoon kosher salt

Vegetable oil, for frying

Pomegranate seeds, for garnish (optional)

Stuffing onions may seem like a lot of work, but this recipe is straightforward and easy. Instead of stuffing whole onions, you separate the layers into little cups. The tangy sauce mixes pomegranate juice and pomegranate molasses to double down on the sweet-tart character.

Slice through the center of each onion as if you are going to cut them in half lengthwise, but don't cut all the way; stop before you cut through the root end. Arrange them in a microwave-safe dish and microwave for 7 to 8 minutes, until the onions are soft. (Alternatively, place the onions in a steamer basket or a strainer set in a saucepan with a tight-fitting lid and steam over simmering water until soft.) Set aside to cool. When cool enough to handle, separate them into cup-shaped "petals" and set aside.

Make the cooking liquid: Stir together all the cooking liquid ingredients in a small bowl; set aside.

Make the stuffing: Combine the ground beef, parsley, cilantro, pine nuts, barberries, and grated onion in a large bowl. Season with the cinnamon, paprika, and salt and knead to blend.

Preheat the oven to 350°F (175°C).

Stuff the onions: Cup one onion petal in your hand and add 1 to 2 tablespoons stuffing (the amount depends on the size of the petals). Roll the onion over the filling to make a football-shaped packet. Place it on a plate seam-side down. Repeat until

you've used all the stuffing; if you have any onion pieces left (especially ones that are too small for stuffing), reserve them.

Pour a thin layer of vegetable oil over the bottom of a large ovenproof skillet–12 inches (30 cm) should be a good size (if you need to, use two pans). Heat the oil over medium heat. Arrange the stuffed onions seam-side down in the pan.

Tuck any leftover onion pieces between the stuffed onions. Cook until the bottoms of the onions are lightly caramelized, 3 to 5 minutes. Pour the cooking liquid over the onions. Cover with a tight-fitting lid or foil and transfer to the oven. Bake for 35 minutes, then uncover and bake until most of the liquid has been absorbed and the onions are very soft and lightly golden, another 25 minutes.

Sprinkle with the pomegranate seeds (if using) and serve. If not serving at once, let cool completely, then cover and refrigerate until ready to serve; reheat the onions gently in a bit of liquid (stock, water, or pomegranate juice).

DRIED MINT

Mint, mostly spearmint, is one of the essential herbs in Middle Eastern cooking. From the ubiquitous mint tea to mint lemonade to garnishes for salads and soups, fresh mint is everywhere. It is readily available year-round and is one of the easiest herbs to grow at home. Yet traditional Levantine cooks, especially in Syria and Lebanon, would often prefer using dried mint to fresh. The reason is twofold. First, in the course of drying, the character of the mint changes somewhat. The cool, slightly medicinal smell of fresh mint gives way to a delicate and distinctive lemony aroma. Even more important, during lengthy cooking, fresh mint loses most of its fragrance and may develop a slightly bitter flavor. Dried mint, on the other hand, holds up nicely; its flavors open up and even a small amount can make a difference, adding a fresh lemony note but without the acidity. Dried mint tones down sweet dishes based on honey, *silan*, or pomegranate molasses and comes in handy in tomato-based sauces or soups, where too much acidity could be an issue.

Cabbage Cake Stuffed with Beef, Rice, Nuts, and Raisins

5 teaspoons kosher salt

1 medium green or savoy cabbage

3 tablespoons extra-virgin olive oil

2 medium yellow onions, finely chopped

1 cup (185 g) jasmine rice, rinsed and drained

1 pound (455 g) ground beef

2 tablespoons pine nuts, fried or toasted (see page 69)

¼ cup (25 g) sliced blanched almonds, fried or toasted (see page 69)

¼ cup (30 g) coarsely chopped shelled pistachios

¼ cup (35 g) coarsely chopped raisins

1 teaspoon Aleppo pepper or hot paprika

1 teaspoon ground cumin

⅛ teaspoon ground cinnamon

Freshly ground black pepper

3 cups (720 ml) homemade or low-sodium store-bought chicken stock or water

Classic Tahini Sauce or Yogurt-Tahini Sauce (page 114), for serving

From plump Eastern European *golabki* to slender Levantine *malfouf mahshi*, cabbage rolls are among the world's most common stuffed vegetable dishes.

Here, individual rolls become a large cabbage "cake"—easier than stuffing lots of little rolls, and visually stunning. Before you begin, make sure you have a suitable pot. It has to be ovenproof, 8 to 9 inches (20 to 23 cm) in diameter, and relatively shallow.

Fill a large pot with about 3 quarts (3 L) water, add 2 teaspoons of the salt, and bring the water to a boil.

With a sharp knife, carefully carve out the core of the cabbage (this will allow the leaves to loosen and cook more evenly). Using tongs or a slotted spoon, gently plunge the cabbage into the rapidly boiling water, cored-side down, and cook over medium-high heat for 4 to 5 minutes.

Using tongs or two large spoons, remove the cabbage from the pot and place it on the counter, cored-side down. (Keep the water in the pot at a simmer.) Using tongs or two forks, peel away as many of the outer leaves as have softened and become pliable enough to remove. Pile the leaves flat in a colander and rinse with cold water.

Bring the water back to a boil, return the cabbage head to the pot, and boil for 2 to 3 minutes. Remove the cabbage from the water and separate more softened leaves. Repeat this process until you have 14 nice leaves.

Check the leaves: If there's still some core attached or their bottoms are a little tough, trim the leaves or shave any thick ribs as needed so the leaves bend easily. Set aside.

Heat 2 tablespoons of the oil in a large skillet over medium heat. Add the onions and sauté until soft and golden brown, 7 to 8 minutes. Add the rice and sauté for 2 minutes longer. Add the ground beef, mix well, and sauté, crumbling the meat with a fork, for 2 to 3 minutes. Remove the pan from the heat and add the pine nuts, almonds, pistachios, raisins, Aleppo pepper, cumin, cinnamon, the remaining 3 teaspoons salt, and several twists of black pepper. Mix everything thoroughly with your hands or a spoon; set aside.

Recipe continues

Preheat the oven to 325°F (165°C).

To assemble the cake: Slick the bottom and sides of an ovenproof 8- to 9-inch (20 to 23 cm) pot (such as a small Dutch oven) with the remaining tablespoon oil. Line the bottom with one nice cabbage leaf, then arrange 8 more leaves in an overlapping fashion over the bottom and up the sides of the pot. If you are using a shallow (4-inch-high/10 cm) pot, the leaves may hang over the rim; that's fine. Pile the beef mixture in the center of the cabbage leaves and smooth it lightly into an even layer. Fold the ends of the cabbage leaves over the beef mixture, then layer the remaining 6 leaves on top to make a tidy cake. Slowly pour in the stock or water, taking care not to disturb the leaves.

Find a smaller pot lid or a plate that will fit inside the pot (anything flat and heatproof will do) and place it on top of the cabbage cake. (This will weigh down the cake as it cooks and keep it flat.) Cover the pot with a lid or aluminum foil, transfer it to the oven, and bake for 1 hour. To check for doneness, open the leaves a little and check the rice: When the rice is tender, everything is cooked.

Take the pot out of the oven, remove the lid and the plate, and heat the cabbage cake on the stovetop over medium heat for about 10 minutes; this will get a little color on the bottom of the cake (which will eventually be the top) and evaporate any excess liquid around the sides. Remove from the heat and leave the cake in the pot to settle the layers for about 10 minutes.

Now get ready for the flip: Place a large flat serving plate (or a cake stand) on top of the pot and, holding the pot and the plate tightly together, flip them with one smooth, decisive swing (watch out for any hot juices). Lift the pot away carefully. Cut the cabbage cake into wedges and serve with tahini or yogurt-tahini sauce.

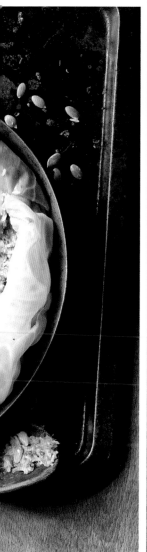

CHAPTER 11

The Couscous Table

Couscous, brought to Israel by North African Jews, is one of our favorite treats. Like busy cooks around the world, most Israelis are happy to use instant microwaveable couscous, except those who grew up eating the real thing—they can spot the instant stuff just by looking at it. Making hand-rolled couscous from scratch takes practice, but the result is spectacular! Real couscous is so good you can eat it plain—the flavor is pure and delicate and the texture airy like a cloud. It's likely that once you've had a taste of the real thing, you won't touch the instant stuff either.

Double-Steamed Hand-Rolled Couscous from Scratch

SERVES 8 TO 10

2 pounds (910 g) coarse semolina (farina or Cream of Wheat)

2½ tablespoons kosher salt

3 tablespoons vegetable oil

3 cups (720 ml) water

I had my first taste of couscous when I was a little kid, in the kitchen of Tova Ben Baruch, a Moroccan Jew who lived next door. One day, I wandered in and found Tova and her mom in the kitchen mixing grains in large bowls, rubbing them between their palms and sifting them through a wooden-rimmed sieve. There was also a big, mysterious-looking pot sitting on the stove. I remember climbing onto a chair and being allowed to help with the rubbing and sifting. A couple of hours later, I had my first taste of hand-rolled couscous and fell in love.

To make proper couscous, you start with semolina—not semolina flour used to make pizza dough, but a slightly coarser variety used to make hot cereal called farina or Cream of Wheat. You will also need two utensils that are probably not in your kitchen. The first is a couscous sieve. It looks like a regular sieve, but with larger holes—about ⅛ inch (3 mm). Order it online or look for it in Middle Eastern shops. The second piece is a two-part steaming pot with a fitted lid called a *couscoussière*. These are also available online but are quite pricey. You can use a regular steamer pot or a tall pot with a colander that fits snugly inside it, in both cases lined with cheesecloth (so that the tiny crumbles don't fall through into the boiling water).

Fill the bottom part of the couscoussière three-quarters full with water and bring the water to a boil. Reduce the heat to low to keep the water at a simmer.

(1) Put the semolina in a large bowl (pick one with a flat bottom, if you can), add the salt, and mix with your hands to distribute the salt. (2) Pour in the oil and (3) mix again thoroughly. You want to make sure all the grains are coated with oil. If there are larger clumps here and there, rub them between your palms to break them down and mix again.

The next step is the most crucial one: (4) Very, very slowly start adding the first cup (240 ml) of water. Pour a little bit over the back of your hand, spreading your fingers, as you mix the grains with that hand. You need to be really patient here–if you add the water too fast, the semolina will become mushy and the whole thing will be ruined. Pour in a bit more water and keep mixing with wide circular movements, spinning the semolina in from the edge to the center. Once the grains form tiny, even crumbles, you can stop–you may not need the whole cup (240 ml) of water. If there are some bigger chunks, rub them between your palms to

break them up. That was the tricky part. From now on, you'll have a smooth ride.

Put the upper pot of the couscoussière (the one with tiny holes) on the counter. **(5)** Transfer the semolina mixture into the sieve and **(6 and 7)** sift it straight into the couscoussière–mix the crumbles with your hands to push them through the mesh. At this point, the mixture will be very fine, crumbly, and pretty dry. Put the pot with the sifted couscous over the simmering water, cover, increase the heat to medium-low, and steam for 40 minutes.

Return the steamed couscous to the bowl and **(8)** gradually pour in another cup (240 ml) of water, mixing, spinning, and rubbing the grains all the while– this time, you may work a bit faster because the hot steamed couscous will absorb the water quickly and efficiently. Once the water is safely incorporated, gradually pour in the final cup (240 ml) water, **(9)** mixing and rubbing the grains between your palms until you have even-sized fine crumbles.

Cover the bowl with a towel and let it sit for 10 minutes–this will let the couscous release some steam and cool it a bit, so you can handle it with bare hands. Pass the couscous through the sieve once again, directly into the couscoussière, and steam for 40 minutes.

Now you have perfectly cooked, fluffy, and airy couscous, and you can be really proud of yourself. Serve at once, or let cool and store in an airtight container in the fridge for up to 2 days or freeze it flat in a zip-top bag for up to 1 month; reheat in a microwave (no need to thaw first) or steam in the couscoussière.

Couscous

Make It from Scratch and Never Look Back

Traditional couscous is made by hand-rolling and steaming semolina with water and oil and coaxing the grains into tiny, soft granules. It is a labor-intensive process that requires practice, and takes a couple of hours. Instant (commercial) couscous is made from the same materials, but the semolina granules are presteamed and dried so they can be cooked in a microwave in 5 minutes or just soaked in boiling water. So the big question is, why bother? Because the difference between hand-rolled and commercial couscous is like the difference between homemade chicken soup and canned chicken broth.

The good news is that once you master the technique, you will discover it is not that complicated. Another piece of good news is that couscous freezes well; you can make a large batch and, when a craving hits you, reheat it in the microwave or steam it—it will be as good as if it were freshly made. You can also experiment with the "cheater" method (see page 272), which yields pretty impressive results and takes less than 20 minutes.

As with all traditional recipes, variations and nuances abound, and recipes and techniques change from country to country and even from household to household. To name a few: Moroccan and Tunisian cooks steam couscous over a broth, while Tripolitans use boiling water. On the other hand, Tripolitans steam their couscous twice (sometimes even three times), as opposed to most Moroccan recipes, which call for just one round of steaming.

There are even bigger differences in the dishes served with couscous. Moroccan couscous stews (tagines) tend to be on the sweet side, while Tripolitan and Tunisian ones are spicier and often quite tart. Moroccan couscous soup is brothy and light, while the Tripolitan variety is thick and—again—quite spicy.

Whatever you choose to cook and serve, remember that couscous is the star (just like pasta in Italian cooking)—don't drown it in the sauce or soup! Serve your stews *next* to couscous, not on it, so diners can appreciate and enjoy the soft golden crumbles you worked so hard to obtain.

T'BECHA B'SALIK

COUSCOU

PANFRIED
CHILES

T'BECHA
B'SALIK
WITH
COUSCOUS

MAFROUM

CHIRSHI

BRAISED CHICKEN
WITH ALMOND
AND CITRUS

MATBOUCHA

MESAYER

HARISSA

RED WINE LAMB
TAGINE WITH
DRIED FRUIT AND
COUSCOUS

MOROCCAN
VEGETABLE SOUP

Cheater's Couscous

2 cups (370 g) coarse semolina (farina or Cream of Wheat)

1½ teaspoons kosher salt

⅓ cup (80 ml) vegetable oil

2 cups (480 ml) boiling water

Different versions of this method have circulated around Israeli food blogs for a while now, but they sounded almost too good to be true. In less than 20 minutes, without any special utensils, you can make couscous that tastes and looks like the real thing? Turns out that yes, it does work (mostly)! This method produces coarser crumbles than couscous made the old-fashioned way (see page 266), but it's still fluffy and delicious, and infinitely better than anything you can get from a box.

Combine the semolina and salt in a microwave-safe medium bowl, then pour in the oil and mix thoroughly with your hands until all the grains are coated with oil. Pour in the boiling water, fluff the mixture with a fork, cover the bowl, and microwave for 4 minutes. At this point, the grains will look like sticky wet sand. Thoroughly mix with a fork again, raking and fluffing the grains as much as possible. Cover and microwave for another 4 minutes. Fluff again with a fork and let cool for about 5 minutes to release some of the steam.

Transfer half the mixture to a food processor and process for 30 to 40 seconds, until the mixture is broken into fine, even-sized crumbles. Transfer to a bowl and repeat with the remaining mixture. Serve at once. If the couscous is not hot enough, reheat for a minute in the microwave. If you don't need the whole amount, store it in an airtight container in the fridge for up to a few days; reheat before serving.

COUSCOUS TWICE A WEEK

In North African Jewish homes, couscous is served twice a week. On Friday, it is the star of the table, accompanied by traditional condiments and pickles and a couple of fish- or meat-based stews. Couscous is also served for Tuesday lunch, but it is a simpler, usually meatless meal. There are all kinds of explanations for this custom. Some claim that bakeries were closed on Tuesdays, so couscous was served instead of bread. Another popular theory is that Tuesday was laundry day (though we have no idea exactly how hand-rolling couscous and washing clothes are connected). Another, more plausible, explanation is that on Sunday and Monday, family members ate leftovers from Shabbat, and on Tuesday everybody was ready for a freshly made, filling meal. Whatever the reason, the curious thing is that Tuesday has become a traditional couscous day in Israel—at workplace dining halls, army canteens, and even in restaurants.

Moroccan Vegetable Soup for Couscous

3 tablespoons extra-virgin olive oil

1 large yellow onion, thinly sliced

2 garlic cloves, thinly sliced

¾ teaspoon ras el hanout, store-bought or homemade (see page 23)

1 teaspoon ground cumin

½ teaspoon ground turmeric

2 celery ribs, cut into 2-inch-long (5 cm) pieces

2 medium carrots, cut on an angle into 1½-inch-long (4 cm) slices

1 small turnip, peeled and cut into 6 to 8 wedges

½ small butternut squash, peeled, seeded, and cut into 2-inch (5 cm) chunks

1 medium russet potato, cut into 6 to 8 chunks

3 quarts (3 L) water or unsalted vegetable stock

1 bay leaf

1 tablespoon kosher salt, plus more as needed

1 medium zucchini, halved lengthwise, then halved crosswise

¼ head green or white cabbage, cored and cut into 2-inch-thick (5 cm) wedges

One 14-ounce (400 g) can chickpeas, drained and rinsed, or 1½ cups (240 g) cooked chickpeas (page 119)

Brothy, bright, and brimming with vegetables, this light and nourishing soup tastes delicious on its own but offers a perfect match for couscous too. Cutting the vegetables into large chunks allows them to retain more of their texture, which plays well off the tender couscous grains. Bring the soup to the table in a separate bowl and allow guests to pile some veggies on the couscous and spoon over a few tablespoons of the broth, just to moisten the grains.

Heat the oil in a large pot over medium heat. Add the onion and sauté until soft and golden brown, 7 to 8 minutes. Add the garlic, ras el hanout, cumin, and turmeric and sauté for another 1 to 2 minutes, until fragrant. Add the celery, carrots, turnip, butternut squash, potato, water or stock, bay leaf, and 1 tablespoon kosher salt. Bring to a boil, then reduce the heat to maintain a simmer and cook until the vegetables are just about tender, 20 to 25 minutes.

Add the zucchini, cabbage, and chickpeas and simmer for another 10 to 15 minutes, until the zucchini is tender, the cabbage has wilted, and the chickpeas are heated through. Taste and season with salt. Serve hot.

Spicy Fish in Cherry Tomato and Harissa Sauce

⅓ cup (80 ml) vegetable oil

10 garlic cloves, smashed

¼ cup tomato paste

1 jalapeño chile, cored, seeded, and thinly sliced

1 tablespoon harissa, store-bought or homemade (see page 26)

3 tablespoons sweet paprika

1 teaspoon ground caraway

1½ teaspoons ground cumin

2 pints (910 g) cherry tomatoes

Kosher salt

½ cup (120 ml) water

1 large bunch fresh cilantro

Freshly ground black pepper

6 (7- to 9-ounce/200 to 255 g) fillets flaky white-fleshed fish (grouper, bass, snapper, and halibut are all nice), skin-on, if possible

Challah or couscous, for serving

Dag hareef, a spicy fish bathed in a flaming-red fiery sauce that begs for a thick slice of challah for dipping, graces almost every North African table on Friday nights. In the Libyan-Tripolitan version, known as *chraime,* the fish cooks in a minimalist sauce of oil infused with cumin, caraway, and lots of paprika. The more elaborate Moroccan version, which is what my aunt would make, contains fresh tomatoes, peppers, and an entire bunch of cilantro. Cherry tomatoes aren't traditional, but they give this gutsy dish a touch of bright sweetness.

This dish is meant to be spicy, but how spicy is up to you. Start with half the amount of harissa and chile, and fire the dish up to your liking.

Pour the vegetable oil into a relatively deep, large skillet. Immediately add the smashed garlic cloves and cook over very low heat just until fragrant, 3 to 4 minutes. Watch the pan closely to make sure the garlic doesn't brown, or it will become bitter.

Increase the heat to medium-high, add the tomato paste, half the jalapeño, 1½ teaspoons of the harissa, and all the paprika, caraway, and cumin, and stir for a minute or two, until fragrant. Add 1½ pints (680 g) of the cherry tomatoes (reserve the rest for later) and season with salt. Reduce the heat to medium and cook, stirring occasionally, until the tomatoes start to break down, 7 to 8 minutes. Pour in the water, bring to a simmer, cover, and cook over low heat for about 30 minutes, or until thick and saucy.

Remove about 3 tablespoons of whole leaves from the cilantro bunch and reserve them for garnish. Tear up the rest of the bunch and toss into the pan. Give it a minute to blend with the sauce, then taste and adjust the seasoning with salt, pepper, and the remaining jalapeño and 1½ teaspoons harissa if you want more heat. Bear in mind that once you add the fish, you won't be able to stir the sauce and play with the seasonings–make sure the flavor and level of spiciness are to your liking.

Add the fish fillets, skin-side up, tucking them gently into the sauce. Sprinkle the remaining ½ pint (225 g) cherry tomatoes on top of the fish.

Bring to a simmer over medium heat. Reduce the heat to low, cover, and simmer, without stirring, until the fish is cooked through, 7 to 8 minutes. Thicker fillets, like halibut, will need 2 to 3 minutes more. To check the fish for doneness, make a small incision in the thickest part of the fish and make sure the flesh is opaque and flaky.

Serve straight out of the pan, garnished with the reserved whole cilantro leaves, with a lot of bread alongside or with couscous.

Braised Chicken with Olives and Citrus

4 chicken legs or 8 thighs or 8 large drumsticks

½ cup (75 g) pitted olives (cracked green, Moroccan oil-cured, Manzanilla, or Kalamata olives)

1 medium yellow onion, halved and sliced

4 wedges preserved lemon, store-bought or homemade (see page 30), pulp and seeds scraped out

2 dried Persian limes, cracked

1 lemon, thinly sliced and seeded

3 tablespoons extra-virgin olive oil

1½ teaspoons honey

1 tablespoon kosher salt

1 cup (40 g) coarsely chopped fresh cilantro, plus a handful of whole leaves for serving (optional)

2 large garlic cloves, smashed

½ teaspoon ground turmeric

1½ teaspoons ground cumin

1 teaspoon sweet paprika

Pinch of chile flakes

1 cup (240 ml) homemade or low-sodium store-bought chicken stock

1 cup (240 ml) fresh orange juice

Cooked couscous (see page 266), for serving

In Israel, chicken with olives is a simple midweek dish, made with tomato paste and the most basic pitted olives, but this version, while still simple to make, is a delicious step up. In place of tomatoes, citrus provides the brightness—fresh and preserved lemons, dried limes, and orange juice. Just mix everything together and put it in the oven, and about an hour later, you have a fragrant, tangy chicken dish that is beautiful as part of the couscous table. If you don't have preserved lemons or dried Persian limes, skip either one or both. The fresh lemons and olives add plenty of flavor.

Preheat the oven to 400°F (205°C).

Put the chicken, olives, onion, preserved lemon, dried limes, lemon slices, oil, honey, salt, cilantro, garlic, turmeric, cumin, paprika, and chile flakes in a large bowl. Using your hands, mix everything thoroughly, making sure the chicken pieces are well coated with the spices and herbs.

Arrange the chicken pieces skin-side down in a deep baking dish in a single snug layer. Arrange the rest of the mixture over the chicken. Whisk the stock with the orange juice in a measuring cup and pour over the chicken.

Cover with aluminum foil and bake for 40 minutes. Remove the foil and, using tongs or a couple of spoons, turn the chicken pieces skin-side up. Bake, uncovered, for another 20 to 25 minutes, until the chicken is cooked through and the skin is nicely browned and crackly. To check for doneness, make a small incision in the thickest part of a chicken thigh and make sure the juices run clear. If they are still pink, baste the skin with the pan juices to prevent the chicken from drying out and roast for another few minutes.

Sprinkle with the cilantro leaves (if using) and serve over couscous.

T'Becha B'Salik

Short Rib, White Bean, and Chard Stew

⅓ cup (80 ml) vegetable oil

2 large bunches Swiss chard, leaves stemmed and coarsely chopped

2 pounds (910 g) boneless beef short ribs, trimmed and cut into 2-inch (5 cm) chunks

2 large onions, sliced

3 potatoes, peeled and cut into chunks

3 garlic cloves, crushed

½ cup (20 g) chopped fresh cilantro

1 jalapeño chile, halved, cored, and seeded

2 teaspoons ground cumin

1 teaspoon ground turmeric

1 tablespoon sweet paprika

1 teaspoon sugar

1 tablespoon kosher salt, plus more as needed

4 cups (960 ml) homemade or low-sodium store-bought chicken stock

2 cups (370 g) dried white beans, soaked in cold water overnight and drained

In this rich winter stew, the Swiss chard and beefy short ribs cook together for hours until meltingly tender, then get mixed with white beans and simmered for a few hours more. While delicious any time you want something hearty, the stew is a traditional partner for couscous. Though it ties up your oven, this mostly hands-off recipe leaves you free to do other things and leaves your kitchen wonderfully warm, cozy, and fragrant.

Preheat the oven to 350°F (175°C).

Heat the vegetable oil in a large skillet over low heat. Add the chard leaves and cook, stirring occasionally, until they turn very soft and almost black, about 20 minutes. Set aside.

Combine the beef, onions, potatoes, garlic, cilantro, jalapeño, cumin, turmeric, paprika, sugar, salt, and the cooked chard with any remaining oil in a large bowl. Toss to make sure everything is evenly mixed. Transfer to a Dutch oven or large heavy ovenproof pot and pour in the stock. Cover and bake for 2½ hours.

Remove the pot from the oven, add the beans, stir gently, cover, and bake for another 1½ to 2 hours, until the beans are completely soft, the sauce is thick and fragrant, and the meat is fork-tender. Toward the end of the cooking time, taste and adjust the seasoning.

Red Wine Lamb Tagine with Dried Fruit

1 tablespoon vegetable oil

2 pounds (910 g) boneless lamb shoulder, cut into 1-inch (2.5 cm) chunks

Kosher salt

1 large or 2 small yellow onions, finely chopped

2 medium carrots, cut into ¼-inch (6 mm) dice

2 garlic cloves, smashed

2 tablespoons tomato paste

2 cups (480 ml) dry red wine

2 russet potatoes, peeled and cut into chunks

6 dried apricots, chopped

6 prunes, pitted and chopped

3 tablespoons golden raisins

1 teaspoon ras el hanout, store-bought or homemade (see page 23)

½ to 1 jalapeño chile, cored, seeded, and chopped

1 teaspoon sweet paprika

½ teaspoon ground cumin

½ teaspoon ground cinnamon

4 cups (960 ml) homemade or low-sodium store-bought chicken stock or water

Lamb, dried fruit, and wine—three hallmarks of festive meals in Jewish Moroccan cooking—give this rich tagine special-occasion flair, but it's actually one of the easiest recipes in this chapter. Many versions of this famous dish (often called Tanziya) exist, most of them so sweet they border on dessert. But not this one, which uses dry wine but no sugar or honey; it lets all the sweetness come from the dried apricots, prunes, and raisins.

Preheat the oven to 375°F (190°C).

Heat a large (preferably cast-iron) skillet over high heat. Add the vegetable oil and heat until it ripples. Add the lamb chunks, season lightly with salt, and sear on all sides until they are nicely browned and have some crust on them, 6 to 7 minutes. Do this in batches if you need to; you don't want to crowd the pan, or the lamb will steam rather than sear. Using a slotted spoon, transfer the meat to a large bowl.

Reduce the heat to medium and add the onion to the skillet. Sauté until it is soft and translucent, about 5 minutes. Add the carrots and garlic and sauté until the carrots start turning golden around the edges, 3 to 4 minutes. Stir in the tomato paste, then pour in the wine. Use a spatula to scrape up the browned bits from the lamb on the bottom of the skillet and stir them into the liquid. Increase the heat to high, bring the wine to a boil, and cook for 2 to 3 minutes, just to reduce it slightly. Transfer the contents of the skillet to the bowl with the seared lamb.

Add the potatoes, apricots, prunes, and raisins to the bowl. Season with the ras el hanout, jalapeño, paprika, cumin, cinnamon, and 1 tablespoon salt, and pour in the stock. Toss everything together.

Transfer the contents of the bowl to a large Dutch oven or a deep, heavy baking dish. Cover (use aluminum foil if you don't have a lid) and bake until the lamb is meltingly tender and the liquids have reduced into a thick sauce, about 3 hours. Serve hot, with couscous.

Mafroum

Beef-Stuffed Potatoes Simmered in Tomato Sauce

6 tablespoons (90 g) kosher
salt

6 to 8 small russet
potatoes

STUFFING

2 cups (100 g) coarsely
chopped challah

1 large onion, quartered

2 garlic cloves, smashed

½ bunch fresh parsley

½ bunch fresh cilantro

1 celery rib, coarsely
chopped

1¼ pounds (565 g) ground
beef

1 tablespoon store-bought
or homemade baharat
(see page 22)

¼ cup (60 ml) water

1 tablespoon extra-virgin
olive oil

Kosher salt and freshly
ground black pepper

FRYING

2 large eggs

1½ teaspoons tomato paste

⅔ cup all-purpose flour

Vegetable oil

Authentic Tripolitan *mafroum* is my favorite comfort food and the reason I opened my couscous restaurant Kish-Kash. It is a potato "sandwich" stuffed with meat, dredged in flour and egg, deep-fried, then slowly braised in a piquant tomato sauce perfumed with baharat and cinnamon and laced with oil. The finished dish is a traditional partner for hand-rolled couscous.

Slitting and filling the potatoes in the traditional manner is tricky, so I like to shape my potatoes into little "boats," which hold plenty of meaty stuffing. They make a fantastic dinner main course, even without the couscous.

Fill a large bowl with 2 quarts (2 L) cold water and add the salt.

Peel the potatoes and halve each one lengthwise. Using a melon baller or a paring knife, scoop out the center of the potatoes to create "boats." Don't worry if the boats don't look picture perfect—the stuffing and coating with egg and flour will cover up all mistakes. Reserve about 3 ounces (85 g) potato scraps to use in the stuffing.

Transfer the boats to the bowl of salted water and set aside.

Make the stuffing: Put the challah, reserved potato scraps, the onion, garlic, parsley, cilantro, and celery in a food processor and pulse until chopped. Transfer to a large bowl. Add the ground beef, baharat, water, and oil and season with salt and pepper. Knead thoroughly to blend.

Pat dry the potato boats, arrange on a tray, and divide the filling among all the potato halves, leaving a little

"belly" on top, pat into place, and smooth the tops.

Preheat the oven to 350°F (175°C).

Fry the potatoes: Whisk together the eggs and the tomato paste in a medium bowl. Pour the flour into a separate bowl or plate. Dip each potato boat, meat-side down, first in the egg mixture and then in flour; make sure you have a light coating only on the meaty side.

Heat about 2 cups (480 ml) vegetable oil in a large (about 12-inch/30 cm) wide pan to about 350°F (175°C). Working in batches, add the stuffed potatoes meaty side down and fry until golden brown, about 2 minutes. Flip and fry for 2 minutes on the other side. Using a slotted spoon, carefully transfer the potatoes to a large Dutch oven or a 9-by-13-inch (23-by-33 cm) casserole dish and arrange them in a single layer stuffed-side up. If there is not enough space for all the boats, use two baking dishes.

COOKING LIQUID

3½ cups (840 ml) water

¾ cup (180 ml) tomato paste

¼ teaspoon ground cinnamon

½ teaspoon baharat (see page 22)

1 teaspoon chile flakes

2 teaspoons kosher salt

1½ teaspoons sugar

2 carrots, quartered

2 celery ribs, quartered

Make the cooking liquid: Whisk together the water, tomato paste, cinnamon, baharat, chile flakes, salt, and sugar in a large bowl. Pour the liquid over and around the stuffed potatoes; if you are using two dishes, make sure to divide the liquid between them.

Tuck the carrot and celery pieces around the potatoes. Cover with a lid or aluminum foil and bake until the potatoes are soft (prick one boat gently with a fork to make sure) and the sauce is thick and rich in flavor, about 1½ hours. If not serving at once, refrigerate and reheat in the oven or on the stove–add a bit of water or stock if there is not enough sauce. Serve with couscous.

Just like french fries are not worth their name without ketchup and mayo, and sausages are kind of pointless without a dollop of good mustard, so a proper couscous needs a few accessories to shine. No matter which main dish you decide to serve with your couscous, consider making at least some of the following little dishes: quick crunchy pickles, a medley of fried chiles, a surprisingly delicious lemony winter squash puree, and a fiery slow-cooked tomato relish.

Chirshi

Spicy Squash Puree

MAKES 4 CUPS (960 ML)

Harissa and lemon juice lift this North African puree out of the sweet zone and turn it into a versatile condiment. Just a spoonful of *chirshi* enlivens a whole bowl of couscous, but that's only the beginning. *Chirshi* goes with any dish that can use a boost of spicy tartness. Serve it with roasted chicken or fish, use it as a sandwich spread, and, if you're feeling adventurous, mix a couple of tablespoons into your next batch of mashed potatoes.

1 small butternut squash, peeled, seeded, and cut into 1-inch (2.5 cm) pieces (4 to 5 cups/460 to 575 g)

1 large or 2 medium carrots, sliced into ½-inch-thick (1.5 cm) coins

2 tablespoons extra-virgin olive oil

Kosher salt

¼ cup (60 ml) water

¼ cup (60 ml) vegetable oil

1 tablespoon plus 2 teaspoons red harissa, store-bought or homemade (see page 26)

3 garlic cloves, grated or minced

3 tablespoons fresh lemon juice

1 teaspoon ground caraway

1 teaspoon ground cumin

Freshly ground black pepper

Preheat the oven to 400°F (205°C).

Toss the squash and carrots with the olive oil and a generous pinch of salt. Transfer to a medium baking dish and add the water. Cover with aluminum foil and roast for 40 minutes, or until the vegetables are fork-tender.

Transfer the vegetables from the baking dish to a large bowl and discard any water that's left behind in the dish.

While the vegetables are still warm, mash them with a fork or a potato masher. Stir in the vegetable oil, harissa, garlic, and lemon juice. Season with the caraway, cumin, 1 tablespoon salt, and several generous twists of pepper. Taste and adjust the seasoning.

Serve at once or let cool and store in an airtight container in the fridge for up to 1 week.

Matboucha

Slow-Cooked Tomato and Pepper Compote

SERVES 8 TO 10

Though often served as part of a meze spread or as a spicy condiment for couscous, *matboucha* can do so much more. Think of this bright red, garlicky, and spicy dish as a North African version of ketchup, but better. Use it as a sauce for shakshuka or a fish stew, or even mix it into pasta.

This version is pretty fiery. If you like, you can use fewer chiles or go for milder varieties.

¼ cup (60 ml) vegetable oil

1 head garlic (about 20 cloves), thinly sliced

4 red bell peppers, cored, seeded, and cut into ½-inch (1.5 cm) dice

4 jalapeño or Fresno chiles (or less to taste), cored, seeded, and thinly sliced

12 ripe plum tomatoes or other sweet tomatoes, halved

Kosher salt

Heat the vegetable oil in a large saucepan over medium heat. Add the garlic and sauté, stirring continuously, just until fragrant, about 1 minute. Add the bell peppers and the chiles, reduce the heat to medium-low, and cook, stirring frequently, until the peppers are soft, 15 to 20 minutes.

Add the tomatoes, season with a bit of salt, and sauté for another minute. Reduce the heat to low, cover, and simmer for about 1½ hours, until the matboucha is thick, shiny, and bright red; depending on how juicy your vegetables are, this could take up to a couple of hours. Every now and then, peek into the pan to check on the matboucha and give it a good stir–you don't want it to stick to or burn on the bottom. If it looks dry, add a bit of water, 1 to 2 tablespoons at a time. Toward the end of cooking, taste and season with salt. Let cool.

Serve at room temperature or store in an airtight container in the fridge for up to 1 week or in the freezer for up to a few months.

VARIATION

If you can't find good fresh tomatoes, substitute one 28-ounce (795 g) can best-quality Italian tomatoes.

Mesayer

Quick Lemony Pickles

SERVES 10 TO 12

You won't need any special canning utensils to make these pickled vegetables, and you won't need a lot of time either. Allow them to marinate for an hour, and they're good to go. The pickles will keep in the fridge for up to a week but will lose some of their crunchy texture.

1 red bell pepper, cored, seeded, and sliced into 2-inch-long (5 cm) strips

1 yellow bell pepper, cored, seeded, and sliced into 2-inch-long (5 cm) strips

2 medium carrots, cut into 2-by-½-inch (5-by-1.5 cm) sticks

1 kohlrabi, peeled and cut into 2-by-½-inch (5-by-1.5 cm) sticks

½ head cauliflower, cut into small florets (about ½ inch/1.5 cm)

1 jalapeño chile, cored, seeded, and thinly sliced

1 cup (240 ml) fresh lemon juice

1 tablespoon white wine vinegar

2 tablespoons kosher salt

Place the peppers, carrots, kohlrabi, cauliflower, and jalapeño in a wide shallow container. Whisk together the lemon juice, vinegar, and salt in a small bowl until the salt has dissolved and pour the mixture over the vegetables. Marinate for at least 1 hour at room temperature. Serve at once or store in an airtight container in the fridge for up to 1 week.

Panfried Chiles

SERVES 8 TO 10

Fiery heat defines many North African meals, but the spice doesn't come from the main dishes as much as it does from the condiments and side dishes, like this one, which you'll always find on the couscous table. Here I use several kinds of chiles—some hot, some not so hot—but you can create your own medley. This recipe makes enough for a big meal—serve them straight from the skillet. Otherwise, store them in the fridge for up to a week and serve cold.

3 tablespoons vegetable oil

4 whole Cubanelle or banana peppers

4 Anaheim peppers

2 poblano peppers

½ teaspoon kosher salt

Fresh lemon juice

Maldon or other flaky salt

Heat the vegetable oil in a large skillet (cast iron works well for this dish) over high heat for 2 to 3 minutes, until it's really hot. Add the peppers and the kosher salt and cook, shaking the pan and stirring the peppers, until they're blistered on all sides, 5 to 7 minutes. Transfer to a serving plate and give them a good squeeze of lemon juice. Sprinkle with flaky salt and serve hot, or let cool and store in an airtight container in the fridge for up to 1 week; serve at room temperature.

MESAYER

PANFRIED CHILES

MATBOUCHA

Shuk Wadi Nisnas/ Wadi Nisnas Market

The story

An elderly woman is squatting on the porch of a greengrocer. There's a crate with tiny summer squash on her left and a large plastic tub on her right. She picks a squash from the crate, hollows it out with a few precise movements, and tosses it into the tub. It's only nine o'clock in the morning, but the tub is almost full. She doesn't like her picture taken but will gladly share a recipe (stuff the squash with meat, bulgur, and chopped dried apricots, then cook them in pomegranate molasses or *tamarindi*).

We fill a large plastic bag with ready-for-stuffing squash and enter the small shop to pay. The squash are expensive. "You pay for the labor," shrugs Elias Nahle, the owner, and adds that if we had come a few weeks earlier, we would have seen the woman shelling fresh fava beans, "but the season is now over." He shows us other seasonal treasures—tiny pink-cheeked apricots that taste like childhood, early summer grapes, and more squash of different shapes and colors. For the last forty years, the Nahleh family has been selling fruit and vegetables, grown on small family plots in their native village of Deir Hanna in the Lower Galilee. In the old days, the villagers were full-time farmers; today most have "modern" jobs, while farming remains a hobby and a source of additional income.

Before we leave, we ask where to buy bulgur and pomegranate molasses, and Elias sends us to The Appetizer. On the floor of this sweet-smelling, overstuffed, and neatly organized little shop, we count eight different kinds of bulgur, including Lebanese red bulgur, considered the best for making fried *kubbeh*, and other interesting stuff such as homemade arak and black nigella paste, which looks like black tahini and, according to the owner, "cures every disease except death."

A vendor peeling and hollowing summer squashes for stuffing (RIGHT); Bulgur wheat and other interesting dry goods at The Appetizer (OPPOSITE)

The vibe

Wadi Nisnas is a villagelike Arab Christian quarter located in a little valley in the town of Haifa, on the slopes of Mount Carmel. Haifa is only an hour's drive from Tel Aviv, but the vibe here is very different—the pace slower, the feel more provincial, the cultural and culinary attractions more limited. On the other hand, Haifa has breathtaking views, it's the only city in Israel with public transportation on Shabbat, and it boasts relatively harmonious coexistence between Jews and Arabs. In the present stormy political climate, this is no small feat. This spirit of coexistence is evident at the Wadi Nisnas shuk, where most businesses are owned by Arabs, while the shoppers are split almost evenly between Arabs and Jews.

As we leave the shop and make our way to Abu Shukra's butchery to buy some of his famous lamb *kofta* mince, we come up with a name for this lovely shuk–*baladi* boutique. *Baladi*, because seasonal, authentic rural produce is its main draw, *boutique* because of its carefully curated artisanal merchandise and hefty prices.

When to come

Because most of the businesses are owned by Christians, Sunday is the weakest day of the week. Fridays and Saturdays are the busiest. On Fridays and Saturdays, many businesses (including groceries and newspaper kiosks on the streets leading to the market) place tables in front of their shops and offer traditional dishes prepared in their family kitchens–stuffed vegetables, freekeh and rice pilafs, pastries, freshly made hummus. Many stalls stay open on Saturdays as well.

Our Favorite Spots

FALAFEL HAZKENIM ("OLD FOLKS' FALAFEL")

18 Wadi Street

Haifa is famous for its falafel stands, and this is one of the most legendary. The original "old folks," Najla and George Afara, opened their shop in 1960 and sold it to brothers Afif and Alif Sabith in 1984, complete with the secret recipe. Afif is in the kitchen and Alif is at the front, doling out smiles, stories, and free falafel balls to customers waiting in line for their turn.

Freshly fried falafel at the famed "Old Folks' Falafel" shop (**TOP AND ABOVE**); *Traditional fare cooked in the shop owners' family kitchens is on offer on Fridays and Saturdays* (**RIGHT AND OPPOSITE RIGHT**); *Nadima, the first restaurant in the Wadi, is still going strong* (**OPPOSITE TOP**)

FALFALA BAKERY

45 Wadi Street

This small bakery delivers pitas and other traditional flatbreads to many restaurants in Haifa, but leaves enough goodies to sell to the market's shoppers. Our favorite is *mankoushe*—a soft, focaccia-like flatbread topped with *gibeneh*, traditional Levantine goat cheese also used to make *knaffeh*.

NADIMA

37 Yohanan Hakadosh Street

Nadima Sabithi, who passed away in 2016 at the age of eighty, was often called the mother of Wadi Nisnas. For almost fifty years, she cooked and served homey Levantine food in a small restaurant right in the heart of the market. Everything was sourced from the market, and the menu was strictly seasonal—tiny stuffed squash in early summer, okra in a lemony sauce in late summer, warm salads made with edible wild greens in winter. Nadima ran the place almost single-handedly, but as the years took their toll, she let the next generation take over, though she would show up in the tiny kitchen almost until the end. Nadima's children and grandchildren honor Nadima's legacy, and the food is still delicious and seasonal. Currently the restaurant is open only on Fridays and Saturdays.

CHAPTER 12

The Flavor of Fire

Israeli barbecue goes by two names: *mangal* ("a grill" in Arabic) and *al ha'esh* ("on fire" in Hebrew), and it combines two of our favorite pastimes: hanging out with large groups of friends and family, and consuming insane amounts of grilled meat, hummus, pickles, and pitas. Israelis, just like their neighbors across the Levant, adore the taste and aroma of grilled food, and since this is not something we can cook at home on a regular basis, it always has a festive feel about it.

Cookout
Israeli-Style

A typical Israeli *mangal* ("cookout") is a potluck affair. It usually starts with a round of phone calls or texts to figure out who will bring fresh pitas, who will take care of beer and soft drinks, who will be in charge of *salatim* (Hebrew for "salads," which is a collective name for all manner of salads, dips, and relishes), and, finally, who will procure the meats.

The dynamics of the Israeli *mangal* are quite different from those of the American barbecue. Most Israelis live in apartments, so *mangal* is usually a picnic that takes place in a park, on the beach, or in a forest. Consequently, the grill (also called a *mangal*) is simple, portable, and quite small–not something you'd use to cook steaks or other large cuts of expensive meat.

Almost everything will be skewered–marinated and cubed boneless chicken thighs (called *pargiyot*; see page 301) and generously spiced lamb *koftas* (locally called kebabs) are popular players. Sausages (usually grilled first and served to the kids so they won't become wild things), chicken wings, chicken hearts, chicken livers, and fresh whole fish are typical for a *mangal*. Chunks of vegetables (onions, peppers, cherry tomatoes) are also skewered, often alternating with bits of meat. If there's some space left, whole eggplants, bell peppers, and tomatoes will be tossed on the grill and served warm and smoky next to the grilled meats. Root vegetables, such as potatoes or beets–which require longer cooking–will be wrapped in foil and buried early on in the smoldering coals. They're so delicious cooked that way; the only problem is that by the time they're cooked, everybody is too full to enjoy them.

Any fair-weather weekend is game for *mangal*, but Independence Day, celebrated in late April or early May, is famous for its heavy *mangal* action. Every patch of grass (and often the adjoining parking lots) is filled to capacity with picnickers, and it looks like the whole country has gone up in smoke.

When we eat out, grilled dishes would be one of our preferred options. A charcoal grill is a must in every restaurant kitchen, from simple market eateries to upscale establishments. One of the most popular restaurant genres in Israel is the *shipudiya* ("skewer house"), where practically everything is chargrilled, including the vegetables used for most of the salads and even the flatbreads, which are quickly seared on a grill or in a *taboon*.

Whole Grilled Fish with Za'atar Chimichurri

ZA'ATAR CHIMICHURRI

1 cup (50 g) coarsely chopped fresh parsley

1 cup (40 g) coarsely chopped fresh cilantro

1 Fresno or other medium-hot fresh red chile, cored, seeded, and finely chopped

1 medium garlic clove, grated or minced

1 tablespoon white wine vinegar

2 tablespoons fresh orange juice

1 teaspoon kosher salt

Freshly ground black pepper

1 tablespoon za'atar

⅔ cup (160 ml) extra-virgin olive oil, plus more for greasing

GRILLED FISH

Three 1-pound (455 g) whole fish (sea bass, snapper, and branzino are good choices), gutted, cleaned, and scaled

Kosher salt

Olive oil

Freshly ground black pepper

1 large lemon, thinly sliced

Small handful of fresh thyme and rosemary sprigs

Easy, impressive, and fun to serve, whole grilled fish—with its crispy skin and juicy flesh—is one of our favorite summertime meals. You can use any large white-fleshed fish that looks good at the market. For the freshest fish, choose one with clear, plump eyes, then ask the fishmonger to clean and scale it for you. The accompanying chimichurri, a legacy of Argentinean immigrants, gets its Levantine slant from the addition of cilantro and za'atar. If you're planning a cookout, make a double batch and serve the chimichurri with other grilled meats, chicken, or fish.

Make the chimichurri: Pulse the parsley and cilantro in a food processor until finely chopped, but stop short of pureeing them. Transfer to a small bowl and stir in the chile, garlic, vinegar, orange juice, salt, several twists of black pepper, the za'atar, and the oil. Taste and adjust the seasoning to your liking. Set aside until ready to use. (You can make the chimichurri up to 1 week ahead and store it in an airtight container in the fridge.)

Grill the fish: Make sure the grill is clean and heat it to high.

Rinse the fish under cold running water, pat dry, and let stand for about 20 minutes, or until it comes to room temperature. Pat the fish dry again with a paper towel and rub with salt inside and out. Rub the fish generously with oil and season with salt and pepper. Fill the cavity with a nice dollop of the chimichurri and tuck in a couple of lemon slices and the thyme and rosemary sprigs.

Oil the grill grates well. Carefully place the fish on the hot grill and cook,

without touching it, for 3 to 4 minutes, which will allow the fish skin to form a slight crust. If you try to flip or move it too early, the skin will tear and the fish will stick to the grill. To test whether it's ready to move, insert a carving fork or other long utensil *under* the grill grate and try to lift the fish from below—if it doesn't lift easily, wait a bit more.

After about 7 minutes, use tongs or a spatula to gently flip the fish and grill on the other side until the flesh is opaque, firm, and easily flaked with a fork. The total cooking time depends on your grill and the size of the fish, but a good rule of thumb is 10 minutes per inch (2.5 cm) of thickness at the fish's thickest point. If you have a meat thermometer, insert it into the thickest part of the fish—when it reads 145°F (65°C), the fish is ready to serve.

Transfer the fish to a large platter and serve at once, with the remaining chimichurri.

Herbed Grouper Kebabs with Chermoula

2 pounds (910 g) skinless fillets grouper or other firm white-fleshed fish, such as red snapper, bream, or halibut

1 large onion, coarsely grated

1 jalapeño chile, cored, seeded, and finely chopped

½ cup (25 g) chopped fresh mint leaves

½ cup (25 g) chopped fresh parsley leaves

½ cup (20 g) chopped fresh cilantro leaves

1 tablespoon extra-virgin olive oil, plus more for greasing

1 tablespoon plus 1 teaspoon kosher salt

¼ teaspoon cayenne

Chermoula (page 33)

Margaret Tayar, owner of a simple restaurant a stone's throw from the pretty Watchtower Square in Jaffa, overlooking the Tel Avivian coastline, is credited with being the first to serve grouper kebabs some twenty-five years ago, and it's still one of the most iconic dishes in Israeli restaurants.

Some consider it a travesty to turn expensive, rare grouper into kebabs, but its firm, slightly fatty flesh is perfect for this dish. You can use whatever fish looks freshest at your market, but no matter what you choose, to make great fish kebabs, you must dice the fish by hand. You'll need a very sharp knife and a bit of patience, but it pays off in superior texture.

Using a very sharp knife, cut the fish into ⅛-inch (3 mm) dice. Transfer to a large bowl and add the onion, jalapeño, mint, parsley, cilantro, oil, salt, and cayenne. Mix well, but use a light hand—you don't want to overwork the delicate fish.

Rub your hands with a bit of oil and shape the fish mixture into 3-inch (7.5 cm) cylinders, setting them on a large plate as you go.

If using a grill: Make sure the grill is very clean and heat it to high.

Grease the grill grates well with oil. Gently place the kebabs on the grill and cook, without moving them, for a few minutes, until they form a slight crust and release from the grates. With tongs, carefully turn them and grill until they are browned on each side and thoroughly cooked.

If using a grill pan: Coat the bottom of a grill pan with oil and heat over medium-high heat until the oil is almost at its smoking point. Working in batches (do not crowd the pan), add the kebabs and cook, without touching them, for a couple of minutes. Move the pan slightly–if the kebabs easily release from the bottom of the pan, carefully flip them using tongs or two forks and sear until they turn golden and have nice grill marks on both sides, about 2 minutes. (If they stick to the pan, cook for a minute longer and test again.)

Serve at once, with chermoula alongside.

TIP *Instead of chopping the fish and the herbs by hand, leave the job to the food processor. The texture will have less bite, but if you are careful, it will come close. First cut each fillet into rough chunks and pulse them very briefly in a food processor. Transfer the fish to a bowl. Put herbs, garlic, and onion in the food processor and pulse until chopped. Combine with the fish. Continue as directed in the recipe.*

Grilled Chicken Pargiyot with Two Marinades

URFA AND SILAN MARINADE

¼ cup (25 g) Urfa pepper

1 tablespoon silan

1 garlic clove, minced or grated

2 tablespoons extra-virgin olive oil

1 teaspoon kosher salt

ONION AND ORANGE MARINADE

1 large onion, cut into rough chunks

2 garlic cloves

Zest and juice of 1 large orange

2 tablespoons honey

1 teaspoon kosher salt

1 teaspoon freshly ground black pepper

1 teaspoon dried mint

1 tablespoon extra-virgin olive oil

1½ pounds (680 g) boneless, skinless chicken thighs

Vegetable oil, for the grill

"Boneless, skinless chicken thighs." No Israeli would use four words every time we ask the butcher for our favorite cut of chicken for the grill—we just ask for *pargiyot* (which means "spring chickens" in Hebrew, though the chickens we use are fully grown). According to popular belief, this catchy name was created way back in the 1970s by the owner of Avazi, a popular skewer house in HaTikva Quarter in Tel Aviv.

With its deeper flavor and higher fat content, the dark meat of a chicken thigh stands up beautifully to the heat of the grill. Sometimes we grill the whole thigh (we call that *pargiyot* steak), but most of the time, we cube the meat and skewer it. In both cases, we marinate *pargiyot* in advance or rub them with a mixture of spices (for example, the shawarma spice rub; see page 24) and oil. If you're going to use wooden skewers (rather than metal ones), make sure you soak them in water for at least 30 minutes before grilling to prevent them from catching fire on the grill.

Sweet yet salty, smoky yet sour, Turkish Urfa peppers are excellent in marinades for grilled meats, and they go wonderfully with earthy-sweet *silan*. The second marinade opts for a tempting blend of orange and dried mint, with a touch of honey for sweetness.

Make the marinades: *For the Urfa and silan marinade*, stir all the ingredients together in a bowl. *For the onion and orange marinade,* put all the ingredients in a food processor and pulse until smooth.

If you're going to grill the pargiyot as steaks, just place the thighs in a bowl, pour over your chosen marinade, and cover and refrigerate for at least 2 hours or up to overnight.

If you want to make skewers, cut the meat into 1½-inch (4 cm) chunks, drop them in a bowl, pour over your chosen marinade, and cover and refrigerate for at least 2 hours or up to overnight. Thread 4 or 5 pieces onto small wooden skewers or 8 to 10 pieces onto large metal ones; discard the marinade.

Make sure the grill is very clean. Heat it to medium-high and oil the grates well.

Grill skewered pargiyot for 5 to 6 minutes on each side; grill whole pargiyot steaks for 6 to 7 minutes per side. To check for doneness, cut into the chicken to make sure there is no trace of redness.

Shawarma-Spiced Grilled Chicken Wings or Drumsticks

2 tablespoons Shawarma Spice Rub (page 24)

3 tablespoons extra-virgin olive oil

8 to 12 chicken wings or 6 to 8 chicken drumsticks

The complex flavor of my shawarma rub elevates this chicken to something more than just "spicy wings." And while wings and drumsticks are ideal for a barbecue, other chicken parts—or even a whole spatchcocked chicken—will be delicious as well. **PICTURED ON PAGE 292**

Combine the shawarma spice rub with the oil in a small bowl and massage the mixture over the chicken, making sure each piece is evenly coated. Refrigerate for at least an hour and up to overnight.

Make sure your grill is clean. Heat it to medium-high.

Arrange the chicken pieces on the grill and cook for about 10 minutes on each side for drumsticks, 8 minutes on each side for wings, until cooked through.

Grilled Lamb and Beef Kebabs

1 pound (455 g) ground beef, preferably 80% lean

1 pound (455 g) ground lamb

1 medium yellow onion, coarsely grated

2 garlic cloves, finely minced or grated

⅓ cup finely chopped fresh cilantro

⅓ cup finely chopped fresh parsley

¼ cup finely chopped fresh mint

2 teaspoons store-bought or homemade baharat (see page 22)

1 teaspoon ground cumin

1 teaspoon sweet paprika

2 teaspoons kosher salt

¼ teaspoon freshly ground black pepper

¼ cup soda water (or cold tap water)

Tahini, hareef, pita, for serving

Grilled tomatoes, for serving

Juicy, bursting with flavor, and begging to be smothered in tahini or warm tomato salsa, kebabs are the hit of the Israeli *mangal*. Adding a splash of soda water (a trick Israelis learned from Romanian immigrants) makes the meat mixture softer and guarantees that the kebabs won't dry out. Kebabs can be round, torpedo-shaped, or formed into skinny sausages on flat metal skewers. Small wooden skewers won't work here. If you don't have metal skewers, shape the mixture into flat round patties and grill as you would burgers. While the kebabs are grilling, toss a few tomatoes on the grill and cook them until they are very soft and the skin is charred. Smash them (no need to peel) and serve warm next to the kebabs with tahini and a bit of *hareef* to your liking (see page 24).

Put the beef and lamb in a large bowl. Add the grated onion (and any juices), garlic, cilantro, parsley, mint, baharat, cumin, paprika, salt, pepper, and soda water, and knead everything thoroughly until the mixture is soft, homogenous, and turns a shade lighter (which means the fat in the meat has melted from the heat of your hands and is incorporated into the mixture).

Transfer the bowl to the fridge for at least 30 minutes to make the meat mixture more stable (you can do this up to 1 day ahead).

Remove from the fridge and knead again to make the mixture super well blended and homogenous; unlike with an Italian meatball, you want the cooked kebab to be firm and springy. Shape 5-inch-long and 1-inch-wide kebabs on metal skewers, or make round patties, about 2½ inches in diameter.

Make sure the grill is very clean and heat it to high. Grease the grill grates lightly with oil. Place as many skewers or patties as your grill allows without crowding them (work in batches). Grill the kebabs for 4 minutes, flip, and grill for 4 minutes on the other side until the meat is cooked throughout. Serve at once with some tahini, hareef of your choice, pita, and grilled tomatoes, if you've made some.

SERVES 6 TO 8

Arayes

Grilled Meat-Stuffed Pitas

1 pound (455 g) ground beef

5 ounces (140 g) ground lamb (the fattier, the better)

2 medium yellow onions, quartered

1 cup (50 g) coarsely chopped fresh parsley

1 tablespoon kosher salt

1 teaspoon freshly ground black pepper

6 small (5-inch/12.5 cm) pitas, halved

⅓ cup (80 ml) extra-virgin olive oil or rendered beef fat (if you can find it)

Grilled meat vendors at Arabic markets in the Galilee have sold these crunchy, meaty treats for years, but somehow they flew under the radar of local foodies, chefs, and media. The concept is simple and brilliant: Rather than grilling kebabs separately and stuffing them into a pita, the raw spiced meat is stuffed into the pita first and the whole thing is grilled together, resulting in a crunchy-outside, juicy-inside scrumptious little meat pie. We're not sure which Israeli chef first served *arayes* in a restaurant, but Jonathan Borowitz of M25 restaurant at Shuk HaCarmel in Tel Aviv definitely made it famous, and this recipe is based on his excellent version of the dish.

Prior to grilling, the stuffed pitas are brushed with rendered beef fat (tallow), which gives them a nice sheen, enhances their crunch, and adds more flavor. Thanks to the Paleo craze, beef tallow is relatively available now. Order it online or look for it in butcher shops. Olive oil works too, but the pitas will seem a bit oilier.

Put the ground beef and lamb in a large bowl and knead until nicely combined.

Put the onions and parsley in a food processor and pulse to create a coarse paste. Wrap the mixture in a clean kitchen towel (no fabric softener, please!), twist the towel like a candy wrapper, and squeeze out as much liquid as you can. Add the onion mixture to the ground meat. Add the salt and pepper and knead again to blend thoroughly.

Stuff each pita half with about ½ cup (125 g) of the meat mixture. Gently press the pita halves between your palms to distribute the stuffing evenly. Make sure it comes all the way to the cut edge of the pita so that the meat can be seared by the grill fire.

Generously brush both sides of each pita with the oil or beef fat (if you're

using beef fat, melt it gently in a small pan until liquid first).

To grill the pitas: Make sure the grill is clean and heat it to high.

Place the stuffed pita halves on the grill and sear until they turn golden brown and have nice grill marks, about 2 minutes on each side. Cut each half into two quarters, return them to the grill, and sear for 2 minutes on each of the sides with the filling exposed. Move the quarters to a cooler spot on the grill, lay them flat again, and continue cooking another 2 to 3 minutes per side depending on your grill heat. By this time, the pitas will have absorbed the fat from the filling and will be juicy inside and crunchy and deep golden brown on the outside, and the meat filling will be perfectly cooked. Total grilling time will be about 12 minutes.

If you're cooking indoors: Preheat the oven to 350°F (175°C). Line a baking sheet with parchment paper.

Heat a large cast-iron skillet over medium-high heat for 3 to 4 minutes to get it really hot. Working in batches, if needed, lay the stuffed pitas flat on the hot skillet in one layer. Sear them until they turn deep golden brown on the first side, 2 to 3 minutes. Using tongs, flip the pitas and sear for 2 to 3 minutes on the second side. Flip the pitas once again so the cut side (with the exposed filling) is now facing the skillet and sear for 2 to 3 minutes, until the filling is set and nicely browned. Transfer to a large plate and repeat to cook the remaining pitas. Let cool for a couple of minutes so you can handle them, then cut each pita in half; you should now have 24 stuffed pita quarters.

Arrange the stuffed pita quarters on the prepared baking sheet and bake for 10 minutes.

Serve at once.

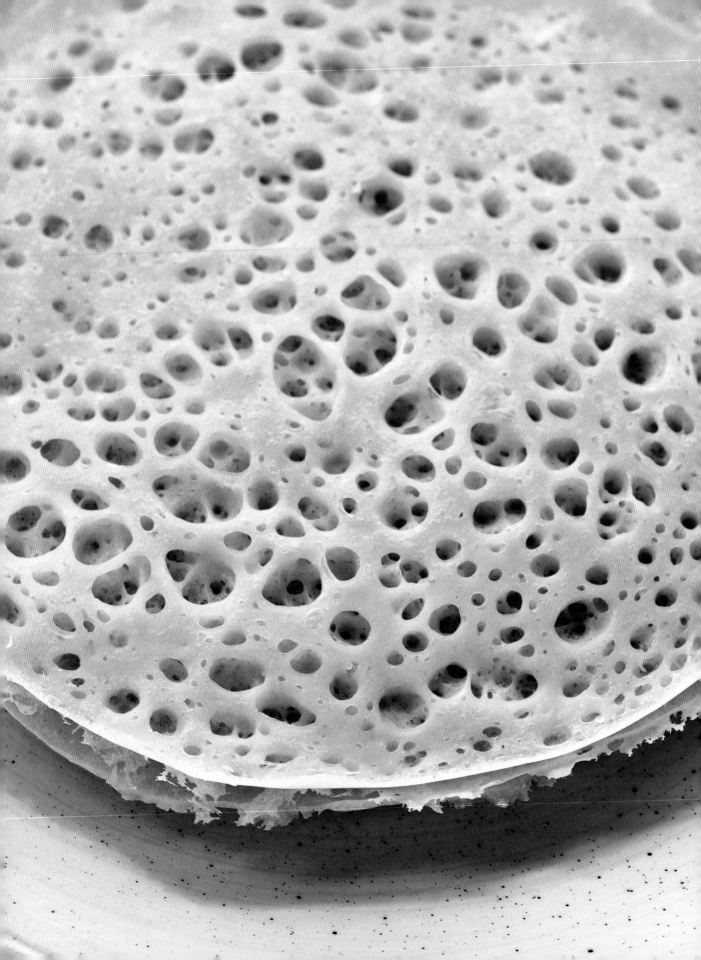

CHAPTER 13

Flatbreads, Traditional Breads, and Savory Pies

A flaky, cheesy pie from the Balkans, meaty "pizza" from Lebanon, crumpet-like pancakes from Yemen, tender Palestinian turnovers bursting with herby freshness—these and other delicacies will fill your kitchen with the lovely smell of baking and offer new and exciting options for entertaining, especially for weekend brunch.

Challah Stuffed with Mushrooms, Leeks, and Za'atar

FILLING

2 tablespoons extra-virgin olive oil

1 leek, white and light green parts only, diced

10 ounces (285 g) button or cremini mushrooms, stemmed and thinly sliced

2 tablespoons plus 1 teaspoon za'atar

¾ teaspoon kosher salt

CHALLAH

2 teaspoons active dry yeast

1 cup (240 ml) lukewarm water (about 110°F/45°C)

¼ cup (50 g) plus ½ teaspoon sugar

3¼ cups (405 g) all-purpose flour, plus more for dusting

1 tablespoon kosher salt

2 teaspoons vegetable oil, plus more for greasing

2 tablespoons honey

2 large eggs

1 teaspoon za'atar

Nothing says "Shabbat" like challah, and every Jewish or Israeli cookbook features at least one recipe for this iconic braided loaf. So I decided to offer something a bit different: stuffed challah. The mushroom-and-leek filling goes beautifully with the pillowy, mildly sweet bread, and with a variety of dishes too. Serve it as a part of your Friday dinner with soup or as a main course, or sliced and spread with good butter or cream cheese for weekend brunch.

Make the filling: Heat the oil in a large skillet over medium heat. Add the leek and sauté until soft and light golden, about 7 minutes. Add the mushrooms and cook, stirring frequently, until they are deep golden and almost dry (mushrooms are 90 percent water, and you don't want any moisture soaking the dough), about 20 minutes. Remove from the heat and stir in the za'atar and salt. Set aside to cool completely, then divide in half.

While the filling is cooling, start on the challah dough: Mix the yeast with ¼ cup (60 ml) of the lukewarm water and ½ teaspoon of the sugar in a small bowl and let stand until foamy, about 10 minutes.

Put the flour in a large bowl. Make a well in the center and pour the yeast mixture into the well.

Whisk together the salt, vegetable oil, honey, the remaining ¼ cup (50 g) sugar, the remaining ¾ cup (180 ml) lukewarm water, and 1 egg in a separate medium bowl.

Gradually stir the liquid mixture into the flour, about ½ cup (120 ml) at a time. When the dough becomes sticky and difficult to stir, turn it out onto a floured surface and knead by hand (adding a little more flour if necessary to keep it from sticking) until smooth and elastic, about 3 minutes.

Grease a large bowl with vegetable oil. Shape the dough into a ball and set it in the bowl. Cover with a damp kitchen towel and let stand in a warm place until it has doubled in size, about 40 minutes.

Line a baking sheet with parchment paper.

Recipe continues

Gently punch down the dough and turn it out onto a floured surface. Divide the dough in half, then divide each half into three equal pieces (you'll be making two loaves). Working with one piece and keeping the other two covered with a damp kitchen towel to prevent them from drying out, roll the dough into a 9-by-3-inch (22.5-by-7.5 cm) rectangle. Position the rectangle with one long side facing you. Sprinkle one-third of your half-batch of mushroom mixture right down the center, leaving about 1 inch (2.5 cm) exposed on each end. Fold the long side closest to you over to meet the other side. Press the edges gently to seal and roll so you have a rope. Be careful not to press too hard, so the filling stays put inside the dough.

Repeat to create three filled ropes that are the same length.

Align the ropes side by side on the prepared baking sheet. Squeeze and pinch the ends together at the top. Braid the ropes loosely—like you're braiding hair—then pinch the ends together and tuck them underneath. Repeat with the other dough and filling.

Cover with a damp kitchen towel and let sit until nearly doubled in size, 20 minutes or so.

Preheat the oven to 350°F (175°C).

Lightly beat the remaining egg with 1 tablespoon water and brush it over the top of each challah. Sprinkle with the za'atar.

Bake the challahs for 25 to 30 minutes, rotating the baking sheet once halfway through the cooking time, until deep golden brown all over—check the bottoms as well. Let cool and serve at room temperature.

VARIATION
To make a regular challah, just skip the filling; everything else is exactly the same. You can still sprinkle some za'atar on top or substitute sesame or poppy seeds.

Pita Bread

4 cups (550 g) all-purpose flour

2¼ teaspoons active dry yeast

1 tablespoon sugar

¾ tablespoon kosher salt

2 cups (480 ml) water

1½ tablespoons canola oil

Pita bread is indispensable to many cuisines of the Middle East, and Israeli cuisine is no exception. But unless you have a good Middle Eastern bakery nearby, your best bet is to bake your pitas at home. This dough is slightly tricky to work with at first, because it is very wet and sticky, but once you get the hang of it, it's a cinch to whip up homemade pita. Tender, puffy, and delicately yeasty, they have more substance and character than anything that comes from a plastic bag.

Put the flour, yeast, sugar, and salt in a large bowl and whisk to blend the ingredients well. Whisk together the water and oil, pour it onto the flour, and mix with a wooden spoon or rubber spatula to form a soft, slightly wet dough. It will be too wet to knead in the normal manner, so just stir and fold the dough on itself a few times, which will develop a bit of the gluten.

Scrape the dough into a neat ball, cover loosely with a cloth or plastic wrap, and leave to rise at room temperature for about 40 minutes; it should double in size.

Generously flour the work surface and dump the dough out of the bowl. Dust the dough with more flour and, with a bench knife or pastry scraper, or a large chef's knife, cut the dough into 10 pieces. Shape each piece into a ball, dusting it with more flour to keep it from sticking to your hands. Arrange the balls on a tray, cover with plastic wrap, and leave to rise a second time for about 20 minutes.

Meanwhile, heat the oven to 550°F (290°C) and put a baking sheet on the bottom rack to heat it up.

When the dough has risen, take a piece and press it to make a 6-inch round; set aside while you make another 2 or 3 rounds. Carefully remove the baking sheet from the oven and flop the pita rounds onto the sheet. Return to the oven and bake the pita until they are puffed and lightly browned on the outside, about 5 minutes. You don't need to turn them during baking, but if you want them evenly browned, you can.

Let the pita cool on a rack while you make the rest of the batch. Eat them the day you make them, or freeze as soon as they are cool.

Kubaneh Stuffed with Caramelized Onions

MAKES 1 TALL LOAF, TO SERVE 6 TO 8

4 cups (500 g) all-purpose flour, plus more for dusting

4 tablespoons light brown sugar

1 tablespoon kosher salt

1 tablespoon active dry yeast

1½ cups (360 ml) lukewarm water (about 110°F/45°C)

Vegetable oil, for greasing

8 tablespoons (1 stick/115 g) unsalted butter

2 teaspoons nigella seeds

1 cup (145 g) Caramelized Onions (page 316)

TO SERVE

Hard-boiled eggs

Grated tomatoes (see page 50)

S'chug (see page 25)

The cuisine of Yemenite Jews is frugal, yet full of surprises, especially when it comes to breads. There are quite a few of them, each one different and unique, but *kubaneh*, sometimes called Yemenite brioche, is one of the most stunning. Made from leavened dough with quite a lot of butter or margarine, this Shabbat bread is baked (or rather, steamed) in a lidded pan in a low oven. Yemenite families traditionally serve flaky, buttery *kubaneh* for Shabbat lunch, along with the accompaniments that so often turn Yemenite breads into a full meal—a few overnight eggs and small bowls of grated tomatoes mixed with *s'chug* for dipping. Guests just tear away chunks until the loaf is gone, which usually happens well before the meal is over.

I decided to enhance my family dish by adding soft caramelized onions. When you pull apart the bread, you get a sweet, savory surprise in some of the bites.

Authentic *kubaneh* is baked in a special aluminum pan with a fitted lid, but a regular 8- to 9-inch (20 to 23 cm; about 3 quart/3 L) ovenproof saucepan with straight walls, a flat bottom, and a tight-fitting lid will do nicely, as will a Dutch oven of a similar size.

Combine the flour, 3 tablespoons of the brown sugar, and the salt in a large bowl. Make a well in the center and add the yeast, the remaining 1 tablespoon brown sugar, and ½ cup (120 ml) of the lukewarm water. Set aside for about 5 minutes, until it starts to bubble.

Gradually mix in the remaining 1 cup (240 ml) water—the dough will be sticky at this point; if it seems dry, add another tablespoon or so of water. Transfer the dough to a floured surface and knead for 7 to 8 minutes, until it is smooth and elastic.

Grease a large bowl with vegetable oil. Shape the dough into a ball and place it in the bowl. Cover with a damp kitchen towel and let stand in a warm place until the dough has doubled in size, 45 minutes to 1 hour.

Preheat the oven to 220°F (105°C). Generously grease a 3-quart (3 L) Dutch oven (or an ovenproof saucepan with straight walls, a flat bottom, and a tight-fitting lid) with 2 tablespoons of the butter and sprinkle 1 teaspoon of the nigella seeds over the bottom.

Divide the dough into six equal pieces. Lightly flatten one piece of the dough with your fingers and smear a bit of butter over the surface. Place about 2½ tablespoons of the caramelized onions in the center and bring up the edges to enclose the filling, then smooth the dough into a ball shape again. Spread a little more butter on the outside of the ball. Repeat to fill the remaining pieces of dough. Use all but a couple teaspoons of the butter for the balls.

Place one ball in the center of the Dutch oven and arrange the rest of them around it, like the petals of a flower. Cover with a damp kitchen towel and set aside to rise for 20 to 30 minutes.

Dot the remaining butter on top of the dough. Sprinkle with the remaining 1 teaspoon nigella seeds. Cover tightly with a lid and bake overnight (9 to 10 hours).

Take the pot out of the oven and remove the lid. Place a large plate over the top of the pot and, holding them together, flip it. The kubaneh should slide out easily. Serve promptly, while still warm, with hard-boiled eggs, grated fresh tomatoes, and a dollop of s'chug.

Caramelized Onions

Countless dishes begin by frying onions—normally for a few minutes, until they turn soft and translucent, sometimes a bit longer, until they are golden. But if you take your time and fry them gently for about an hour, you end up with a treasure: Very slow frying releases and gently caramelizes the onions' sugars without burning them and renders the onions meltingly soft and jammy. You can use them to top a pizza or a tart, sprinkle them on mashed potatoes or rice, or simply eat them with a spoon—they are that good. And the brilliant thing is that they freeze well (you'll have leftovers from the *kubaneh*). The technique is simple—all you need is patience. **MAKES ABOUT 4 CUPS (580 G)**

3 tablespoons vegetable oil

3 tablespoons extra-virgin olive oil

6 large onions, thinly sliced

Heat both oils in a very large skillet or Dutch oven over medium heat. Add the onions, increase the heat to medium-high, and cook, giving them a good stir every couple of minutes, for 20 minutes. Stick around to make sure the onions don't burn.

Reduce the heat to low and cook, stirring occasionally, for another 40 minutes, or until a deep brown color has developed. As you stir, scrape up any browned bits from the bottom of the pan so they don't burn, and stir so they add their deep, sweet flavor to the mix. Remove from the heat and let cool completely. The onions can be stored in an airtight container in the fridge for up to 1 week or frozen in zip-top freezer bags for up to 2 months.

Laffa

Pan-Seared Flatbreads

½ teaspoon active dry yeast

½ teaspoon sugar

¼ cup (60 ml) lukewarm water (about 110°F/45°C)

1 cup (125 g) all-purpose flour, plus more for dusting

½ teaspoon kosher salt

2 teaspoons extra-virgin olive oil, plus more for greasing

2 tablespoons soda water

Laffas are traditional Middle Eastern flatbreads that fall somewhere between thin focaccia and thick wheat tortillas. In Israel, they're also called Iraqi pita (we have no idea why), and in Jerusalem, they go by the name *esh-tanur*, meaning "oven fire." *Laffas* are great for mopping up hummus, labneh, or tahini and are often used as wraps (especially for shawarma, kebab, and koftas). They can also serve as edible plates (see, for example, the recipe for *musahan* on page 180). *Laffas* are usually made in a *taboon*, but at home a cast-iron skillet will do a good job. If you're having a cookout, sear the *laffas* on a hot, clean, oiled grill. During picnics and outings, we like making *laffas* on an inverted wok heated over a bonfire.

Combine the yeast and sugar in a small bowl, pour over the lukewarm water, and let sit for about 10 minutes, until the yeast is foamy and bubbling.

Combine the flour and salt in a large bowl and make a well in the center. Add the oil, yeast mixture, and soda water and mix with your fingers or a rubber spatula until a dough starts to come together. Dump the dough onto a lightly floured surface and knead until smooth, 3 to 4 minutes.

Grease a large bowl with oil. Transfer the dough to the bowl, cover with a damp kitchen towel, and let sit until it has doubled in size, about 1 hour. (At this point, the dough can also be wrapped in plastic wrap and refrigerated for up to 1 day before using.)

If you're using the *laffa* dough to make *lahmajun* (page 319), stop here and continue with the *lahmajun* recipe, beginning with "Divide the dough in half and roll each half into a ball."

If you're making *laffa* as a flatbread, divide the dough into 2, 3, or 4 pieces (according to the number of breads you want) and roll each piece into a ball. Let sit for another 10 minutes.

Using a lightly floured rolling pin, roll each dough ball into rounds about ¼ inch (6 mm) thick or thinner (the actual diameter depends on how many *laffa* breads you want to make).

Heat a 9- or 10-inch (23 or 25 cm) cast-iron skillet over medium-high heat. Brush the skillet lightly with vegetable oil and flop one dough disc onto the skillet. Sear until you have plenty of nice scorch marks, about 3 minutes. Flip and cook the second side in the same way, making sure the dough is cooked through. Continue with all the dough rounds.

Serve at once–*laffas* are best when they are served straight from the skillet. If you have leftovers, wrap them in plastic wrap and store at room temperature for up to 1 day or freeze for up to 1 month and reheat for a few minutes in a hot oven.

Lahmajun

Savory Beef–Topped Flatbread

2 tablespoons extra-virgin olive oil

1 large yellow onion, chopped

2 garlic cloves, grated or minced

¼ jalapeño chile, cored, seeded, and chopped

½ pound (225 g) ground beef

2 teaspoons tomato paste

2 ripe tomatoes, finely chopped (about 1 cup/ 180 g)

Pinch of sugar

1 teaspoon kosher salt

1 teaspoon ground cumin

Freshly ground black pepper

Several fresh mint leaves

¼ cup (35 g) pine nuts, toasted or fried (see page 69)

1 recipe Laffa dough (page 317)

Vegetable oil, for greasing

Lahmajun, "bread and meat" in Arabic, is a famous Levantine open-faced meat pie also known as Armenian pizza. Traditionally baked in a special oven called a *taboon*, *lahmajun* doesn't translate easily to regular home ovens. Often the meat topping will overcook and dry out before the dough bakes through, so in this version, I sear the dough in a smoking-hot skillet before topping and baking.

Heat the olive oil in a large skillet over medium-high heat. Add the onion and sauté until soft and translucent, 5 to 6 minutes. Add the garlic and jalapeño and sauté for 1 to 2 minutes.

Add the ground beef, increase the heat to high, and cook, crumbling the meat with a fork as it cooks until it's broken into tiny pieces and lightly browned, 5 to 6 minutes. Using a slotted spoon, transfer the meat mixture to a bowl and set aside.

In the same pan, combine the tomato paste, chopped tomatoes, and sugar. Cook, stirring continuously, for 1 to 2 minutes (this will help cut the acid in the tomatoes). Return the meat to the pan and season with the salt, cumin, and pepper to taste. Remove from the heat and stir in the mint and pine nuts. Set aside. (The topping can be prepared, cooled, and stored in the fridge for up to a few days before using.)

Divide the dough in half and roll each half into a ball. Let sit for another 10 minutes.

While the dough is resting, preheat the oven to 425°F (220°C). Line a baking sheet with parchment paper.

Using a lightly floured rolling pin, roll each round of dough into an 8-inch (20 cm) disc, about ¼ inch (6 mm) thick or even thinner.

Heat a 9- or 10-inch (23 or 25 cm) cast-iron skillet over high heat until smoking hot. Brush the skillet lightly with vegetable oil and flop one dough disc onto the skillet. Sear until you start seeing bubbles on the surface of the dough, about 2 minutes, then flip and sear on the second side for 2 minutes. Transfer to the prepared baking sheet and repeat with the second dough disc.

Divide the topping between the dough discs and spread it evenly, leaving about ⅔ inch (1.75 cm) exposed around the edges. Bake just until the meat is nicely browned and lightly crispy, 10 to 12 minutes.

Cut the lahmajun into wedges or slices using a pizza cutter. Serve at once.

Lachuch

Yemenite Pancakes

3½ cups (440 g) all-purpose
flour

1 tablespoon semolina
(optional)

1 tablespoon sugar

1 tablespoon kosher salt

2¼ teaspoons (1 packet)
active dry yeast

3½ cups (840 ml) warm
water

Vegetable oil, for frying

Early in the morning at Tel Aviv's HaTikva Market (see page 132), you can find one of the very last *lachuch* makers in town juggling a dozen skillets, cooking up a storm of spongy, crumpetlike pancakes as customers gather around. Some buy fresh *lachuch* to take home; others eat it right on the spot, dipped in *hilbeh*, a Yemenite fenugreek sauce, or filled with an entire Israeli breakfast: an omelet, chopped salad, cheese, and hummus.

Spongy like a crumpet on one side, smooth like a pancake on the other, this distinctive Yemenite bread gets fried on only one side and requires a cold nonstick pan to cook properly. This means you have to cool down the pan after each round or work with two pans, letting one cool while the other is doing the work.

Serve *lachuch* to dip in hot soups and stews, or serve it for breakfast with butter, honey, and even cream cheese. **ALSO PICTURED ON PAGE 306**

In a large bowl, combine the flour, semolina (if using), sugar, salt, and yeast. Stir in the warm water until well combined. The mixture should resemble pancake batter. Cover the bowl with a kitchen towel and set aside in a warm place for 1½ hours. At this point, the batter should have lots and lots of tiny bubbles–this is a good sign.

To cook the lachuch, you want to start with a cold pan–the opposite of what you would normally do. Line a plate with paper towels. Grease a 9-inch (23 cm) nonstick pan with a bit of vegetable oil (no additional oil will be needed during frying). Add ½ cup (120 ml) of the batter and only

then turn the heat to high. Fry for 3 minutes, cover with a lid, and cook for another 1 to 2 minutes, until the bottom is golden brown and smooth and the top is set and full of little bubbles. Slide the lachuch onto the paper towels. Remove the pan from the heat, rinse the bottom with cold water to cool the pan, and dry. When the pan is completely cool, repeat to cook the remaining batter, stacking the finished lachuch on top of one another.

Serve fresh, warm or at room temperature. You can also freeze them, wrapped well in plastic wrap, for up to 1 month; reheat gently in a microwave.

Boureka Pie with Chard and Four Cheeses

**CHEESE AND CHARD
FILLING**

1 bunch Swiss chard

3 tablespoons extra-virgin
olive oil

1 large yellow onion,
chopped

1 garlic clove, grated or
minced

5 ounces (140 g) feta
cheese, crumbled

5 ounces (140 g) goat
cheddar, Manchego, or
other firm cheese, cut
into chunks

8 ounces (225 g) fresh
mozzarella cheese,
torn into large chunks

2 tablespoons cream
cheese

¼ teaspoon freshly grated
nutmeg

¼ teaspoon freshly ground
black pepper

PIE

12 sheets frozen phyllo
dough, thawed in the
package overnight in the
fridge

8 tablespoons (1 stick/115 g)
unsalted butter, melted

Nigella seeds, for topping

Bourekas arrived in Israel with Bulgarian and Turkish immigrants and became a national food symbol, on a par with falafel and hummus. Made from puff pastry or phyllo dough and usually stuffed with cheese (but also greens, mushrooms, eggplants, meat, or potato puree), they're everywhere—sold at market stalls and neighborhood bakeries, served at wedding receptions, and featured on breakfast menus in cafés.

This version, a big, beautiful *boureka* pie, can only be found in homes (usually Balkan ones). It's always the star of the party at Shavuot, the most laid-back Jewish holiday, when you're supposed to wear white, put some flowers in your hair, and stuff your face with cheesecake and other dairy-based delights.

Store-bought phyllo makes this version easy to put together. Even if you haven't worked with phyllo before, you will find it quite user-friendly. Just remember it's made from only water and flour rolled out into paper-thin sheets. Without any fat, the sheets dry up fast, turn brittle, and break. Thaw the phyllo slowly in its packaging, preferably overnight in the fridge. And when you work with one sheet, keep the rest covered with a barely damp towel (damp, but not wet, so that the sheets don't get wet and stick to each other).

Make the cheese and chard filling: Trim off the dried ends of the chard and cut or strip the ribs from the leaves. Slice the ribs thinly crosswise (you should have about 2 cups) and cut the leaves into thin ribbons. Heat the oil in a large skillet over medium heat. Add the onion and sauté until soft, 3 to 4 minutes. Add the chard ribs and cook for another couple of minutes. Add the garlic and cook for another minute. Add the chard leaves and cook, stirring frequently, until it wilts and gives up its excess moisture, about 10 minutes. Remove from the heat and let cool.

While the chard mixture is cooling, put the feta, goat cheddar, mozzarella, cream cheese, nutmeg, and pepper in a food processor and process until blended but still crumbly. Transfer to a bowl, add the chard mixture, and stir gently to blend.

Make the pie: Preheat the oven to 350°F (175°C).

Unwrap the thawed phyllo sheets, gently unroll them, and keep them ready in a stack, covered with a barely damp kitchen towel.

Brush the bottom of a deep round 10-inch (25 cm) baking pan (a springform pan works well) with melted butter and drape a sheet of phyllo over the pan, letting the edges hang over the sides. Brush with more melted butter. Continue layering the phyllo sheets, brushing each with butter and rotating each layer so you don't have any open spaces around the edge, until you have eight layers. If your phyllo sheets tear, don't worry, just try to patch them together.

Add the cheese-chard mixture to the pan and spread it evenly. Fold the overhanging phyllo over the topping. Top with the remaining 4 sheets phyllo, brushing each one with butter before adding the next. Crumple them slightly so they fit in the pan and create a slightly frilly surface.

Brush the top with the remaining melted butter and sprinkle with nigella seeds. Bake until the top turns deep golden, about 40 minutes. The pie is at its best hot and fresh from the oven, but you can also store it, covered, in the fridge for up to 3 days; reheat at 325°F (165°C) for a few minutes.

Fattayers

Spinach and Pine Nut Mini Pies

DOUGH

2 cups (250 g) all-purpose
flour, plus more for
dusting

¼ teaspoon sugar

¼ teaspoon kosher salt

½ teaspoon active dry yeast

¾ cup (180 ml) warm water

¼ cup (60 ml) extra-virgin
olive oil, plus more for
greasing

FILLING

3 tablespoons extra-virgin
olive oil

1 large onion, diced

2 garlic cloves, minced or
finely grated

¼ teaspoon ground allspice

¼ teaspoon ground
cinnamon

1¼ teaspoons kosher salt

Freshly ground black pepper

10 ounces (285 g) baby
spinach, finely chopped

1 tablespoon fresh lemon
juice

¼ cup (35 g) pine nuts,
toasted or fried (see
page 69)

Ground sumac, for topping

In the winter, Palestinian cooks fill these tiny pies with foraged edible plants, such as wild spinach, hyssop, mallows, or borage leaves; the rest of the year, they use regular spinach. Either way, the juicy, fresh, and slightly tart filling provides a bright contrast to the delicate, flaky crust.

Fattayers make great finger food for parties, or add them to your weekend brunch table along with a bowl of yogurt and a salad. The soft dough can be tricky to work with, so I suggest shaping the pies directly on the baking sheets so you move them as little as possible.

Make the dough: Mix together the flour, sugar, and salt in a large bowl. Make a well in the center and add the yeast and warm water to the well (do not stir). Let sit for 10 minutes, until the yeast starts to bubble.

Add the oil and mix the flour and liquids with your fingers just until a dough starts coming together–it will be wet and runny, but don't worry, just plop it onto a lightly floured surface and start kneading. If it's too wet to work with, add a bit more flour, keeping in mind that the dough is meant to be a bit sticky; be careful not to add too much flour or the dough will be heavy. Knead until you have a smooth, slightly sticky ball of dough.

Grease a bowl with oil. Transfer the dough to the bowl, cover with a damp kitchen towel, and let sit in a warm place until it has doubled in size, about 1½ hours.

While the dough is proofing, make the filling: Heat the oil in a large skillet over medium heat. Add the onion and sauté until soft and translucent, about 5 minutes. Add the garlic, allspice,

cinnamon, salt, and several twists of pepper and sauté for another minute.

Add the spinach, starting with a few handfuls and adding more as the spinach wilts–it will shrink considerably. Sauté until all the spinach is totally wilted but still bright green, 2 to 3 minutes. If the spinach mixture seems watery, transfer it to a plate lined with paper towels to absorb the excess liquid or let it cool enough to handle, then squeeze out the liquid using your hands. Transfer to a bowl, stir in the lemon juice and pine nuts, and let cool.

Preheat the oven to 350°F (175°C). Line two baking sheets with parchment paper.

Assemble and bake the pies: Turn the dough out onto a lightly floured work surface and cut it in half. Cover the half you're not using with plastic wrap. Dust your rolling pin with a little flour and roll out the dough as thinly as you can (ideally ⅛ inch/3 mm thick). Using a glass or a cookie cutter, cut out 3½-inch (9 cm) discs. Arrange the discs on the prepared baking sheets and cover with plastic wrap to prevent them from drying out. Repeat with the remaining dough. Gather the scraps into a ball, roll them out again, and cut out a few more discs. You want to end up with about 15 discs.

Place 1 tablespoon of filling in the center of each disc. Now you have two options to shape the pies: the first more traditional, the second a little bit easier.

Traditional: Bring three sides of each disc together in the center and pinch firmly to seal.

Envelope (easier): Bring the top and bottom of each disc to the center and pinch to seal. Then bring the two open sides to the center and pinch all four sides together, making sure the dough is completely sealed.

Sprinkle the pies with a little sumac and bake until golden brown on their tops and bottoms, 20 to 25 minutes.

Serve warm or at room temperature. Store leftovers in an airtight container in the fridge for up to a few days; reheat at 350°F (175°C) for 5 to 6 minutes just before serving. The unbaked fattayers can be frozen on a baking sheet until firm, and then transferred to a zip-top freezer bag or airtight container. When ready to serve, transfer the frozen fattayers directly from the freezer to a baking sheet and bake as directed, adding 10 minutes or so to the cooking time.

Jerusalem Bagel Stuffed with Scallions and Feta

DOUGH

3 tablespoons sugar

4 teaspoons active dry yeast (from two ¼-ounce/7 g packets)

1¾ cups (420 ml) lukewarm water (about 110°F/45°C)

4½ cups (560 g) all-purpose flour, plus more for dusting

1 tablespoon plus ½ teaspoon kosher salt

3 tablespoons vegetable oil, plus more for greasing

1 tablespoon plus 1 teaspoon milk

FILLING

1 tablespoon extra-virgin olive oil

2 bunches scallions, chopped (about 2 cups/ 110 g)

1½ cups (225 g) crumbled feta cheese

Pinch of chile flakes

2 large eggs, for the egg wash

½ cup (75 g) sesame seeds, for topping

Good-quality olive oil, for serving

Za'atar, for dipping

Let's be clear—this is not a bagel as you know it. Oval shaped and sesame dotted, these delicious breads were made for centuries by Palestinian bakers. Israelis who discovered them in the Old City of Jerusalem after the Six-Day War gave them this name, and it stuck. The bread carts in the Muslim Quarter of the Old City market still boast the best Jerusalem bagels (supposedly baked according to a top-secret recipe), but you can find them at markets around the country and even at highway junctions, where they are stacked on huge wooden trays that vendors carry on their heads. Their flavor is somewhat sweetish, and their texture is light, bready, and a bit chewy. Freshly baked Jerusalem bagels are delicious on their own, dipped in olive oil and za'atar (the latter is offered at no extra price, wrapped like a candy in a small piece of newspaper). They are also terrific for cheese toasts, which gave me the inspiration for this recipe. If you want to make the original Jerusalem bagel, without the filling, I have that covered too (see the variation).

Make the dough: Combine 1 tablespoon of the sugar with the yeast in a small bowl and pour over ¾ cup (180 ml) of the lukewarm water. Let the mixture sit for 5 to 7 minutes, until the yeast starts to get bubbly and foamy.

Combine the flour, salt, and remaining 2 tablespoons sugar in a large bowl and make a well in the center. Pour the yeast mixture into the well and add the remaining 1 cup (240 ml) water, the vegetable oil, and the milk. Mix with your fingers or a rubber spatula until the dough starts to come together.

Dump the dough onto a lightly floured surface and knead until it comes together in a smooth ball, adding more flour if necessary–possibly up to another ⅓ cup (40 g) or so–3 to 4 minutes. Slick a bowl with a little oil. Place the dough in the bowl. Cover with a clean kitchen towel and let rest for 1 hour, or until doubled in size.

Transfer the dough to the lightly floured work surface and divide it into eight equal pieces. Shape each piece into a ball and place on a baking sheet. Cover with a towel or plastic wrap and refrigerate for at least 30 minutes or up to 1 hour (this will make the bagels easier to shape).

While the dough is resting, make the filling: Heat the oil in a medium skillet over high heat. Add the scallions and cook, stirring occasionally, until slightly softened, about 3 minutes. Remove from the heat, transfer to a medium bowl, and set aside to cool. Add the feta and chile flakes to the bowl and stir to combine. No salt is needed–the feta is plenty salty.

Preheat the oven to 325°F (165°C). Line three baking sheets with parchment paper and oil them lightly.

Remove the dough from the fridge. Set a ball of dough on a lightly floured work surface (keep the others covered). Flatten it and roll it into a long rope, starting from the center and rolling outward, about 18 inches (45 cm) long. Press down on the dough and flatten it until you have a 2-inch-wide (5 cm) strip. Repeat with the remaining balls of dough.

Sprinkle 2 to 3 tablespoons of the filling along the middle of the strip, from one end to the other. Gently lay your finger on the filling to hold it in place, and pull the sides of the dough to the center. Press to seal the filling inside the dough. Roll again so you have a long tube. Join the two ends of the tube, pressing them to seal. Place it seam-side down on one of the prepared baking sheets and, if needed, reshape by pulling slightly on the inside hole to create a long, slender oval bagel. Repeat to fill and shape the remaining dough strips.

Beat the eggs until well blended, and then brush the bagels with egg wash and sprinkle each generously with about 1 tablespoon of the sesame seeds. Bake for 20 to 25 minutes, rotating the baking sheets halfway through, until the bagels are a light golden brown with a dark brown underside.

Serve warm or at room temperature, with a side of oil and za'atar for dipping. The bagels are best oven fresh. If you are not serving them within a few hours, it is best to wrap tightly in several layers of plastic wrap and freeze them for up to 1 month; reheat them in a preheated 350°F (175°C) oven for about 10 minutes.

VARIATION

Classic (Unfilled) Jerusalem Bagels: Skip the stuffing and shape the bagels as directed (there's no need to flatten the tube, as there is no stuffing). Bake at 350°F (175°C) for 15 to 20 minutes. Serve warm with za'atar and olive oil.

Savory Knafe with Pistachios and Red Pepper Sauce

KNAFE

¾ cup (1½ sticks/170 g) unsalted butter

Small pinch of saffron

One 1-pound (455 g) box shredded phyllo dough, thawed overnight in the fridge

3 teaspoons kosher salt

8 ounces (225 g) goat cheese, at room temperature

16 ounces (455 g) whole-milk ricotta cheese

1 teaspoon chopped fresh rosemary

1 teaspoon chopped fresh thyme

1 teaspoon finely grated lemon zest

½ teaspoon freshly ground black pepper

People love *knafe*, a classic Levantine dessert especially popular among Palestinians, for its contrast between crunchy, syrup-doused pastry and soft, mildly savory cheese filling. Here I've turned the dessert into an elegant entrée, skipping the syrup in favor of fiery red pepper sauce and adding a contrasting sprinkle of pistachios. Like *boureka* pie (see page 322), *knafe* uses ready-made dough, this time a shredded phyllo called *kadayif* in Turkey and *kataifi* in Greece. Look for it in the frozen aisle at Middle Eastern groceries and specialty stores.

Make the knafe: Preheat the oven to 375°F (190°C).

Put the butter in a small saucepan and crumble the saffron between your fingers into the pan. Melt the butter over medium heat (you can also do this in the microwave). Give it a good stir; the saffron should dissolve into the butter and give it a deep golden color.

Unwrap the shredded phyllo and transfer about one-third to a food processor. Pulse for a few seconds to separate the dough into smaller strands. Transfer the phyllo strands to a large bowl and repeat with the rest of the shredded phyllo. Stir in the melted butter, season with about 2 teaspoons of the salt, and toss thoroughly but with a gentle hand–you want to make sure that all the strands are coated with butter, but you don't want to mash them.

In a separate bowl, combine the goat cheese, ricotta, rosemary, thyme, lemon zest, the remaining 1 teaspoon salt, and the black pepper, or to taste. Mix until smooth.

Arrange half the phyllo strands in a 12-inch (30 cm) cast-iron skillet or in a round baking pan (but not a springform pan, which could allow the butter to leak out). Add the cheese mixture in dollops and smooth the top with a spatula. Cover with the remaining phyllo, patting down the strands to make sure you have a smooth and uniform layer. Bake until the phyllo is deep golden brown, 40 to 45 minutes.

Recipe continues

RED PEPPER SAUCE

2 red bell peppers, roasted, cored, seeded, peeled, and cut into large chunks (see page 155)

2 red Fresno or other medium-hot fresh red chiles, or ½ long red chile, roasted, cored, seeded, and peeled (see page 155)

1 tablespoon fresh lemon juice

2½ tablespoons extra-virgin olive oil

1 tablespoon sweet paprika

1 teaspoon kosher salt, or more to taste

½ cup (15 g) coarsely chopped shelled raw pistachios, lightly toasted

While the knafe is in the oven, make the sauce: Put all the ingredients for the sauce in a food processor or blender and puree until smooth. Taste and adjust the seasoning. The sauce should be bright red and quite spicy. Set aside.

To serve: Let the knafe cool for a few minutes to set up a bit, then flip it onto a large serving plate and top with the pistachios. Cut into wedges using a bread knife. Serve with the red pepper sauce on the side.

TIPS *Flipping* knafe *is optional–it will make the dish look more attractive, because the beautifully golden brown underside will be exposed, but if it makes you nervous, you can skip it and serve the pie right out of the pan.*

If you don't have a 12-inch (30 cm) round pan or skillet, use a 9-by-13-inch (23-by-33 cm) rectangular pan. Cut the knafe *into squares rather than wedges to serve.*

VARIATIONS

Individual knafe pies: Divide the shredded phyllo and the cheese filling evenly among six 5-inch (12.5 cm) tartlet pans. The baking time will be considerably shorter, about 20 minutes.

Classic dessert knafe: Follow the recipe above, but omit the thyme, rosemary, salt, and pepper from the cheese mixture. As soon as you remove the *knafe* from the oven, drizzle it with about 1 cup (240 ml) cold sugar syrup (use the recipe for orange blossom syrup on page 352). Top with chopped toasted pistachios. And of course you won't need the red pepper sauce.

Shuk Akko/Old Akko Market

The story

Israel is a small, narrow country with a long Mediterranean coastline, so you would expect a thriving fishing industry and an abundance of fresh fish and seafood. The reality, sadly, is different. The marine population in the eastern Mediterranean basin is relatively poor, the situation made worse by chronic overfishing. Most of what is sold at the markets or served in restaurants comes from aquaculture, and a significant part is imported. Still, there are a few enclaves of traditional fishing, and the northern coastal town of Akko (aka Acre) is their shining star.

Dozens of boats sail at sunset from the pretty Fishermen Harbor and return at the crack of dawn. Within a few hours, the better part of their catch ends up at Old Akko Market, making it the only true fish market in the country. The fishmongers, not the most reliable folks, will promise you that everything you see at their stalls was swimming in the Mediterranean the previous night, but seasoned shoppers, many of whom travel here from afar to buy fish, know better. They know that even here, freshly caught ocean fish is in the minority, sold alongside less romantic merchandise that comes from fish farms.

They also know that fish, like vegetables, have seasons. And just like vegetables, as the summer dies out and the temperatures drop, the bounty grows more varied and plentiful. September brings shrimp, Spanish mackerel, and the first amberjacks, one of our favorite local fish. Come October and November, you'll see more squid and blue crabs. These crabs, locally called blue sailors, are, in fact, new immigrants. Originally from North America, these sturdy crustaceans arrived in the area as larvae in the bilges of cargo ships and more or less wiped out the local crab population, but we forgive them because they're so delicious. In winter, the fish stalls are at their very best, selling fresh cod, monkfish, small barracuda, grouper, red mullet, and more. A whole freshly grilled fish may be the food we crave most in July and August, but the fishing is at rock bottom during these sweltering months. Many fishermen don't even bother to take to the sea, using this time of the year to repair their boats and get ready for the next season.

While the fish stalls are the gems of the Akko market, they're not the only reason to visit. The walled ancient city is breathtakingly beautiful and steeped in history that goes back thousands of years. A gateway to northern Israel and the Galilee, Akko was an important port during Hellenistic, Roman, and Byzantine times, but reached the peak of its glory in the twelfth century, when it was the capital of the Crusader Kingdom of Jerusalem. In the thirteen century, it fell into the hands of the Mamluks and later became part of the Ottoman Empire, which built most of the present-day walled town. In 2001, the old city of Akko was named a UNESCO World Heritage Site, which spurred a wave of restoration and excavation projects.

The vibe

The market itself consists of a few shaded roofed streets in the heart of the ancient town. Thousands of tourists stroll through them every day on their way to the Templars Tunnel, the Knights' Halls, or the newly restored Hospitaller Fortress, but most of the shop owners don't count on those visiting tourists as potential buyers.

Except for a few souvenir shops, the market caters to the few-thousand-strong Arabic population that still lives within the city's walls and to those who come from out of town to buy fish. There are only three vegetable stalls (compared to nine fish stalls), and the produce they offer is strictly seasonal, mostly *baladi* (local) and tailored to the preferences of local cooks. For example, you won't find chard, leeks, or zucchini. Though all three are extremely popular in Israel, Arabic Galilean cooks never use them; they prefer spinach (large-leafed Turkish spinach, if possible) and *kar'a*–crookneck squash. Aside from the fish, the market is famous for its spice shops and sweets shops selling baklava, *knaffeh*, honeyed nuts, and other delightful diet-busters. Last but not least–hummus. There are hummus places at every corner, and at least three of them compete for the title of best hummus place in Galilee.

When to come

The market is open and active all week. Tuesdays and Thursdays are the best for fish, because the trawlers unload their catch on these days, resulting in a wider variety.

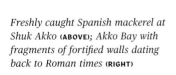

Freshly caught Spanish mackerel at Shuk Akko **(ABOVE)**; *Akko Bay with fragments of fortified walls dating back to Roman times* **(RIGHT)**

Our Favorite Spots

HUMMUS SAYID
Akko Marketplace

ABU SOHIL
24 Salah-a-Din Street

EL ABED ABU HAMID
Old Akko Lighthouse

Sayid is consistently considered one of the best hummus places in Israel. Although the restaurant is relatively large for a *hummusiya*, you'll still need to wait for a table, but hummus is something you eat fast, so the line moves briskly. Sayid's hummus is thick, creamy, and generously laced with olive oil. The oil, which comes from the family press, is an attraction in its own right (you can buy a bottle to take home). When we visited during olive-picking season, our hummus was drizzled with olive oil pressed just a few days earlier. Very young olive oil tends to be bitter and feisty, but paired with earthy, velvety hummus, it was beautiful. Sayid is equally famous for its *mashaushe* (the Galilean version of *masabacha*; see our recipe on page 126) and *makhlouta* (fava bean and olive oil stew served with tahini). To taste all three, ask for a triple (*meshuleshet* in Hebrew).

Shuk Akko is famous for sweets (TOP); *It's fun to get lost in the maze of passageways surrounding the market* (ABOVE); *At Kurdi Spices and Coffee, the prices are high but so is the quality* (RIGHT)

know your spices, you'll smell the difference. He also treats to you a cup of strong black coffee, brewed from beans roasted on the premises and scented with a bit of cardamom, and tells you funny stories about spices and Old Akko—and without noticing it, you end up buying twice as much as you originally planned.

The other two places may not be as famous as Sayid, but they are just as good. Both restaurants are run by women, a very rare phenomenon in the local hummus world and another reason to support them. Sohila of Abu Sohil took over the family business in 1993 and expanded the menu to include fried *kubbeh*, tabbouleh, and even falafel, freshly fried at the adjacent falafel stall.

Arin Abu-Hamid Kurdi's menu is even more interesting and includes homey dishes rarely seen in restaurant kitchens, such as *saydiya* (a traditional rice-and-fish pilaf favored by fishermen) and *tridi* (layers of chickpeas, crunchy pita, yogurt, and clarified butter, perfumed by cinnamon). The spice blends Arin uses in her kitchen come from her husband's shop, which brings us to our next stop.

KURDI SPICE & COFFEE

Akko Marketplace

Literally drowning in all kinds of knickknacks, such as model ships, fishing nets, huge conch, and other marine paraphernalia, the place looks like a tacky souvenir shop. In fact, however, this is one of the best (and most expensive) spice shops in Israel. The founder, Hamudi Kurdi, passed away several years ago, and the shop is now run by his son Marwan. To explain why everything costs twice as much as anywhere else, Marwan opens a jar of cinnamon or cumin and lets you take a sniff. If you

Dried herbs for culinary and medicinal uses (TOP); *Arin Abu-Hamid Kurdi, serving freshly made hummus and sautéed foraged mallows with yogurt* (ABOVE)

CHAPTER 14

Sweet Endings

Ein hagiga bli uga—"This is not a party if there is no cake," claims a famous children's song. Our passion for sweets almost equals our love of vegetables. Cake baking is a time-honored tradition in Israeli homes, especially on Shabbat and holidays; but even during weekdays, a jar of cookies or a loaf of cake will be waiting for someone who might drop by for *kafe ve uga* (a cup of coffee and a slice of cake).

Coconut Malabi with Macerated Berries

MALABI

Two 13½-ounce (380 g) cans coconut milk, unopened

½ cup (120 ml) water

¼ cup (50 g) sugar

3 tablespoons cornstarch

1 tablespoon rose water

BERRY SAUCE

12 ounces (365 g) ripe strawberries, hulled and quartered lengthwise, and blueberries

2 tablespoons crème de cassis

¼ cup (50 g) sugar

1 tablespoon fresh lemon juice

FOR GARNISH (OPTIONAL)

Coconut flakes, toasted

Peanuts, toasted and chopped

Israelis over the age of sixty still remember *malabi* vendors riding their tricycles around town or parking at the entrance to the food markets, their carts filled with small tin cups of quivering snow-white pudding nestled in crushed ice. Clearly we have a long-standing love affair with this milky rose-scented pudding from the Balkans, but for years it remained strictly in the realm of street food. Then in the 1990s, a new wave of Israeli chefs transformed it into an elegant restaurant dessert. Still, even today some of the best *malabi* is found in little hole-in-the-wall shops (where it is the only dish on offer) or makeshift snack trucks parked near highways.

Proper *malabi* pudding is unsweetened, but doused with bright red and very sweet syrup. It is usually topped with coconut flakes and chopped peanuts, though many *malabi* purists prefer their pudding without the crunchy add-ons. This version uses juicy macerated strawberries and blueberries instead of syrup and substitutes coconut milk for the dairy milk to make the dish vegan.

Make the malabi: Shake the cans of coconut milk before opening them. Pour the contents into a medium saucepan. Add ¼ cup (60 ml) of the water to the empty cans and give them a good swish to remove any coconut left in the cans, then pour the water into the pan. Add the sugar, stir, and bring the mixture to a boil over medium-high heat, stirring occasionally.

Meanwhile, mix the cornstarch, rose water, and remaining ¼ cup (60 ml) water in a small bowl to make a slurry.

When the coconut milk mixture is boiling, reduce the heat and, while whisking vigorously, slowly pour in the cornstarch slurry. The mixture will turn thick and lumpy–don't worry, just keep whisking until it is smooth again; this should take less than a minute. Remove the pan from the heat and pour the pudding into small bowls, glasses, or ramekins, or into a large glass bowl if you prefer to serve your malabi family-style. Shake the bowls lightly and tap the bottoms on the counter to pop any large air bubbles and cover each tightly with plastic wrap. Refrigerate overnight.

Make the berry sauce: Put the berries in a medium saucepan, add the crème de cassis and sugar, and cook over medium-high heat, stirring frequently, until the berries collapse a bit and start releasing their juice, 3 to 4 minutes. Remove from the heat and stir in the lemon juice. Let cool completely. (The sauce can be made a day ahead and stored in an airtight container in the refrigerator.)

To serve, spoon the sauce over the chilled malabi and, if you like, garnish with toasted coconut flakes and chopped peanuts.

Creamy Israeli Cheesecake with Homemade Labneh and Pistachios

CRUST

7 tablespoons (100 g) unsalted butter, melted, plus room-temperature butter for greasing

One 7-ounce (200 g) package petit beurre biscuits (we like Leibniz)

2 tablespoons granulated sugar

¼ teaspoon kosher salt

FILLING

2½ (8-ounce/225 g) packages cream cheese, at room temperature

1½ cups (300 g) granulated sugar

1 cup (240 ml) sour cream or crème fraîche, at room temperature

1 teaspoon finely grated lemon zest

1½ teaspoons pure vanilla extract

2 tablespoons cornstarch

3 large eggs, separated, at room temperature

We love cheesecakes in Israel, but ours use a very different cheese than their American counterparts. Simply called *gvina levana*, or "white cheese" (see page 138), it's low-fat, soft, and acidic, similar to German quark. Since *gvina levana* is difficult to find abroad, I use cream cheese combined with sour cream for this cake, then top it with tangy labneh to balance the rich, sweet filling.

To make the cake even more Israeli, swap the ubiquitous graham crackers for buttery, not-too-sweet petit beurre biscuits, the go-to for cookie crusts in Israeli home baking.

Make the crust: Preheat the oven to 375°F (190°C). Grease a 9-inch (23 cm) springform pan with butter, making sure to grease all the way up the sides.

Pulse the cookies in a food processor until they turn into fine crumbs. Add the granulated sugar, salt, and melted butter and pulse until the mixture is fully combined and resembles wet sand. Press the cookie mixture evenly over the bottom of the prepared pan (use the bottom of a glass to help you apply even pressure, if you like). Bake the crust until lightly golden brown, 10 to 12 minutes. Remove the pan from the oven and let the crust cool completely. Reduce the oven temperature to 325°F (165°C).

Make the filling: In the bowl of a stand mixer fitted with the paddle attachment, beat the cream cheese on medium speed until fluffy. Add 1 cup (200 g) of the granulated sugar and

beat until incorporated. Scrape down the bowl and add the sour cream, lemon zest, vanilla, and cornstarch. Beat again until the mixture is smooth and thick. With the motor running on low, add the egg yolks one at a time, stopping to scrape down the bowl after each addition. Transfer the mixture to a separate large bowl and clean and dry the mixer bowl thoroughly.

In the clean mixer bowl using the whisk attachment, whip the egg whites on medium speed until foamy. With the motor running, gradually add the remaining ½ cup (100 g) granulated sugar and whip until firm peaks form. Add about ½ cup (120 ml) of the egg whites to the cream cheese mixture and stir to combine—this will lighten up the texture a bit. Gently fold in the remaining egg whites in two or three batches until fully combined.

Recipe continues

TOPPING

2 cups (480 ml) soft unsalted homemade labneh (see page 140; made from 4 cups/ 960 ml yogurt)

4 teaspoons powdered sugar

¼ teaspoon kosher salt

½ cup (65 g) shelled pistachios, toasted

½ teaspoon ground cardamom

Pour the filling into the fully cooled crust and gently tap the pan on the counter to remove any air bubbles. Bake the cheesecake for 45 to 50 minutes, checking halfway through to make sure the top isn't getting too brown; if it is, cover it loosely with a sheet of aluminum foil to prevent further browning. The cake is ready when the filling is set but still jiggles slightly in the center. Set the cake on a wire rack and let cool for 10 minutes. Run a paring knife between the cheesecake and the side of the pan to make it easier to remove the cake later, and let the cheesecake cool completely in the pan. Do not skip or rush this step; the texture will be so much better if you give the cheesecake proper time to cool before putting it in the fridge. Cover with plastic wrap or foil and refrigerate overnight.

Make the topping: In the bowl of a stand mixer fitted with the paddle attachment, beat the labneh until fluffy. Add 2 teaspoons of the powdered sugar and the salt and beat until combined.

Pulse the pistachios in a food processor until very finely chopped. Remove and mix with the remaining 2 teaspoons powdered sugar and the cardamom.

Remove the plastic wrap from the cheesecake and, with the cake still in the pan, spread the topping evenly over the top. It's possible that the center of the cake will have sunk slightly—the labneh topping will cover it up nicely. Cover the cheesecake tightly and return it to the fridge for at least 1 hour and up to 2 days before serving.

Shortly before serving, sprinkle the top of the cheesecake with the pistachios while the cake is still in the pan. Release the sides of the springform pan, set the cake on a serving plate, and serve cold.

Lazy Cook's Baklava

ROSE SYRUP

1 cup (240 ml) water

2 cups (400 g) granulated sugar

¼ cup (60 ml) honey

One 3-inch (7.5 cm) strip orange zest (peeled with a vegetable peeler)

1 cardamom pod, cracked

2 teaspoons rose water or orange blossom water

BAKLAVA

2 cups (about 8 ounces/ 240 g) unsalted raw peanuts

2 cups (about 8 ounces/ 240 g) shelled pistachios

2 cups (about 8 ounces/ 240 g) walnuts

½ cup (50 g) powdered sugar

1 egg white, lightly beaten

1 teaspoon rose water

⅛ teaspoon ground cardamom

½ teaspoon ground cinnamon

6 tablespoons (¾ stick/ 85 g) unsalted butter, melted

⅓ cup (80 ml) vegetable oil

One 16-ounce (455 g) package frozen phyllo dough (about 18 sheets), thawed overnight in the fridge

Traditionally, these dainty delights are made by building layer after layer of pastry and filling, making them pretty labor-intensive. This version takes a shortcut, rolling up a few sheets of buttered phyllo with crushed nuts, then slicing, baking, and drizzling them with rose-scented syrup. That's it. For the complete Middle Eastern experience, serve them with small glasses of mint tea.

Make the syrup: Combine the water, granulated sugar, honey, orange zest, and cardamom pod in a medium saucepan. Bring to a simmer over low heat and cook, stirring occasionally, just until the sugar has completely dissolved. Remove from the heat, discard the orange zest and cardamom pod, and stir in the rose water. Transfer the syrup to an airtight container and refrigerate for at least 1 hour and up to 1 day.

Make the baklava: Put the peanuts, pistachios, and walnuts in a food processor. Add the powdered sugar, egg white, rose water, cardamom, and cinnamon and pulse until finely chopped and almost pasty.

Combine the melted butter with the oil in a small bowl (the addition of oil will help keep the butter liquid).

Remove the phyllo dough from the fridge and set it on your work surface, covered with a damp kitchen towel to prevent the sheets from drying out.

Place one sheet of phyllo on your work surface with one short side closest to you and lightly brush the whole sheet with the butter mixture. Top with another sheet of phyllo and brush lightly with the butter. Top with a third sheet, and this time be generous with the butter.

Spread about 1 cup (120 g) of the nut mixture over the bottom third of the phyllo stack and firmly tamp it down. Tightly roll the phyllo away from you until you reach the end. The roll should be about 1½ inches (4 cm) in diameter. Put the roll on a tray, seam-side down. Repeat with the remaining phyllo sheets and nut mixture, using 3 sheets of phyllo for each roll; you should end up with 4 or 5 rolls. Freeze the rolls for 10 to 15 minutes–this will harden them a bit and make them easier to cut.

Preheat the oven to 350°F (175°C). Line a baking sheet with parchment paper.

Remove the baklava rolls from the freezer, put one roll on a work surface and, using a very sharp knife, cut it into 1-inch-wide (2.5 cm) pieces–use a ruler to be precise. You should get 12 or 13 pieces from each roll. Arrange the pieces, cut-side up, on the prepared baking sheet (no need to space them apart, but they should not be touching). Repeat with the rest of the rolls.

Bake the baklava for 30 to 35 minutes, until golden. Remove from the oven. Gently spoon the chilled syrup over the baklava, making sure all the pieces are covered. Let cool before serving. Store at room temperature, tightly wrapped in plastic wrap, for 3 to 4 days.

Fresh Orange Pound Cake

1 medium orange (about 7 ounces/200 g; choose a thick-skinned variety), unpeeled, quartered

½ cup (120 ml) vegetable oil, plus more for greasing

½ cup (120 ml) fresh orange juice

2 large eggs

1 egg yolk

1 cup (200 g) granulated sugar

1¾ cups (220 g) all-purpose flour

1 heaping teaspoon baking powder

Grated zest of 1 lemon

Grated zest of ½ orange

Powdered sugar, for garnish (optional)

Sliced almonds, toasted or fried (see page 69), for garnish (optional)

Crème fraîche or creamy yogurt, for serving

Pound cakes with orange juice are the epitome of Israeli home baking, so much so that we sometimes call them *ugot safta*, or "grandma cakes." In addition to fresh orange juice, this cake incorporates a whole crushed orange into the batter, making the cake taste and smell like fresh fruit.

Put the orange in a small pan and add water to cover. Bring the water to a boil, drain, cover the orange with fresh water, and bring to a boil again. Drain again and let cool.

Preheat the oven to 350°F (175°C). Grease a 12-inch (30 cm) loaf pan with vegetable oil.

Pick the seeds from the cooked orange, place it in a food processor with 3 tablespoons of the orange juice, and pulse until you have a smooth orange slush.

In the bowl of a stand mixer fitted with the whisk attachment, beat the eggs, egg yolk, and the granulated sugar on medium speed until pale, fluffy, and shiny, 4 to 5 minutes. Reduce the speed to low and slowly stream in the vegetable oil.

Combine the flour, baking powder, lemon zest, and orange zest in a large bowl and fold in the egg mixture.

Fold in the crushed orange until just incorporated–be careful not to overwork the batter, which would make the cake tough. Pour the batter into the prepared pan and bake until a toothpick inserted into the center comes out dry, with a few crumbs clinging to it, 40 to 50 minutes.

While the cake is still hot, brush it with the remaining orange juice. Wait a minute between brushings to let the juice soak gradually into the cake without making it soggy. Let the cake cool completely in the pan, then store wrapped in plastic wrap at room temperature. The cake is at its best the day after it is baked but can be stored for up to 3 days at room temperature. Before serving, remove from the pan and dust the cake with powdered sugar and/or top with sliced almonds. Slice and serve. The cake goes beautifully with a dollop of thick creamy yogurt or crème fraîche.

Strawberries and Citrus

The Flavors of Israeli Winter

When we peel our first tangerine of the season (usually in late September), we can smell the rain, even if the air is still heavy with summer heat. As the short Israeli autumn melds into winter, the markets are colored in every shade of gold and green.

Oranges, notably the famous Jaffa oranges, are one of the most iconic local fruits and symbols of modern Israel. Once one of the major Israeli exports, they are now mostly sold locally and used primarily for juice, cooking, and baking. When it comes to snacking, most of us would go for an easy peeler, especially the tangerine (Israeli tangerines are fantastic!).

As you stroll around the shuks in winter, amid the fields of golden citrus you'll spot unexpected islands of red—these are strawberries, which, surprisingly, are another defining feature of the Israeli winter.

Almost everywhere in the world, strawberries represent the beginning of summer, but not so in Israel. Early varieties of strawberries planted in late September get picked in November and December, just in time to ship to Europe for Christmas (which is why these varieties were developed in the first place). Truthfully, these early berries look better than they taste, so we usually wait for February, when the markets overflow with juicy red berries and the prices come down.

Strawberries stay with us until April, which is very convenient, considering spring in Israel is virtually fruitless. We're saying good-bye to winter's oranges and tangerines, summer fruits have yet to arrive, and apples and pears come from cold storage. But by this time, strawberries are at their sweetest and make their way into almost every dessert and pastry.

Apricot Semolina Cake with Almonds

SYRUP AND APRICOT SAUCE

2 cups (400 g) sugar

1½ cups (360 ml) water

1 cinnamon stick

One 3-inch (7.5 cm) strip orange zest (peeled with a vegetable peeler)

4 cardamom pods, cracked

2 teaspoons orange blossom water

2 fresh apricots, pitted and halved

CAKE

1 cup (240 ml) vegetable oil, plus more for greasing

Butter, for greasing (optional)

2 cups (360 g) semolina

¾ cup (95 g) all-purpose flour

4 teaspoons baking powder

6 large eggs

1¼ cups (250 g) sugar

1½ cups (360 ml) almond milk

1 cup (85 g) shredded sweetened coconut

6 fresh apricots, pitted and quartered

1 cup (100 g) sliced almonds

Semolina cakes (aka *basbousa*, *revani*, *makrout*, or *tishpishti*) are very popular across Levantine and North African cuisines, and despite their many differences, they all share a unique crumbly texture reminiscent of corn bread. Traditionally cooks douse the still-warm cakes heavily in syrup, making them very sweet and somewhat sticky. But this recipe takes a lighter, fresher approach, mixing fresh apricots and crunchy sliced almonds into the batter and giving the baked cake just a light drizzle of orange blossom syrup. A delicious apricot sauce served on the side adds a burst of juicy fruit. In fact, the sauce tastes fantastic with a host of other desserts, from crêpes to a bowl of vanilla ice cream, so you might want to make a double batch.

PICTURED ON PAGE 355

Make the syrup and the sauce: Put the sugar and water in a small saucepan; add the cinnamon stick, orange zest, and cardamom; and bring to a boil over medium-high heat. Reduce the heat to low and cook, stirring occasionally, until the syrup is very thick, about 10 minutes. Remove from the heat and discard the cinnamon stick, orange zest, and cardamom. Pour about ¾ cup (180 ml) of the syrup into a cup or a small bowl and stir in 1 teaspoon of the orange blossom water; set aside to cool.

Add the apricots to the pan with the remaining syrup and return the syrup to a boil. Reduce the heat to medium-low and simmer until the apricots are soft and starting to break down, 7 to 8 minutes. Stir in the remaining 1 teaspoon orange blossom water and let cool. Transfer the apricot mixture to a blender and puree until smooth and orange colored. Set the sauce aside until ready to serve. (Both the syrup and the apricot sauce can be made a few days ahead and stored in airtight containers at room temperature.)

Make the cake: Preheat the oven to 350°F (175°C). Line the bottom of a 10-inch (25 cm) springform pan or 9-by-9-inch (23-by-23 cm) baking dish with parchment paper and grease the sides with oil or butter (if using).

Combine the semolina, flour, and baking powder in a medium bowl. Set aside.

In the bowl of a stand mixer fitted with the whisk attachment, beat the eggs and sugar on high speed until pale and fluffy, about 8 minutes. Reduce the speed to low and slowly stream in the vegetable oil and the almond milk.

Gradually add the flour mixture and beat just until smooth. Fold in the coconut, apricots, and ½ cup (50 g) of the almonds by hand.

Pour the batter into the prepared pan. Give it a light stir to make sure the apricots are distributed more or less evenly. Bake until a toothpick inserted into the center of the cake comes out dry, with a few crumbs clinging to it, about 35 minutes.

Meanwhile, toast or fry the remaining ½ cup (50 g) sliced almonds as directed on page 69.

Remove the cake from the oven and, while hot, drizzle the cake with the reserved syrup. If not serving at once, wrap well and store at room temperature for up to 2 days.

Cut the cake into wedges and pour about 3 tablespoons of the apricot sauce onto each slice. Garnish with the toasted sliced almonds and serve.

VARIATION

If you can't find fresh apricots, use dried ones by soaking 16 dried apricot halves in the syrup until swollen and soft, about 1 hour. Cut into small chunks.

TOMORROW, WHEN THERE ARE APRICOTS

There is an old Arabic adage, *Bukra fil mish-mish*, which translates to something like "Tomorrow, when there are apricots" and describes something that has been postponed indefinitely and will probably never happen.

Experienced shuk shoppers know that when a seasonal fruit first hits the market stalls, you shouldn't rush to buy it–it will be overpriced and underripe. This doesn't work with apricots, however. When they finally arrive, in late May or early June, there's no waiting for the high season. The season is *now*, and it will be over before you know it.

For years, we've been hearing rumors about groundbreaking agricultural research that will make apricots stay with us for longer periods as other summer stone fruit (peaches, plums, nectarines) do, but so far, no luck–apricot season is still fleeting, about one month, which makes this early-summer fruit even more precious. This is also the reason why preserving apricots is so important. Dried apricots are very common in the region, and so is delicious apricot leather (we call it *leder*)–pureed fruit, spread out and dried in thin, leatherlike sheets.

Tahini Shortbread Cookies with Sweet Hawaij and Almonds

MAKES ABOUT 24 COOKIES

¾ cup (150 g) granulated sugar

1 cup (2 sticks/225 g) unsalted butter, at room temperature (but not too soft)

1 cup (240 ml) best-quality raw tahini

1 teaspoon pure vanilla extract

2⅓ cups (290 g) plus 1 tablespoon all-purpose flour

2 teaspoons baking powder

1 teaspoon Sweet Coffee Hawaij (page 23)

¼ teaspoon kosher salt

Marcona almonds or blanched whole almonds

Powdered sugar, for dusting

You might as well call these halva cookies, because once you add something sweet to tahini (like honey, sugar, maple, or *silan*), it tastes just like halva. And like halva, these crumbly, soft, nutty cookies are utterly delicious and work wonderfully with a variety of spices, especially cinnamon and cardamom, or sweet *hawaij*, the redolent Yemenite spice blend, which was the fragrance of my childhood. Be sure to use good-quality raw tahini without any trace of bitterness (see our recommendations on page 112).

In the bowl of a stand mixer fitted with the paddle attachment, combine the granulated sugar, butter, tahini, and vanilla and beat on medium speed until pale and fluffy, about 5 minutes.

Meanwhile, combine the flour, baking powder, hawaij, and salt in a medium bowl and whisk together. Reduce the mixer speed to low and gradually add the flour mixture. Mix until the dough just comes together; be sure not to overwork the mixture or the cookies will be tough.

Transfer the dough to a lightly floured work surface and shape it into two logs, each about 6 inches (15 cm) long. Put each log on its own sheet of plastic wrap 4 inches (10 cm) longer than the logs and roll them up tightly in the plastic. Roll the logs under the palms of your hands to remove any creases and bumps, twist both ends closed (like a candy wrapper), and roll the dough back and forth to eliminate air pockets. Once secure, continue to roll the logs with your palms, pushing the ends of the log toward the center, until the logs are about 1½ inches (4 cm) in diameter. Refrigerate for at least 30 minutes and up to 1 day. (You can also make a double batch and freeze the logs for up to 2 months. Thaw in the refrigerator overnight before continuing.)

When you're ready to bake the cookies, preheat the oven to 350°F (175°C). Line two baking sheets with parchment paper.

Unwrap the logs of dough and, using a very sharp knife, slice them crosswise into ½-inch-thick (1.5 cm) discs (see Tip). Arrange the cookies on the prepared baking sheets, spacing them at least ½ inch (1.5 cm) apart, and gently press an almond into the center of each one.

Bake until the cookies just start turning golden, about 15 minutes. Be careful not to overbake; the cookies should be just lightly browned around the edges and on the bottom. Remove from the oven, but don't touch the cookies until they cool completely, or they'll crumble and break.

Dust the cookies with powdered sugar, eat a few, and store the rest in a cookie jar for up to 1 week.

TIP *To slice the cookies evenly, place a ruler next to the roll to use as a guide.*

Kadorei Shokolad

Crumbled Biscuit and Chocolate Balls

½ cup whole milk

Pinch of kosher salt

7½ ounces good quality dark chocolate pieces (aim for 70% cacao), chopped

2 ounces unsalted butter, softened at room temperature

½ teaspoon vanilla extract

8 ounces petit beurre cookies or other plain butter biscuits such as Kedem

½ cup unsweetened cocoa powder

1 cup toasted and finely shredded sweetened coconut

½ cup finely chopped pistachios

Coated in coconut or sprinkles and served in tiny paper cups, sometimes with a little flag stuck into them, these nostalgic bonbons that were all the rage in the eighties are still a hit at kindergarten birthday parties, often made by the kids themselves. Despite their name, the original recipe doesn't have a shred of chocolate, just cocoa powder mixed with crushed biscuits, sugar, and butter (or oil). Using good-quality chocolate turns them into a real treat fit for grown-ups too.

Put the milk and salt in a medium saucepan and heat until hot but not simmering. Remove from the heat, add the chocolate and butter, and stir until the chocolate is melted. If you need to put the pan back on the heat for a minute to get the chocolate to melt, that's fine. Add the vanilla and stir until the mixture is smooth and creamy. Chill until thick but not fully firm, about 45 minutes.

Put the cookies in a heavy plastic bag and crush them with a rolling pin or heavy pot. You want a mix of fine crumbs and little pieces, the largest about the size of a Cheerio. Fold the cookie crumbs into the chocolate mixture.

Refrigerate until the chocolate has set, about 1 hour. Scoop the mixture into little balls using a small ice cream scoop or tablespoon. Gently roll to make the balls evenly round.

Roll the balls either in the cocoa powder, coconut, or chopped pistachio until nicely coated, then keep cool until time to serve. These will last in an airtight container for up to about a week . . . if they aren't eaten before then. You can also freeze them and let them thaw for 5 minutes before serving. They taste delicious half-frozen.

VARIATIONS

For a vegan version, use almond milk instead of regular milk and ¼ cup vegetable oil instead of butter.

Tuck a whole Amarena cherry inside each ball.

Add about ⅓ cup finely diced dried fruit to the chocolate, such as prunes, apricots, pineapples, or raisins.

Thanks

To our amazing publisher, Lia Ronnen. You navigated the *Shuk* ship through choppy waters and brought it to a safe haven with your vision, fortitude, and unwavering faith in the project.

To Martha Holmberg, our editor extraordinaire—for being so wise and savvy and never losing your sense of humor.

To Quentin Bacon, for mouthwatering photographs and cheery vibes.

To the entire Artisan team, especially Zach Greenwald, Bella Lemos, Carson Lombardi, Michelle Ishay-Cohen, Jane Treuhaft, Hanh Le, and Nancy Murray, who put everything together in such a masterly way.

To the past and present Balaboosta team: Sarah Stanton, who makes everything look brighter; Tomer Avital; Jeremiah Del Sol, the most accurate recipe tester; Lizzy Singh-Brar; Jaime Velázquez Diaz; Christie Zierolf; and Hadley Assail.

To Ilan and Steph, our better halves and best friends, who stood beside us throughout this journey as they always do.

Last but not least: to all the men and women—in Israel and around the world—who open their hearts and their kitchens so we can learn and be inspired.

Index

Note: Page numbers in *italics* indicate photographs.

Michelle Gevint

Einat Admony is the author of *Balaboosta* and chef/owner of New York City's popular Balaboosta, Kish-Kash, and Taïm restaurants, which have been featured in *The New Yorker*, the *New York Times*, and *New York* magazine, among many other newspapers, magazines, and websites. When Admony is not at her restaurants, she can be found at her home in Brooklyn, cooking for the crowd of family and friends who regularly gather around her dining table.

Dan Peretz

Janna Gur was born in Riga, Latvia, and immigrated to Israel in 1974. She is the founder of *Al Hashulchan*, the premier Israeli food and wine magazine, which she edited for almost 30 years. Gur is the author of *The Book of New Israeli Food* and *Jewish Soul Food: From Minsk to Marrakesh*. She has published and edited nearly 40 cookbooks, many of them national bestsellers in Israel. She lives in Tel Aviv.